Southeast Asia Under the New Balance of Power

edited by
**Sudershan Chawla
Melvin Gurtov
Alain-Gerard Marsot**

The Praeger Special Studies program—
utilizing the most modern and efficient book
production techniques and a selective
worldwide distribution network—makes
available to the academic, government, and
business communities significant, timely
research in U.S. and international economic, social, and political development.

Southeast Asia Under the New Balance of Power

PRAEGER SPECIAL STUDIES IN INTERNATIONAL POLITICS AND GOVERNMENT

Praeger Publishers   New York   Washington   London

Library of Congress Cataloging in Publication Data

Chawla, Sudershan, 1924-
    Southeast Asia under the new balance of power.

    (Praeger special studies in international politics
and government)
    "Appendix: treaties, declarations, and statements
of policy": p.
    Bibliography: p.
    1. Asia, Southeastern—Foreign relations. 2. World
politics—1945-   I. Gurtov, Melvin. II. Marsot,
Alain-Gerard. III. Title.
DS518.1.C484   327'.11'09047   73-19441
ISBN 0-275-28826-9
ISBN 0-275-88850-9 (pbk.)

PRAEGER PUBLISHERS
111 Fourth Avenue, New York, N.Y. 10003, U.S.A.
5, Cromwell Place, London SW7 2JL, England

Published in the United States of America in 1974
by Praeger Publishers, Inc.

Printed in the United States of America

CONTENTS

APPENDIX: TREATIES, DECLARATIONS, AND
STATEMENTS OF POLICY

Southeast Asia Under the New Balance of Power

1

A NEW ASIAN
BALANCE OF POWER
Melvin Gurtov

It is by now almost a commonplace to talk about the new multipolar balance of power in Southeast Asia. Changes in the landscape of international politics have made several old and inaccurate descriptions of the region—such as American dominion, a Chinese sphere of influence, or East-West (U.S.-Soviet) competition—obsolete. The actions of the major powers, and the reactions of the Southeast Asian governments since the end of the 1960s are responsible for these changes. This book studies the region from the perspective of the four major powers (the United States, USSR, China, and Japan) and India. The conclusion indicates how their behavior and the changes they have promoted are being assessed in Southeast Asia.

Each of the next five chapters will elaborate on those policies and developments that have brought about this threshhold in Southeast Asian international relations. However, a brief summary here may be useful. Perhaps the starting point was President Lyndon Johnson's offer of negotiation to the Democratic Republic of Vietnam (North Vietnam) in March 1968, which opened the long road to the Paris Accords of January 1973. The reduction of American military strength in Indochina and, under the Nixon Doctrine, elsewhere in Asia, clearly had a major impact on strategic calculations within the region, all the more so after the presidential visit to Peking in Febuary 1972.

Outside Southeast Asia, the start of Sino-American diplomacy had significant impact in Japan. It quite quickly led to the establishment of diplomatic relations between China and Japan and to a new basis for Sino-Japanese trade. An even more far-reaching effect may be that Japan henceforth will conduct foreign policy with greater independence and an unwillingness to react constantly to U.S. initiatives. Japan's break with the United States in 1973 on policy toward the Middle East, during the energy crisis, was the first clear sign that Japanese support can no longer automatically be assumed in Washington. Japan is not yet a superpower; but it has become one of Asia's major powers.

A third cluster of events that affected Southeast Asia was Sino-Soviet tension and the return of stability to Chinese politics. Armed clashes along the Sino-Soviet border in March and August 1969 threatened to escalate into a major war. The two sides were able to negotiate successfully, and to resume trade and diplomatic relations; but the basic issues remain unresolved. A large and increasing Soviet force along the border makes the USSR China's primary security problem. Since the culmination of the Cultural Revolution in 1969, the Chinese leadership has had a more stable domestic base on which to conduct foreign relations. China was then able to resume an active diplomacy, leading to entry into the United Nations in 1971 and to Premier Chou En-lai's search for counterbalances to the perceived Soviet threat.

The USSR's military pressure on China's northern and western frontiers is only one measure of Moscow's increased attentiveness to and involvement in Asia. Other bench marks are the Tashkent Agreement, which Premier Aleksei Kosygin helped bring about between India and Pakistan in January 1966; Party First Secretary Leonid Brezhnev's proposal in June 1969 for an Asian "collective security" agreement; and the Soviet-Indian friendship and cooperation treaty of August 1971, in the midst of the Bangladesh struggle for independence. These developments, together with an activist diplomacy in Southeast Asia, have thrust the Soviet Union for the first time into regional politics as a major actor.

The overall significance of these events for the Southeast Asian states seems to be a need to reconsider foreign policy alignments (as discussed in Chapter 7), and, for the major external powers, a new pattern in their relationship to each other and to the states of the region. Southeast Asia, for these major powers, must be considered in the context of a quadrilateral relationship, that is, an intersection of the interests of four major powers. And now more than ever the major powers will also have to take account of the interests of the region's governments, expressed both independently and in association with one another.

The ability of this quadrilateral relationship to promote an equilibrium in Asia and produce the enduring stability that is supposed to be the hallmark of a balance-of-power system cannot be taken for granted. For it needs to be stressed that the term "balance of power" has been so differently used, and abused, by political scientists, statesmen, and journalists alike that we cannot assume that all those who talk about a new power balance in Asia are referring to or anticipating the same thing. There are different types of balances; there are many meanings of power; there are numerous possible conditions to the operation of a balance of power; and, most important of all, there may be very diverse expectations about and degrees of interest in a balance of power held by the major and minor powers that are (supposedly) involved in it. Because of these complexities, and the contradictions they occasion, we need to give some theoretical perspective to the chapters that follow.

CLASSICAL BALANCE OF POWER

Most writers accept that the balance of power was the central mechanism regulating international relations in Europe between 1812, at the height of

Napoleon's power, and 1914, when World War I began. During that approximately hundred-year period, despite major convulsions (such as the 1848 revolutions) and changes in the distribution of power (the French bid for primacy under Napoleon III and the Second Empire between 1848 and 1870, and the ascendancy of Bismarck's Germany after the Congress of Berlin in 1878), a balance-of-power system is generally believed to have operated successfully.[1] It functioned well because it was a system of independent states that included five major powers (Britain, France, Russia, Prussia/Germany, and Austria), each of comparable strength, and several lesser powers. No state was predominant, nor could attempt to become predominant without inviting formation of a coalition to resist it. Secondly, the system had recognized territorial limits and a fixed number of members, which meant that European political developments could be easily assessed as possible threats to the balance of power. Thirdly, the system was held together by a homogenous culture and similar military, diplomatic, and legal codes. This homogeneity not only gave cohesiveness and stability to the system; it also made each state's behavior more understandable to the others, hence to some extent also more predictable. Finally, it was easier than it is in present times to measure national power. Therefore, assessments of a state's intentions, evaluations of increases in national capabilities, and determination of terms for settling a war could be accomplished without the anguish and protraction to which we have become accustomed.[2]

Perhaps the crucial attribute of the classical balance of power was that the five major powers were willing to act in concert to maintain the system.[3] Beginning in the Napoleonic period, checking aggression was accomplished through several bilateral and trilateral alliances that served as counterweights to a neighboring state or alliance. At times this function was undertaken by a balancer power, usually Great Britain, which was able and willing to step into disputes between two other powers or power blocs.

Of great relevance to an evaluation of the so-called multipolar balance in Southeast Asia today is that the pre-World War I balance worked on the basis of a subordination of nationality and state interest to the principle of equilibrium.[4] For the sake of balance, the major powers were prepared to forgo efforts to strengthen themselves to the point of predominance in Europe. Their interest in a stable relationship among themselves was paramount. An important implication of that interest, noted in Edward Vose Gulick's analysis, is that the powers were prepared to move toward higher forms of collective effort—from action by alliance to coalitions and ultimately to some form of federation.

In recent years, an ambitious reformulation of the balance-of-power theory has been made by Mortan A. Kaplan.[5] He has set down rules for a balance-of-power system based on five "essential" powers, or actors. These rules are worth reciting in view of recent developments in Asia.

Under Kaplan's theoretical system, a main actor will always seek to increase his capabilities "even at the price of war." But each will also prefer negotiation to fighting, and will oppose attempts at predominance by another actor or combination of actors. A defeated essential actor will either be allowed to rejoin the system or be replaced by a secondary actor (lesser power). In short, as in the real system of 1812-1914, major powers accept certain constraints on their national power for the sake of system maintenance and balance.

Questions can be raised about the workability of such a system, especially against the background of the European experience. For instance, can a major power for long be expected to exercise the called-for restraints—to negotiate all disputes, to maintain rather than destroy a major-power adversary, and to avoid trying to form an all-powerful coalition? Are five powers essential? What about four? Is the measurement of national power certain enough so that when a major power increases its capabilities, qualitatively or quantitatively, there is little likelihood of its intention being misinterpreted? At what point can a major power be presumed to prefer fighting to negotiating, that is, to give priority to self-interest over maintenance of the balance system? If the risks of war include mutual annihilation, can it be assumed that an alliance or coalition of powers will always act to check aggression? (And what is "aggression"?) Finally, what about the "nonessential" actors? Are they, today, passive on-lookers, or do their interests and behavior count in calculations of where power resides and how the balance tilts?

ASIAN BALANCE OF POWER?

These questions, it should be obvious, are asked not as an intellectual exercise but because aspects of Kaplan's theoretical balance of power can be discerned in contemporary Asia. The Soviet Union, while increasing her military capability along the border with China, has so far been willing to negotiate differences rather than (for example) to carry out a preemptive strike against China's nuclear facilities. China and the United States have agreed, in the Nixon-Chou Shanghai communiqué of February 1972, that they oppose any attempt by a state to achieve predominance in Asia, and oppose collusion by either power with a third country against the other. In June 1968, three of the four Security Council members with nuclear weapons (the United States, USSR, and Britain) subscribed to a resolution that promises protection to any non-nuclear weapon state against attack or threat of attack by a nuclear weapon state, commonly presumed to mean China. And during the conflict over Bangladesh in 1971, the Nixon Administration played balance-of-power politics by opposing India and backing Pakistan, mainly because (in this writer's view) the President viewed any increase in Indian influence as an extension of that of the Soviet Union.

We need to inquire, however, whether these developments are consistent with each other and with a particular kind of power balance, or whether they are merely interesting sidelights, singular events that are not part of a pattern. It may be too early to attempt a definite answer, but it is not too early to reflect on the many meanings and types of balances of power, and then ask if any of them describes what is happening in or around Southeast Asia. For unless the "players" are in general agreement about the "rules of the game," an Asian balance of power will exist in name only, and unwarranted expectations of positive benefits from it will be aroused.

One basic distinction, emphasized by Inis L. Claude, Jr.,[6] is between balance of power as a *system*, a *policy*, and a *situation*. In Asia, are we witnessing an arrangement for conducting international relations in accordance with certain rules and mechanics (that is, under a system)? Or is balance of power the policy of certain key powers in order to promote their separate interests while preserving stability? Or is the concept descriptive of an objective situation that is, in fact, a true balance of equals; or, descriptive of an imbalance of power—a "balance" favorable to one power; or, descriptive of a distribution, not really a balance, of power?

There are other ways of distinguishing balances of power. For instance, *internal versus external* balance—a balance developed and maintained by states within a system (as in the nineteenth century), contrasted with a system maintained by states outside the system. One may make a distinction based on the character of the major powers involved: is the "balance" truly that, or is it "equal shares for the great powers at the expense of the lesser?"[7] In other words, balance of power may be a cover for *trade-offs among the major powers* of territorial or political interests at the expense of third countries. The question of what is being balanced—power or influence—is important. Is the balance one of military or economic equals, or is it primarily one of psychological and political influence? Lastly, does the balance of power provide for, or accept, a role for a *balancer power*, a modern-day Britain?

Circumstances in Asia would seem most nearly to approximate a balance-of-power policy rather than a system or situation. To promote their separate interests, the American, Soviet, Chinese, and Japanese governments now find it desirable to stabilize the competition for influence and advantage in Asia. Steps to normalize relations have continued between Moscow and Washington and have begun between Washington and Peking and between Peking and Tokyo. But it would be unrealistic to elevate these developments to the status of a system. The major powers have not yet established or accepted specific procedures for collective action to preserve a balance against efforts by a major power or lesser powers to disrupt it. United States-USSR differences during the Bangladesh conflict, and the continuation of intense fighting in Vietnam and Cambodia despite the Paris Accords, illustrate the absence of procedures for enforcing a balance of power. The current reliance on diplomacy to prevent the direct involvement of the major powers in local wars is not the equivalent of a balance system. And the realization of such a system will require, in addition, that Sino-Soviet relations become peaceable, and that the remaining points of contention in Soviet-Japanese, Sino-American, and Sino-Japanese relations be removed or muted.

Nor do present circumstances warrant the conclusion that there is already a balance-of-power situation in Asia. Certainly, the relationship of the major powers there cannot be considered a balance of equals. Japan lacks the military capability and reach of the other major powers, but far exceeds China and the USSR in economic penetration. The United States still is the dominant military (as well as economic) power in Asia, notwithstanding the Nixon Doctrine's emphasis on retrenchment. And China's objective power remains quite weak. There is, then, an imbalance of power or, still more accurately, an uneven distribution of power, and that situation is likely to continue for many years to come.

It should be noted in this connection that bipolarity remains an important feature of international and regional politics.[8] The United States and the Soviet Union are still the only two superpowers—Chinese leaders publicly disclaim any intention of joining them—in the sense that only they have the capacity to be globally involved militarily, politically, and economically. Moreover, their decisions are essential to the prevention and settlement of major international conflicts, and to the effective disposition of issues such as arms control, nuclear proliferation, and space exploration. Their military power is of far greater significance than that of, say, China: only Washington and Moscow have the nuclear strength which by itself can effectively deter enemies, and which can credibly guarantee the security of allies.

Additional problems arise when we consider the other distinctions mentioned above. The present so-called balance of power involves powers both inside and outside Asia. Economic, political, and strategic developments in the region are much more vital to the well-being of China and Japan than that of the United States or the Soviet Union. This circumstance creates another kind of imbalance, one of involvement and prolonged interest. Unlike the classical European balance of power, in Southeast Asia and Asia as a whole, not only (to state the obvious) do the four major powers lack a similar culture—the end of ideological differences is not in sight—and parallel institutions, but also they differ widely in their histories as Asian powers, hence in the kinds and degrees of interests in the region, and in the depth of influence they have exerted and can expect to exert.

Moreover, although three of the major powers (the United States, USSR, and China) have subscribed in general terms to the view that the powers should not collude with one another in order to disadvantage third countries,[9] the reality seems to be different. China sees U.S.-Soviet political collusion in the Middle East and Soviet-Japanese economic collusion in the joint development of Soviet Asia. It was the "Nixon shock"—the sudden opening of Sino-American diplomacy—that led Japan's prime minister, Tanaka, to follow Nixon to Peking. The Cambodian rebel government of Prince Sihanouk implies that the U.S.-China detente has led to a deliberate reduction of Chinese aid to Cambodian insurgents. On Taiwan, the government sees (mainland) Chinese-American diplomacy undercutting its political viability. The so-called multipolar balance may indeed be nothing more than a glorified name for old-time power politics.

Finally, let us examine the concept of a balancer power. Certainly, none of the major powers has been acknowledged by any of the others to be a balancer. Yet this fact may not keep one or the other of them from trying to play that role. The Japanese government, during most of the 1950s and 1960s, thought of itself as a bridge between China and the West. It may so regard itself again. In the past, American intervention in Asia has been rationalized in balancer terms. More recently, U.S. diplomacy over Bangladesh, and the Nixon-Kissinger strategy of simultaneously broadening détente with Moscow and Peking while Sino-Soviet tensions persist, also may indicate presumptions of the United States as a balancer power. If so, or indeed if any one of the major powers should seek to play the balancer in ways that are unacceptable to the others, disputes are as likely to grow larger as to be settled.

We should extend our skepticism about an Asian balance of power to a reevaluation of its past success. Claude's analysis suggests a cautious appraisal of what the classical European balance actually accomplished. The "stability" of the classical balance was of a special kind: it provided a framework for the maintenance of a state system in which the great powers could coexist without any one power dominating, but it did not provide the means of preventing wars, annexations, broken settlements, and the dismemberment of smaller powers.[10] That kind of balance of power seems to have appeal for the major-power governments, but in reality the historical record provides little comfort to the lesser powers in Southeast Asia and elsewhere.

Even insofar as relations among the major powers are concerned, the stability that is frequently presumed to be a benefit of the new multipolar balance may be more transitory than is expected. If, as I have suggested, the Asian balance of power is, using Claude's definition, a matter of national policy, neither institutionalized nor descriptive of a genuine balance, then it is subject to all the vagaries of shifting interests and sudden opportunities. As Claude reminds us, even in the nineteenth century, the balance of power was not usually an *equilibrium* of power. "More normally, states give evidence of the desire to possess power superior to that of their rivals or potential enemies. . . . The system breeds competition; it is pervaded by a spirit of rivalry."[11] Today's major powers seem far from accepting the primacy of equilibrium or any other kind of balance of power over state interest. What they do accept is that, for the moment, state interests are best served by balance-of-power politics. Furthermore, it is a balance of unequals—powers not equal by any objective indicators of national strength, nor equal in involvement and interest in the region, nor in capabilities. And because their relationship has been marked for so long more by tension and conflict than by cooperation or even competitive coexistence, there are further reasons for doubting that a real balance exists or, if it does exist, that it will prove long lasting.

Alastair Buchan has written that, on a global scale, international politics have become more balanced because:

> all the major participants in it are more politically introverted, more concerned with the organization, order, and prosperity of their own large societies and social systems, less disposed to impose their standards on others, with less energy available for scoring a point off their adversaries, than was the case in the 1950s and 1960s.[12]

If he is correct, then the root cause of what he too calls a multipolar balance of power is not a deep-seated and far-reaching interest in a stable balance, but rather the exhaustion, defeat, or inescapable domestic problems of the major-power governments. Such a conclusion can only reinforce skepticism that these powers have arrived at a common understanding of the inherent virtues of balance, much less equilibrium. "Stability," no less now than in the past, means different things to different governments—the neutralization of an external threat, the suppression of a revolutionary movement, the widening of economic markets, or the attainment of a new weapons system. All this is not to suggest that an Asian balance of power cannot be or should not be formed. It does suggest that today's stability may be illusory—that the quadrilateral "balance" may increase the difficulties of policy-making, make the consequences of imperfection more hazardous, and make the competition for influence more (or no less) intense.

NOTES

1. The history of the nineteenth-century European balance of power is exhaustively recounted in A. J. P. Taylor, *The Struggle for Mastery in Europe, 1848-1918* (London: Oxford University Press, 1954).

2. Edward Vose Gulick, *Europe's Classical Balance of Power* (New York: Norton, 1955), ch. 1. Gulick's discussion concerns the balance-of-power system of the Napoleonic period (1812-1815), but the system's characteristics apply as well to the remaining years before 1914.

3. Ibid., pp. 60-61.

4. Ibid., pp. 303-304.

5. Morton A. Kaplan, *System and Process in International Politics* (New York: Wiley, 1957), pp. 22-24.

6. Inis L. Claude, Jr., *Power and International Relations* (New York: Science Editions, 1962), pp. 13-21.

7. Alastair Buchan, *Power and Equilibrium in the 1970s* (New York: Praeger Publishers, 1973), p. 65.

8. See Stanley Hoffmann, "Weighing the Balance of Power," *Foreign Affairs*, 50, no. 4 (July 1972), pp. 620-626.

9. U.S.-China agreement on this point was in the 1972 Shanghai communiqué. U.S.-USSR agreement occurred in the Statement of Basic Principles of U.S.-Soviet Relations signed in Moscow on 26 May 1972.

10. Claude, op. cit., p. 69.

11. Ibid., p. 88.

12. Buchan, op. cit., p. 42.

U.S. STRATEGY IN SOUTHEAST ASIA IN THE POST-CEASE-FIRE PERIOD
Sudershan Chawla

When Henry Kissinger took over the stewardship of American foreign policy in 1969, it was generally expected that under his influence the Vietnam War would end quickly and that the United States would begin a phased withdrawal from most of South and Southeast Asia. Many nursed these hopes on the basis that Kissinger was primarily Europe oriented, and thus he would set U.S. policy on the right course by turning its focus toward the area where the real American interests rested. There were others who were of similar belief but for different reasons. In their view the lesson of the long and painful Vietnam War was clear. Americans would never again submit to an experience where their lives and resources were wasted in the cause of a people who neither had any use for nor understood the Western political and social values.

Kissinger only failed partly in fulfilling these expectations. He succeeded in negotiating a cease-fire in Vietnam in January 1973; a cease-fire that was some four years late in coming and cost untold additional casualties for Vietnam, South and North, and also many more for America. Soon thereafter Kissinger turned his attention toward Europe and delivered his "Year of Europe" speech in April 1973. This also was possibly too late, for Europe was disinterested and to Kissinger's chagrin grumbled that it was not about to be led by another "Bismarck." A British ambassador commented ironically: "I wonder if there isn't some subliminal resentment in Kissinger against Europeans—you know, the emigrant who left Europe behind and then made it to the top in the world's most competitive intellectual society, now making decisions which affect our lives."[1]

By and large Kissinger did pursue the course expected of him. But if things went awry, it is because there were other forces that played their own special role in molding the outcome. In the turmoil of the Vietnam War years, few took time to note that there were legacies as well as internal and external constraints upon American foreign policy, which were beyond the control of any foreign policy maker. Aside from the fact that he was operating under the command of President Nixon, who had his own political concerns as well as definite ideas about other states and their leaders, Kissinger was at the same time dealing with the collective and individual wills of other states, especially Russia and China. Therefore, U.S. policy followed a direction which from the policy maker's point of view was dictated by the limited alternatives available, but which from the outside observer's point of view was a projection of the Nixon-Kissinger personality and perspective.

Nixon and Kissinger never approved of unilateral withdrawal from Vietnam; nor were the American people ever guaranteed freedom from Asian involvement in the future. If the American community and the world community were shocked when American forces invaded neutral Cambodia in April 1970; if all watched with disbelief the intensive bombing of North Vietnam, it is because the new Administration was expected to bring relief not greater suffering to the peoples of America and Indochina. If the Kent State University tragedy cast a pall of grief all over the land, it was because the tired and wounded spirit of men at home and abroad had built up hopes for peace with the change of administrations. On the other hand, the new leadership could shout down all criticism with statements pointing to the fact that it had never contemplated compromising national honor or the welfare of the armed forces in the field. Writing in *Foreign Affairs* in January 1969, Kissinger had said:

However we got into Vietnam, whatever the judgment of our actions, ending the war honorably is essential for the peace of the world. Any other solution may unloose forces that would complicate prospects of international order. A new administration must be given the benefit of the doubt and a chance to move toward a peace which grants the people of Vietnam what they have struggled so bravely to achieve: an opportunity to work out their own destiny in their own way.

Similarly, President Nixon in laying down the guidelines of his foreign policy in an interview in Guam in July 1969 stated:

First, the United States will keep all of its treaty commitments.
Second, we shall provide a shield if a nuclear power threatens the freedom of a nation allied with us or of a nation whose survival we consider vital to our security.
Third, in cases involving other types of aggression, we shall furnish military and economic assistance when requested in accordance with our treaty commitments. But we shall look to the nation directly threatened to assume the primary responsibility of providing the manpower for its defense.[2]

Clearly there was a gap between what many Americans expected from the new administration, and what the new administration saw as its duty. The gap was never bridged. But the fact that President Nixon was reelected in 1972 with a resounding majority without bringing an end to the Vietnam War in his first four years of office, is a commentary on the U.S. policy makers as well as the American public. However, the year 1972 was not without some unusual accomplishments on the part of the President. Reversing the policy of more than two decades, Nixon was successful in establishing a diplomatic dialogue with the Peoples Republic of China. The United States struck a détente with the Soviet Union that has not only become the dominant note of world politics in the seventies, but which has resulted in a consultative relationship between the two superpowers that grates on the nerves of even the closest allies.

January 1973 did see the end of the Vietnam War for America. The cease-fire brought the withdrawal of American combat forces from South Vietnam. It also brought the prisoners of war home. But it did not end American involvement in Vietnam or Southeast Asia as a whole. This was neither intended, nor was it ever considered desirable by the U.S. policy makers in terms of the overall objectives of American foreign policy. Therefore, to understand U.S. strategy in Southeast Asia in the post cease-fire period, it is well to examine a number of factors surrounding American involvement in and withdrawal from the theater of action.

THE UNITED STATES IN VIETNAM

It is generally accepted now that the United States became heavily involved in the affairs of Southeast Asia in general and Indochina in particular in the aftermath of the Geneva Conference of 1954. As one writer has put it:

In 1954, we were just a year beyond a painfully achieved Korean truce, after three years of bloody fighting. The communists had won the civil war in China, a result which brought severe psychological shock to Americans, who had nurtured sentimental notions of the Chinese people and of U.S.-Chinese relations. . . . Chinese communist intervention in the Korean war . . . reinforced our perception of a precarious coalition of free states under assault across the entire glove by a seamless international conspiracy. In the circumstance, it was almost inevitable that the United States would view the impending French departure from Indochina as merely the opening of another avenue for communist expansion in Asia.[3]

John Foster Dulles, then Secretary of State, said in June 1954:

At the moment, Indochina is the area where international Communism most vigorously seeks expansion. . . . The problem is one of restoring tranquility in an area where disturbances are fomented from Communist China, but where there is no invasion by Communist China.[4]

In view of such perceptions it is not surprising that not only did the United States refuse to sign the Geneva Agreement, but she proceeded to take certain actions calculated to further the objectives of American foreign policy that sought to "contain" communism. Since containment policy attempted to halt the spread of communism beyond certain boundaries in the East and the West, it was a natural consequence that Dulles, totally hostile to the spirit of the Geneva Agreement, encouraged and supported the Diem regime of South Vietnam to violate the agreement, which called for internationally supervised elections in 1956, in North and South Vietnam, with the aim of bringing about peaceful unification of the entire land. It was clear that had elections been held, Vietnam would have been reunited under the communist regime of the North, led by Ho Chi Minh. Denied the avenue of elections, Ho Chi Minh turned to military means to unite his country. It is at this point that the United States started its military assistance program to South Vietnam to build her defenses against what became known in American circles as "communist aggression." How this relatively small scale military assistance program escalated into a massive commitment of American men and material is a long and complex account that cannot be dealt with here. Military assistance under President Eisenhower rose to an additional 16,500 military advisers under President Kennedy and half a million combat soldiers under President Johnson. At the time that the demands for disengagement from this theater reached a peak at home, there were about 549,000 members of the U.S. armed forces on Vietnamese soil and the government was spending approximately 25 billion dollars per year on this military venture.

It is now known that before the Johnson administration initiated steps to deescalate American involvement, the field commanders had submitted the estimate that the United States could achieve a military victory only by invading North Vietnam and committing some 700,000 American soliders to battle.[5] But the Tet offensive carried out by the National Liberation Front in February 1968 brought to the surface the reality of the situation for the first time. It revealed that optimistic appraisals of the situation in the past were baseless. It was clear that there was a gross misjudgment of enemy capabilities and his will to fight. The NLF had launched a major offensive on a wide front. Its forces had succeeded in penetrating not only Saigon and other provincial capitals, they had even penetrated the American Embassy compound, demonstrating that half a million American soldiers plus a larger South Vietnamese force had together failed to bring security and stability to South Vietnam.

As students and university professors were joined by a growing number of political commentators and some prominent senators in opposing the war, it began to dawn upon Americans that prolonged conflict in Vietnam had cost heavily in human lives, taxes, delaying of domestic reform and disruption of internal unity, with no visible returns. Resistance to the administration's line of thought grew louder day by day. Then in March 1968, in a televised speech to the nation, President Johnson laid the basis for talks to begin in Paris between the United States and North Vietnam toward negotiation of a peace settlement. At the same time he declared that he would not run for another term of office. This was judged as a sign that finally public disapproval of government policy had made an impact.

Even though Johnson's new approach was a welcome relief in most circles, it was clear that the road to peace was long and hazardous. The fact that a new president was to be elected in November did not help the prospects for peace. The Paris talks had a slow start, but they moved at an even slower pace as Washington, Hanoi, and Saigon kept one eye on the U.S. presidential elections.

NIXON-KISSINGER POLICIES AND PERCEPTIONS

Elections in November 1968 transferred power to Richard Nixon. President Nixon laid bare an outline of his foreign policy in an interview with the press in Guam in July 1969, and also in an address to the nation in November 1969. He presented the blueprint of his policy in greater detail on 25 February 1971, in "U.S. Foreign Policy For The 1970s: A Report To The Congress by Richard Nixon." The guidelines and principles defining the new American role in world affairs came to be known as the Nixon Doctrine.

Among other things the doctrine stated: "We are not involved in the world because we have commitments; we have commitments because we are involved. Our interests must shape our commitments, rather than the other way around." Yet the doctrine emphasized support of all treaty commitments. It further conveyed the message that an exit from Vietnam could not take place without a guarantee that the Saigon regime would not be overthrown once the American forces departed from the scene.[6] As the President saw it:

> If the United States withdrew quickly, the events it had fought to prevent might well occur; if South Vietnam collapsed and Hanoi unified Vietnam under its control . . . the credibility of the 'imperial center's' commitments and power would be weakened, perhaps gravely so. For the stability of the state system and deterrence depended . . . not only on American arms but upon the country's reputation in Moscow, Peking, and other capitals.[7]

Therefore, a speedy withdrawal of American forces at a time when South Vietnamese forces could not yet cope with Hanoi's forces and the NLF by themselves was not considered the most advisable course of action by the new President.

Nixon did introduce a different approach to deal with the Vietnam issue; an approach that would pacify the public at home and would keep the enemy engaged abroad. American ground troops were to be gradually withdrawn, thus cutting the cost of war and making continued hostilities more palatable for the American public. Vietnamization of the war or shifting the major burden of the battle to Vietnamese shoulders, was to proceed only with such speed that would neither jeopardize the welfare of the retreating American soldiers nor undermine the Saigon regime. At the same time U.S. air bombardment and naval support would continue both to prevent the enemy from overwhelming the South Vietnamese forces, and to remind for North Vietnam that the matter had to be settled at the negotiation table. President Nixon and his chief foreign policy adviser Henry Kissinger thus made it clear that under their guidance the

United States was in no haste to extricate itself from Vietnam. Moreover, they felt certain that their approach would be acceptable to the large number of Americans who would not tolerate unconditional withdrawal.

If the American public did not expect a precipitous retreat, then it did not expect a return to pre-Tet conditions either. This became evident when widespread dissent engulfed the new Administration after American and South Vietnamese troops invaded Cambodia in April 1970, presumably to wipe out North Vietnamese sanctuaries in Cambodia—South Vietnamese border areas. Campus protests erupted all over again. In one such demonstration at Kent State University, National Guardsmen fired into the crowd killing four students. Bills were introduced in the Senate to cut off funds for military operations in Cambodia. One amendment sought to cut off funds for all operations in Vietnam after June 1971.

Renewed turmoil on the domestic scene, which the President had successfully arrested by his policy of troop withdrawals, was a warning that while America was prepared to wait in search of a reasonable settlement, the people and the Congress had no intention of giving the new Administration the blank check that had been misused by the previous Administration.

As the 1972 elections approached, the situation reached a point where the President offered "the complete withdrawal of all American forces from Vietnam within four months" if all prisoners of war were returned and an internationally supervised cease-fire was imposed. Hanoi rejected the offer, suggesting that unless a change of government in Saigon was a part of the settlement, no agreement could be reached. As the contest to see whose will would prevail dragged on, certain developments beyond the control of both parties appeared on the international horizon, which influenced the conduct of both the United States and North Vietnam—leading finally to a cease-fire in January 1973.

Signs of a rift between the People's Republic of China and the Soviet Union had surfaced as early as 1959. There was much speculation at the time, and during the years to come, whether this cleavage meant a permanent division within the world communist movement, or whether it was a temporary breach which would mend before long. A decade passed; the leadership in the Soviet Union changed hands; but there were no indications that the two communist giants intended again to present the united front that prevailed between 1949 and 1959. Their denunciations of each other became more frequent and vitriolic. Rivalry between the two reached a new peak in the sixties. Ironically, while the United States watched the struggle between the two, because of intense distrust and fear of communism she could neither believe that the split was permanent nor did she exploit the situation to her advantage. America was so deeply involved in Vietnam that the only thing which seemed to impress her was the fact that Hanoi received military assistance and encouragement from both China and Russia.

Two events occurred in 1968 and 1969 that forced a change in this pattern. In 1968 the Soviet Union marched into Czechoslovakia and crushed the rising tide of opposition to the manner of Soviet control. This was a manifestation of Russian resolve not to permit public criticism of the official system in the USSR beyond a certain point. It reflected a determination to put a stop to emerging signs of self-assertion in Eastern Europe. It was another demonstration that Soviet might would be used, with all the ruthlessness necessary, in any confrontation that directly threatened or challenged Soviet strategic and ideological interests. The invasion of Czechoslovakia appeared to bring to an end the officially tolerated post-Stalin liberalism. This seems to have raised a serious question for the rulers of China. Would the Soviets contemplate a similar action toward China, given the fact that relations between the two had been steadily deteriorating?

A partial answer appeared in 1969. There were a series of clashes all along the border between the Sino-Soviet troops, in March and then again in August, which threatened to escalate into a major war. While the two sides succeeded in halting the potentially explosive situation through negotiations, this did not put to rest the mutual suspicion and fear that had now become a reality.

North Vietnam was caught in the middle of the contest between the two communist giants, her prime supporters, as both sought to influence Hanoi according to their respective interests. While China counselled Hanoi to continue the struggle against the "imperialists," the support China rendered was hardly adequate for the task. While Peking supplied conventional arms and ammunition, it could neither supply the sophisticated weapons that Hanoi needed badly to persist in its efforts to compel U.S. withdrawal, nor was China prepared to dispatch volunteers to fight side by side with Hanoi's soldiers.

The Soviet Union on the other hand furnished the sophisticated weapons, but she was not totally opposed to some form of negotiated settlement between Washington and Hanoi, especially if it could result in serving Russian interests on the western front, as Moscow sought to make progress in SALT talks and establish economic and technical cooperation. Such an approach made all the more sense in the aftermath of the armed clashes with the People's Republic of China.

By 1970, then, the Sino-Soviet split had become an undeniable fact. Cracks in the once presumably impregnable communist wall were deep enough to reflect the emergence of an outline of a new world order. This not only influenced the course of the Vietnam War, it set a pattern for new relationships among nations all over the globe, and it led to major shifts in American foreign policy. As Kissinger put it in August 1970:

> The deepest international conflict in the world today is not between us and the Soviet Union, but between the Soviet Union and Communist China. . . . Therefore, one of the positive prospects in the current situation is that whatever the basic intentions of Soviet leaders, confronted with the prospect of a China growing in strength and not lessening in hostility, they may want a period of détente in the West, not because they necessarily have changed ideologically, but because they do not want to be in a position in which they have to confront major crisis on both sides of their huge country over an indefinite period of time.[8]

Responding to the new international situation, Nixon-Kissinger policies in 1971 and thereafter aimed mainly at realizing two objectives: on the one hand they sought to capitalize on the rift between China and Russia; on the other hand they reached for a settlement of the Vietnam War that would both not seriously impair American credibility, and also preserve America's global role.

Nixon-Kissinger perceptions led to a secret trip by Kissinger to Peking in July 1971. At the end of his visit it was announced that President Nixon would journey to China before May 1972, to hold talks with Mao Tse-tung and Chou En-lai. This was a stunning reversal of American policy of the previous two decades. There was widespread disbelief because the initiative had been taken by an American President who, prior to his election in 1968, had written:

> The common danger from Communist China is now in the process of shifting the Asian governments' center of concern. During the colonial and immediately post-colonial eras, Asians stood opposed primarily to the West, which represented the intruding alien power. But now the West has abandoned its colonial role, and it no longer threatens the independence of the Asian nations. Red China, however, does, and its threat is clear, present and repeatedly and insistently expressed.[9]

Nixon's visit to Peking in February 1972, was followed by a visit to Moscow in May 1972. Even though these meetings did not bring an end to hostilities in Vietnam, several important trends did flow from these summit talks, which had a significant impact on world politics.

A face-to-face meeting between top leaders of China and America brought to an end the American quarantine of China over the years. While the People's Republic of China was seated in the UN much before Nixon's arrival in China, and strangely enough, over strong U.S. opposition, Nixon's visit gave to the Peking regime the stamp of approval and legitimacy that the new leaders of China had searched for, ever since their assumption of power on the mainland. Further, the visit allayed the fears of China that the United States might possibly join the USSR in impeding Chinese advancement toward the goal of becoming a full-scale nuclear power. The Shanghai communiqué issued at the end of the Nixon-Mao-Chou talks did not pledge U.S. withdrawal from Taiwan or abrogation of the United States-Taiwan defense treaty. It did extract the concession from the United States that Taiwan was a part of mainland China, while obligating China not to use force to bring back Taiwan into the Chinese fold.

Conversations with the Soviet leaders, while promising noninterference in Sino-Soviet quarrels, brought about the détente that opened up a period of cooperation leading to several agreements in the area of SALT talks, discussion on mutual arms reduction on the part of members of NATO and Warsaw pacts, exchange of information in space technology, and establishment of better trade relations.

But more important, the actions taken by Nixon and Kissinger were calculated to improve the U.S. strategic position in Asia and Europe, without increasing economic burdens at home and without jeopardizing U.S. global role or commitments abroad. In Asia, the United States had turned China, for long considered a potentially troublesome adversary, into an ally in thwarting Soviet attempts to dominate the area as the United States rearranged her relationships in this theater. Furthermore, friendly gestures toward China on the part of the United States reduced the chances of a quick reunion between the two communist giants, which always loomed large as the greatest threat to future U.S. strategic and economic interests. Also, the Soviets now had two fronts to contend with, one in the East and one in the West. Concern and tensions related to the Eastern front would always compel the Soviet Union to pursue a moderate course in her relations with the Atlantic powers. And, of course, the United States hoped that in the aftermath of the summit talks both China and Russia would exert influence on Hanoi to agree to some accommodation, which would permit American policy makers to claim that they had won a peace with honor.

Thus the efforts to end the war in Vietnam became part of a bigger package. It was the beginning of a new global posture and strategy for U.S. policy. As Nixon and Kissinger saw it, this was far more in tune with the prevailing international power structure than the earlier anticommunist theme that had clearly failed, especially in Asia, and which no longer held any relevance. The new approach permitted the United States greater freedom of diplomatic maneuver in Europe, the Middle East, and Latin America, in consultation with the Soviet Union.* It also allowed America continued presence and involvement in Asia, not opposed but approved by China, who now saw Russia as the greatest threat to her security.

The new balance of power, as the U.S.-USSR-China relationship came to be characterized, did not stop the war in Vietnam. However, it gave impetus to moves and countermoves that finally produced an agreement in Paris, leading to a cease-fire in January 1973. The cease-fire brought home the POWs and the U.S. combat troops in South Vietnam. But by no means did it end American involvement in Vietnam or Southeast Asia as a whole, because this was not the goal Nixon-Kissinger sought as a part of American foreign policy objectives under their direction.

It is significant to note that in seeking accommodation with Russia and China, U.S. policy makers did not change all the previous characteristics of American foreign policy. They brought an end to the doctrine of "containment," which stood for involvement anywhere in the world where threat of communist expansion was perceived; they brought an end to the belief that the United States could never conduct normal relations with states espousing communist ideology; they brought an end to the conviction that all communist states, bound together by a revolutionary ideology, would pursue a common policy toward all capitalist and noncommunist states; and they also brought an

---

*European powers have begun to show resentment against the American practice of consulting the Soviet Union on all major issues, without extending the same privilege to their NATO allies. The Brezhnev-Nixon San Clemente declaration of June 1973 stated that the United States and the USSR had agreed to avoid a nuclear war and cooperate in resolving political issues. The NATO allies were neither consulted nor informed in advance about such a declaration. This led many European diplomats to ask, "Which comes first with Kissinger and Mr. Nixon—the NATO Treaty or their new coziness with the Soviet Union?" Los Angeles *Times*, 24 February 1974.

end to the myth that communist states formed a monolithic structure that prevented any dealings with individual states on a separate basis. Nixon-Kissinger policies did eliminate all that, and with a stroke bold enough to catch the world gasping.

On the other hand, what the U.S. President and his chief foreign policy adviser did was to replace the doctrine of "containment," which emphasized ideology, with the doctrine of "balance of power," which emphasized power. This shift in emphasis required an adjustment, but it did not call for withdrawing into fortress America. It required paying greater attention to countries with superpower status and potential superpower status. It required deemphasizing certain alliances and changing the nature of some others. It required a preference for bilateral relationships rather than bipolar relationships. It required a reassessment of commitments to different regions and different nations. But it did not require scrapping of multilateral or bilateral defense treaties that the United States had executed in the post World War II period; it did not require a noninterference or noninvolvement pledge. As Kissinger spelled it out in his address at the Pacem in Terris conference in Washington, D.C., in October 1973:

> We will oppose the attempt by any country to achieve a position of predominance either globally or regionally.
>
> We will resist any attempt to exploit a policy of détente to weaken our alliances.
>
> We will react if relaxation of tensions is used as a cover to exacerbate conflicts in international trouble spots.[10]

Quite clearly then disengagement from Vietnam did not mean disengagement from global responsibilities or if necessary global involvement. Therefore, it was not strange that the overall objectives of American foreign policy and the worldwide strategy designed by Nixon and Kissinger had many familiar features. America's position vis-à-vis the countries of Southeast Asia has to be looked at from this perspective.

United States policy in Southeast Asia in the post-Vietnam period has three dominant and identifiable features. First, America proposes to continue her presence in select areas of Southeast Asia. Second, America will not discourage pacts of mutual cooperation and defense among the nations of the area, as long as these pacts do not include either China or Russia. Third, America will not become directly involved in a conflict that might occur between any two parties in the region, as long as China and Russia observe the same restraints, and as long as American presence in areas of her choosing is not under attack.

Whether this is what President Nixon really meant when he said, "I think it will be a safer world and a better world if we have a strong, healthy United States, Europe, Soviet Union, China, Japan, each balancing the other, not playing one against the other, an even balance," is something which has been the subject of much debate. Nonetheless, U.S. actions in Southeast Asia since the cease-fire in Vietnam lend credence to the belief that America, far from contemplating a wholesale exit from the area, does not intend to permit China or Russia to challenge the United States for predominant influence.

American commitments in Southeast Asia, originally born out of attempts to contain communism, resulted in American military presence in many more states than Vietnam alone. At the time of the cease-fire in Vietnam, American military advisers and armed forces were present in the territories of Thailand, the Philippines, Taiwan, South Korea, New Zealand, Japan, and Okinawa. They were sent there as a consequence of defense agreements that the United States had signed with each one of them in the 1950s. While some modifications had occurred by mutual consent, these agreements did not change their fundamental character in the 1970s.

THE UNITED STATES AND THAILAND IN THE 1970s

Close relations between Thailand and America grew out of the multilateral mutual defense pact, SEATO, which came into being in 1954. SEATO was conceived by the former U.S. Secretary of State John Foster Dulles shortly after the French defeat in Indochina. While the stated aim of the pact was to prevent aggression against the full members of the treaty—Australia, France, New Zealand, Pakistan, the Philippines, Thailand, the United Kingdom and the United States—the real aim of the agreement was to stop the rising power of mainland China from overwhelming Southeast Asia. It was because of this that the treaty members by a unilateral declaration extended the protection of the treaty to Cambodia, Laos, and Vietnam. Soon after the treaty came into force, Cambodia rejected the SEATO protection in favor of a policy of neutralism. Laos was neutralized by an international agreement in 1962. While this left South Vietnam alone under the SEATO umbrella, all the members of the pact never agreed to support U.S. action on behalf of South Vietnam.

The pact did not hold much promise from the beginning. Most of the nations of Southern Asia opposed being drawn into an anti-Chinese security treaty. Even the few who did respond to the persuasions of Secretary Dulles, did not totally agree with the aims and objectives of the pact as interpreted by the United States. As each state sought to use the pact to serve its interests— Britain in Hong Kong and Malaya, Pakistan against India, and the United States in Vietnam—it became clear that prospects for concerted military action on the part of the group were very slim. While Secretary General Sunthorn Hongladarom of Thailand told a news conference in November 1973 in Bangkok that SEATO was scrapping its activities as a military deterrent, the treaty was a dead letter long before that.

Nonetheless, out of this pact was born a tie between the United States and Thailand that not only survived the shock of disintegration, but became a crucial source of support for American presence in Southeast Asia and American military campaigns in Vietnam.

As the weakness of the SEATO pact began to surface, Thailand sought to negotiate a separate security arrangement. In the spring of 1962, the then

Secretary of State Dean Rusk negotiated an agreement with the Thai Foreign Minister that pledged America to come to the aid of Thailand if she were attacked, regardless of the reaction of the other SEATO members. While Thailand considered this bilateral arrangement a more dependable source of security, in later years Thailand proved to be one of the most dependable forward bases for U.S. military action in Vietnam. It was from there that the United States carried out her heaviest air raids in North Vietnam, Laos, and Cambodia in the course of the protracted war. It was from there that the United States was able to provide some crucial logistical support to her combat troops. The end of the Vietnam engagement did not change the nature of U.S.-Thai relations.

The importance of the Thai military bases in the past and in the future can be gauged by looking at some of the statistical information available publicly. In numbers, the U.S. armed forces stationed in Thailand constitute the largest American military contingent based abroad, next to West Germany. At the height of the Indochina war, America had in Thailand 48,000 servicemen and more than 1,000 planes. The American air fleet consisted of the big strategic B-52 bombers, jet powered flying service stations, jet fighters, cargo, and transport planes. While it was highly publicized that the Thai government sought a reduction in American military presence in August 1973, available information indicates that no serious pullout has taken place to this date. The figures revealed in 1974 place the current American military strength in Thailand, consisting mostly of airmen, at about 35,000 men and 500 planes.

Distributed among six separate military bases on Thai soil, these men and their machines perform functions that are considered essential to the interests of America. American officers on one of these bases, Utapao, expressed the belief that "Utapao-Sattahip complex will remain indefinitely in American hands, whether peace is restored in Indochina or not."

Utapao base and the nearby military seaport of Sattahip, hold special significance. Utapao is the only American-held airport in Asia which has landing facilities for the eight-engine Stratofortresses, the biggest fighter-bomber craft in the American air arsenal. It is the base that still receives the U-2 spy planes, which continue their secret flights. Transport planes from the United States land high-priority cargo here. This cargo is then dispatched to the battlefields of Indochina, which remain alive more than a year after the cease-fire. The Navy uses this base as a stopover for its antisubmarine patrol planes, which cover a wide range of sea lanes in this area. Utapao has recently acquired another highly sensitive function. As America seeks to build a high-powered naval base at Diego Garcia atoll in the Indian Ocean, Utapao has become the aerial resupply point for the construction needs of this naval base. No wonder then that the Utapao airfield's 18 miles of perimeter is defended by a highly trained security force, which is nearly half American and half Thai.

In addition to being a formidable air base, Thailand has also served as a home for a large contingent of Central Intelligence Agency, and Special Forces. Intelligence gathered by the CIA staff has been used by both the Thai and U.S. governments. Under the guidance of the CIA, a group of American linguists and analysts based in Bangkok has for quite some time intercepted and interpreted foreign-language broadcasts from hostile and friendly nations. Both governments have shared this information and put it to use. CIA agents have also been involved in gathering information about rebellious elements in Thailand, at the request of the host government, which helped the government in power to deal with unfriendly forces at home.

The Special Forces, consisting of some 3,500 Green Berets at the height of their strength, operated under the guidance of the CIA. They were a small force serving a limited function when they came to Thailand in 1960. By the late sixties, however, their numbers had grown substantially and so had their activities. To begin with they trained Thai police and Thai soldiers to deal with guerrillas within the boundaries of the state. But with developments in Vietnam, the Special Forces took over the duties of training Cambodian soldiers for special missions, and training Lao elite troops and Thai "volunteers" to fight in Laos. They were accused by some members of the U.S. Congress of being involved in clandestine activities, but if so these were never brought to the surface.[11]

Nearly all of the Special Forces have been withdrawn from Thailand. It is also expected that the Thai government will demand further reductions in U.S. military buildup in the coming years. But the American military presence in Thailand will continue. This is visible evidence that not only is America prepared to engage in a future military conflict in Southeast Asia if necessary, but also that American interests in Southeast Asia are of an abiding nature.

THE NEW RELATIONSHIP BETWEEN THE UNITED STATES AND TAIWAN

American military presence in Taiwan is at a much lower level than in Thailand. But is has to be noted that the Mutual Defense Treaty signed between the United States and Taiwan in 1954 remains intact despite the Nixon visit to Peking. Some 3,000 U.S. servicemen continue to be based on Taiwan. The Seventh Fleet, which was interposed between Taiwan and mainland China by President Truman immediately after the Korean war began, roams from the East China Sea to the Bay of Bengal and the Indian Ocean, not only guarding Taiwan against any attack, but guarding American interests all over Southern Asia. The yearly multimillion dollar military aid program to Taiwan continues ($120 million in 1971), which provides for the modernization of Nationalist armed forces, the training of naval personnel in submarine warfare, and also for the purchase of military supplies such as jets, artillery, and other equipment.

Furthermore, the Pentagon, with an eye to the future, apparently would like to increase American use of Taiwan. It has become public knowledge that the Pentagon has advocated transferring U.S. nuclear weapons storage facilities from Okinawa to Taiwan, where there already is a small stockpile. Taiwan's air base runways, which the Nationalists have been expanding since the late 1960s to accommodate B-52s, may also be attractive to Defense Department planners. . . .[12]

Mutual defense pacts signed by America with the Philippines in 1951 and with South Korea in 1953 are still very much alive. While American armed forces are not represented in significant numbers in these states, their influence is still heavy and unmistakable in the form of military advisers and substantial military aid programs. In the case of the Philippines, after she received her independence from the United States, she continued to permit American air and naval forces to remain on her soil. The status of these forces was not affected by the 1951 treaty. In 1958 the U.S.-Philippines Mutual Defense Board was established to provide consultation and cooperation between the two countries on defense matters, outside the framework of SEATO. This cooperation was very much in evidence when POWs were brought home from Vietnam recently. Clark Air Base served as a crucial stopover in their journey from South Vietnam to the United States. Similarly, when the Pentagon moved the 24-plane squadron of EB-66 twin-jet electronic jamming and monitoring aircraft from Korat Air Base in Bangkok in January 1974, it was transferred to Clark Air Base in the Philippines.

These activities may not be eye-catching, but they should not leave any doubt in one's mind that the U.S. considers this area as her extended frontier in the Pacific. As Richard Nixon wrote before becoming President:

The United States is a Pacific power. Europe has been withdrawing the remnants of empire, but the United States, with its coast reaching in an arc from Mexico to the Bering Straits, is one anchor of a vast Pacific community. Both our interests and our ideals propel us westward across the Pacific, not as conquerors but as partners, linked by the sea not only with those oriental nations on Asia's Pacific littoral but at the same time with occidental Australia and New Zealand, and with the island nations between.[13]

U.S. RELATIONS WITH INDONESIA UNDER SUHARTO

Continued existence of Mutual Defense Pacts bears testimony to the fact that U.S. does not consider détente with China and Russia by itself an adequate source of guarantee for the security interests of Southeast Asian states. Moreover, Washington probably would not discourage other Asian states from relying on America for security purposes. In this regard it is noteworthy that the growing presence of the Soviet Union in the Indian Ocean and other border areas has prompted the United States to strive for closer ties with Indonesia, and to establish a naval base in the Indian Ocean.

The geographical location of Indonesia, situated between the Indian and Pacific Oceans, holds great appeal for American military strategists. President Nixon, before assuming office, said in one of his writings: "Indonesia constitutes by far the greatest prize in the Southeast Asian area." Until the overthrow of the Sukarno regime in 1965, the United States had no standing in Indonesia. It was in August 1965 that the then President Sukarno announced plans for the formation of an Indonesian-mainland Chinese axis whose objective would be to drive America and Britain out of Southwest Asia. But the following September Sukarno was overthrown, the Peking-oriented Communist Party smashed by the forces of General Suharto, who took over complete control of the government in March 1966. While the United States started a program of economic aid at this time, relations between the general and America remained cool between 1966 and 1970. Marshall Green, American ambassador to Indonesia during most of this period, advised Washington that American assistance to Indonesian armed forces should be limited to "engineering equipment for civic action projects only."

After the visit of General Suharto to Washington in 1970, however, there was a major change in U.S. policy. The Pentagon, which has always favored modernizing Indonesian armed forces, considering it essential for Indonesian security as well as the defense of Southeast Asia, is now busy taking steps in this direction. The U.S. military, logistical, and advisory group in Indonesia, which stood at 20 men in 1970, has increased to more than 100 officers and enlisted personnel in 1974. America supplied $5 million worth of military equipment and weapons to Indonesia in 1971. This figure has risen to $18 million today. The Indonesian high command, which includes many officers trained in U.S. military staff colleges, is being assisted by American teams to modernize the army, train the air force, and build the navy. The 40,000 man Indonesian Air Force has been supplied with F-86 Sabrejets, P-51 Mustangs, and C-47 transport planes by the United States. The navy has been given a destroyer escort, and flotillas of patrol craft to build enough strength so that it can now conduct coastal maneuvers jointly with some of the neighboring states.

Indonesia continues to purchase military hardware from the Soviet Union. But the growing influence of America becomes apparent when it is recognized that Indonesia has trained Cambodian soldiers for action in Cambodia, "and the 11 nation conference of foreign ministers that convened in Djakarta in May 1970 and called for the withdrawal of all 'foreign' forces from Cambodia acted in accord with American wishes."[14]

U.S. INTERESTS IN THE INDIAN OCEAN

The current military budget presented by the White House to the Congress includes a request for $29 million dollars to build the first permanent U.S. naval base in the Indian Ocean. In a confidential memo to the Congressional leaders, the State Department said:

> In our judgment, an adequate U.S. presence in the Indian Ocean provides a clear signal to the Soviets of our resolve to insure a credible military capability there. . . . The opening of the Suez Canal will obviously increase the Soviet ability . . . to show force to influence events where major U.S. interests are at stake.[15]

America seeks to build this naval base on the island of Diego Garcia, a part of the Chagos archipelago, located some 1,200 miles south of the tip of India in the Indian Ocean. The American government showed interest in this area in the sixties, when the British made it known that they intended to phase out their military presence in the Indian Ocean. In 1966 the United States and the United Kingdom signed a 50-year agreement whereby the British-owned island was leased to the United States, rent free, for joint defense purposes. The United States now has only a minor communications facility on the island. But reports of increasing Soviet presence in the Indian Ocean, and the possibility of the Russians securing a naval base on India's east coast, have spurred the demand for a matching presence on the part of America. During the "global alert" called by President Nixon in October 1973, with a view to challenging a potential Soviet military intervention in the Middle East conflict, a U.S. aircraft carrier task group was sent to the Indian Ocean. When the alert was over, it was revealed by the Defense Secretary that the U.S. Navy will not be called back, and that it will continue to patrol the area from now on. This has provided the navy with the opportunity to seek a permanent base in the Indian Ocean, because maintaining ships in this area with logistic support coming from the Subic Bay in the Philippines is considered impractical.

It is expected that were Congress to approve the appropriation, and already there are indications that it will, Diego Garcia will be turned into a base that will have a harbor to receive nuclear submarines, and runways to permit all types of U.S. planes to land there. It will also have fuel and storage facilities for both ships and planes. In addition there will be living facilities, which will be able to accommodate an American force of 500 to 600 men.

Some Congressmen are of the opinion that Diego Garcia is bound to become one of America's major naval bases abroad, and that the $29 million appropriation is only an initial investment. This is exactly what the littoral states in the area fear. India has been highly vocal in demanding that both the Soviet Union and the United States keep out of the Indian Ocean. She has been joined by Malaysia, Indonesia, Australia, New Zealand and Sri Lanka (Ceylon), whose representative introduced a resolution in the United Nations in 1971 that asked that the Indian Ocean be declared a "Zone of Peace." The super-powers have ignored all protests.

This leads one to conclude that the "New Balance of Power" as conceived by Nixon and Kissinger, on the one hand allows for extension of U.S. commitments beyond the level at which they stood at the time of the cease-fire in Vietnam, and that on the other hand accommodation and adjustment are instituted only when the interests of Russia or China come into direct collision with those of the United States. Interestingly enough, even though Japan has emerged as one of the major economic powers of the world, and her geographical location is a compelling reason for involvement in Southeast Asian affairs, she appears to be playing little or no role in the power plays of the United States, Russia, and China in this region.

THE UNITED STATES AND JAPAN

The U.S. policy makers seldom fail to mention that an effective balance-of-power system today demands the participation of Japan. But Japan is not a nuclear power. Even as a close ally she was neither consulted nor informed about U.S. intentions to normalize relations with China in 1971. Ironically, Japan continues to refuse to build sufficient armed strength to shoulder the burden of her own defense or the defense of the Southeast Asian region.

The American bilateral security pact with Japan, which came into force in April 1952, still remains the bulwark of protection for Japan against any attack from outside. Under the provisions of this treaty American forces remain on Japanese soil. These armed forces can also be deployed in any manner seen fit by the United States to keep peace in East Asia and Southern Asia. There was speculation in the sixties that the Japanese people would call for major revisions in the treaty when it came up for review. In 1960 and then in 1970, the treaty was revised; but the revisions were minor. The major provisions of the treaty remain intact. It is, however, now stipulated that there will be prior consultation between the two governments before American forces stationed on Japanese soil are used for "peacekeeping" operations abroad. But otherwise the United States still remains Japan's shield against any potential aggressor. Thus militarily speaking if there is such a thing as a balance of power in Southeast Asia, it is tripartite in its dimensions.

The president and the secretary of state have made statements to the effect that they encourage regional cooperation on security and economic matters. The efforts made in this direction by countries involved have borne some fruit in the economic and cultural sphere, but the matter of security appears beyond the reach of these states. At the time when the Asia and Pacific Council was born in June 1966, there were some who hoped that in the future the council might serve as a foundation stone for a regional security arrangement. In the eighth year of existence, ASPAC shows no signs that its objectives will extend beyond the limits of cooperation in economic, cultural, and social matters. At the Bangkok meeting in 1967, Japan's Foreign Minister Takeo Miki expressed the hope that ASPAC's activities would not be of a kind to arouse the suspicion in any circles that this regional association was created out of a perceived threat from any quarters and nurtured fears of aggression from any source. But if this body has ignored the security aspect, it is not difficult to understand why. With the exception of Malaysia, whose defense is now guaranteed by Britain through a Five Power Agreement, which went into effect in November 1971, all the members of ASPAC—Australia, Japan, New Zealand, the Philippines, South Korea, South Vietnam, Taiwan, and Thailand—are bound to the United States by mutual defense pacts or other security guarantees. Since the United States has repeatedly said that she will not break these bonds, prospects of self-reliance or mutual reliance for security purposes on the part of these states are nil. They have neither the collective will nor the capability to survive on their own.

THE UNITED STATES AND INDOCHINA
SINCE THE CEASE-FIRE

As the cold war tensions fade, neutrality and nonalignments have become acceptable foreign policy postures. But like China and Russia, the United States has not encouraged or initiated efforts toward turning Southeast Asia into a neutral zone by physically vacating the area and providing a tripartite guarantee for its stability and security. The fact of the matter is that mutual suspicion and fear among the great powers is still strong, détente and balance-of-power strategy notwithstanding. Cambodia and Laos are tragic examples of this.

Cambodia's Prince Sihanouk had succeeded in maintaining a measure of security and stability in his state under the umbrella of proclaimed neutralism all through the sixties. Bending with the reality of the geographical location of his state and its limited capabilities, he tolerated communist troops and supply lines supporting the Viet Cong in the border areas of South Vietnam. In March 1970 his regime was overthrown, with the blessing of the United States. Field Marshall Lon Nol, who took over the government of Cambodia, not only wanted the communist troops out of the country, but he was also ready to welcome American military aid and advisers to accomplish his goal. Soon after his assumption of power, American and South Vietnamese troops moved into Cambodia in April 1970, allegedly to wipe out the North Vietnamese sanctuaries in the Cambodia-South Vietnam border areas.

Cambodia was not a party to the Paris agreements; nor do these agreements deal with the question of a Cambodian political settlement. But since March 1970 this nation has remained in constant state of war between forces that seek to reinstate Prince Sihanouk, who is in exile in Peking, and the forces of General Lon Nol.

American air strikes in Cambodia, which began with the other operations in 1970 in support of Lon Nol's armies, continued until August 1973 when a congressional amendment ordered an end to American air activities in Indochina. With American help Cambodian troops are being trained in Thailand for combat readiness. While the Pentagon admits to the presence of a 27-man army attaché staff in the American Embassy in Cambodia, and also confirms that a 76-man military equipment delivery team is there, it insists that all U.S. "advisers" and "combat troops" have been withdrawn. The Pentagon neglects to explain that these Americans continue to perform advisory functions, and that it pays foreign nationals to do the jobs Americans previously did.*

The foreign aid bills signed by President Nixon in January 1974 contained $2.4 billion in emergency aid for Israel and Cambodia. The Pentagon was unhappy that this would not permit them to supply $200 million worth of extra arms for Cambodia. It should be noted that the United States pays for all Cambodian oil supplies needed for civilian and military use, at the cost of $1.4 million a month. As of the spring 1974, the total military and economic support of government forces in Cambodia was costing the Americans $1.5 million daily.

Laos was guaranteed neutrality by an international agreement in 1962. Civil war has raged in Laos between the Pathet Lao and American backed Royal Lao forces since 1963. Repercussions of the Vietnam War led to heavy involvement in Laos on the part of the United States. American air strikes

---

*Congressional order limits the military and diplomatic staff in Cambodia to no more than 200 persons.

against supply lines coming along the Ho Chi Minh trail situated in Southeastern Laos, began as early as 1966. A steady increase in the bombing ensued, and under Nixon-Kissinger policy heavy bombing on a daily basis against virtually every conceivable target became a regular feature of U.S. action in Laos. The Vietnam cease-fire did not change the picture. Only when Congress acted firmly against this in August 1973 did the American bombing come to a halt.

Formally, the civil war ended in Laos on 4 April 1974. King Savang Vatthana signed a decree appointing a new Laotian coalition government in which the Vientiane and Pathet Lao will share power equally. Whether this will bring an end to outside intervention in the affairs of Laos is yet to be seen. In the meantime some 1,000 U.S. military and civilian personnel, of whom nearly one-third are military advisers and trainers, continue to stay in Laos. No plans for their departure have been announced thus far.

The Paris agreements stated that "foreign countries shall put an end to all military activities in Cambodia and Laos." It was also agreed that the internal affairs of these states "shall be settled by the people of each of these countries without foreign interference." The situation in Laos and Cambodia has not even come close to meeting the spirit and the stated objectives of the Paris peace talks. In reality, what was negotiated in January 1973 was the release of American prisoners in exchange for total withdrawal of American combat troops in Vietnam. Even there, however, 16,000 Americans in various advisory capacities are still in Vietnam; and the war has by no means ended for the Vietnamese. During the fiscal year ending in June 1974, the Congress allocated $1.12 billion for military aid to South Vietnam. While the House turned down a request by the Pentagon for supplemental funds to the tune of $474 million, Representative Otis Pike (Democrat, N.Y.) made the statement: "The American people are not in a mood to abandon South Vietnam, but they're in a mood to question how much money they should pay."[16] At about the same time that Congress was dealing with the issue of increased military aid to Saigon, it was reported by the press that in a letter to Senator Edward Kennedy, Secretary of State Henry Kissinger said that the United States is morally and politically committed to long-term military assistance to South Vietnam.

These are the stark realities of American activities in Southeast Asia in the aftermath of the cease-fire in Vietnam. There is one restraint which has been imposed by the Congress on all future action. The Congress passed a joint resolution in November 1973, overriding the veto of President Nixon. The "War Powers Resolution," as it is formally known, places limitations upon the prerogatives of the Executive branch in the "introduction of United States Armed Forces into hostilities, or into situations where imminent involvement in hostilities is clearly indicated by the circumstances, and to the continued use of such forces in hostilities or in such situations." Among other things this resolution mandates that the president inform the Congress within 48 hours if American troops become involved in hostilities abroad. It further enjoins the president to terminate engagement of troops after 60 days, unless the Congress has declared war.[17]

How much effect this will have on presidential initiative in American involvement abroad, only time will tell. In the immediate future what it says is that the American public and Congress are in no mood to accept again a massive military commitment in Southeast Asia—which, of course, is no guarantee against other types of involvement and commitment.

Nation-states and policy makers are given to wrapping up their foreign policy postures in general phrases such as "balance of power." It spares them the agony of telling the public and the world in straightforward terms what their real intentions are, or what deeds they will lead to. The policy maker will, of course, claim that this is done to introduce that element of secrecy and uncertainty in foreign policy that is the hallmark of astute diplomacy, and which also reserves for the nation the benefit of flexibility. But these are subjects of perennial debate in world politics.

As discussed by Melvin Gurtov in Chapter 1, it is difficult to determine exactly what a statesman means when he employs the term "balance of power" to describe a foreign policy, certain goals, or certain actions or intentions. On close scrutiny, the Nixon-Kissinger designs in Southeast Asia turn out to be:

1. Defense ties will continue and shall be honored.
2. Military assistance programs will not be halted; they will continue and might very well be extended.
3. While ground troop involvement will be shunned, unless there is a direct attack on territory where troops are present or where the United States has an explicit defense commitment, air and naval intervention will be executed whenever deemed necessary.
4. A direct clash between the U.S. forces and Chinese or Russian forces will be avoided.
5. U.S. interests will be considered as involved in any instance in which a Southeast Asian state is threatened by a major hostile power or, in the case of Indochina, by North Vietnam.
6. The United States will continue to pour economic and military aid into the area to sustain friendly regimes, and to thwart revolutionary efforts.

Thus U.S. intervention and containment will continue in Southeast Asia, only in less obvious forms than in previous Administrations.

NOTES

1. As quoted in Los Angeles *Times*, 24 February 1974.

2. *U.S. Foreign Policy For The 1970's* (Washington, D.C.: Government Publications Office, 1971), pp. 12-14.

3. Townsend Hoopes, "Legacy of the Cold War in Indochina," *Foreign Affairs* 48, no. 4 (July 1970): 604.

4. Ibid.

5. Consult *The Pentagon Papers* for a detailed account of American military effort.

6. Government Publications Office, op. cit., pp. 13, 62-63.

7. John Spanier, *American Foreign Policy Since World War II* (New York: Praeger Publishers, 1973), p. 253.

8. Text of background briefing, San Clemente, 24 August 1970, as quoted by David Landau in *Kissinger: The Uses of Power* (Boston: Houghton Mifflin, 1972), p. 106.

9. Richard M. Nixon, "Asia After Vietnam," *Foreign Affairs* 46, no. 1 (October 1967): 113.

10. Los Angeles *Times*, 14 October 1973.

11. Statistics and related information have been drawn from reports of Jack Foisie as they appeared in Los Angeles *Times* on different occasions.

12. Melvin Gurtov, "Security by Proxy: The Nixon Doctrine and Southeast Asia," in Mark Zacher and Stephen Milne, eds., *Conflict and Stability in Southeast Asia* (New York: Doubleday, 1974), p. 232.

13. Richard M. Nixon, op. cit., p. 112.

14. Gurtov, op. cit., p. 229.

15. As quoted in *The New Republic*, 9 March 1974, p. 7.

16. Los Angeles *Times*, 5 April 1974.

17. *United States Code: Congressional and Administrative News* (St. Paul: West Publishing Co., 1973) no. 11, 15 December 1973, pp. 4064-4067.

CHAPTER
3
THE SOVIET
PERSPECTIVE
Robert C. Horn

During the late 1950s and the early 1960s Southeast Asia was the scene of considerable rivalry between the Soviet Union and the Chinese People's Republic. Their striving for influence in the area may well have begun as early as the Asian-African conference in Bandung, Indonesia, in April 1955, when uninvited Moscow had to watch helplessly from the sidelines as Peking's Chou En-lai appeared to score great successes. Thereafter, into the 1960s, the two communist competitors focused their attention primarily on Indonesia as the most significant (considering strategic location and potential power) and most anticolonial state in the region, and to a lesser extent on Burma and the states of Indochina.

This direct competition endured until the anticommunist, anti-Chinese aftermath of Indonesia's *Gestapu* of 1 October 1965. Destruction of the powerful, CPR-aligned Indonesian Communist Party (PKI) and the political demise of President Sukarno meant a radical alteration of the country's foreign policy and, particularly, an abrogation of the Djakarta-Peking axis. Moscow's response to this Chinese setback was a more active and diversified Southeast Asian policy. No longer were relations with Malaysia and Singapore precluded because of Soviet identification (however reluctant and equivocal) with Sukarno's *konfrontasi*. Thailand and the Philippines also came to receive increased Soviet attention. Meanwhile, Peking began to turn away from regional and other foreign policy concerns in favor of the inward focus of the Great Proletarian Cultural Revolution. Until 1969, competition between the USSR and the CPR slackened as the latter focused its very limited international attention on communist-led insurrections and the spread of Mao Tse-tung thought. Since early 1969, however, particularly because of China's gradual

Portions of this chapter are from the author's article "Changing Soviet Policies and Sino-Soviet Competition in Southeast Asia," *ORBIS* 17, no. 2 (Summer 1973): 493-526. By permission.

reemergence into world politics, accompanied by more traditional forms of behavior, it has been renewed. The confluence of national and regional (endogenous) and international (exogenous) determinants beginning in that year have only intensified this Sino-Soviet competition for influence. The likely continuation of this rivalry significantly structures the possibility of balance in Southeast Asia. The genuine equilibrium aspect of a balance, then, seems remote so long as two of the main external powers, the Soviet Union and China, view each other with hostility and distrust and base their policies largely on competition with the other.

SOVIET PRIORITIES AND GOALS
IN SOUTHEAST ASIA

Southeast Asia does not seem to contain an interest considered "vital" by Moscow. In the initial years after 1964, the Brezhnev-Kosygin regime lowered the priority of the Third World as a whole and replaced the Khrushchevian optimism with a more realistic view of the prospects for Soviet gains there.[1] Moreover, even within the developing world, the Middle East and South Asia seem to rank as areas of greater Soviet interest than Southeast Asia. Pursuit of the Soviet goal of the reduction of American influence would seem to be promisingly and crucially affected in the Middle East, Western Europe, and Japan than Southeast Asia. By the same token, in the effort to contain Chinese influence, South Asia and Japan are clearly seen as more significant than Southeast Asia in the Soviet perspective. Nevertheless, while the post-Khrushchev leaders have approached the Third World with greater caution and with lesser expectations than their enthusiastic predecessor did in the 1950s, they have reversed Khrushchev's policy of disengagement from Southeast Asia (especially Vietnam). Moreover, given the record to be examined below it would seem that Southeast Asia does not rank very far below the Middle East and South Asia in Soviet priorities in the Third World. Most importantly, the USSR considers itself an Asian power as well as a major world power and, at minimum, seeks recognition by other Asian powers and by the Southeast Asians themselves of this fact and a granting by all of them of a substantial Soviet voice in the region's affairs. This minimal Russian objective would seem to indicate that Southeast Asia will continue to be viewed as an important region even if not of vital interest to Soviet policy.

Given the aggregate of Soviet goals in world politics, then, Southeast Asia still looms as a significant arena for Moscow. While it is difficult to assess the precise ranking of various goals, it certainly seems that beyond the fundamental one of gaining recognition as a world and Asian power, the USSR seeks in the region primarily the containment of China. From the Soviet perspective, China aspires to attain political and ideological leadership in Southeast Asia (and elsewhere). Chinese influence in Southeast Asia historically and potentially, of course, makes the region that much more significant to Moscow as far as the Chinese pursuit of this goal is concerned. Second, the Soviets seek to reduce the influence of the United States in the area. Although it is likely that the

United States is viewed as much less of a threat in the region than the CPR, as part of the global struggle against capitalism, the anti-American effort must be continued everywhere, including Southeast Asia. Another Russian goal is the limitation of growing Japanese influence in the area. Soviet concern has deepened as Japanese economic involvement increases. The rapidly expanding Soviet navy has given Moscow further incentives in Southeast Asia (as well as Soviet interest in the area being one cause of the naval buildup in the first place) for influence in the region. These include bases or at least docking and repair facilities, as well as free access through such bodies of water as the Straits of Malacca, in order to increase the Soviet presence in the Indian Ocean, the Persian Gulf, and elsewhere. Finally, the Russians have economic interests in Southeast Asia and Japan and seek expanded opportunities for trade and markets. It is, then, a mix of these goals along with the basic effort to expand the Soviet presence regionally as befits a superpower and an Asian power, which has conditioned Soviet behavior in Southeast Asia over the last several years.

NEW INCENTIVES FOR SOVIET POLICY

A large number of far-reaching developments have combined to produce the vastly changed and still changing picture of Soviet involvement in Southeast Asia. The Soviet leadership change in 1964 and the substantial expansion of the Soviet navy during the 1960s are conspicuous on the Soviet level, but shifts have also occurred on other levels: within the Southeast Asian states, regionally, and in international politics. Taken together, these interrelated modifications have created a radically new environment for Southeast Asians and for the Soviet Union and other powers.

Among the changes within the states of the region, the abrupt turn in Indonesia in 1965-66 was undoubtedly the most significant, standing as a bench mark in virtually any study of Southeast Asia. *Gestapu* and its aftermath drastically transformed the international relations of the area. While it hardly led to a warm embrace between Moscow and Jakarta, it allowed the Soviets somewhat to restore relations with Indonesia and it destroyed what had been thought to be a brilliant success of Chinese foreign policy. Furthermore, it facilitated a renewed role in Indonesia for the United States and led to the end of Sukarno's confrontation against Malaysia, thus removing a destabilizing factor and encouraging the Southeast Asian countries to investigate regional cooperation once again.

The new atmosphere of decreased tension also afforded the countries in the area the opportunity to consider greater independence from outside powers and this became, in varying degrees, a noticeable aspect of their internal and foreign politics. A parallel development was the increasing assertion of nationalism in many of the region's states. While fueled by changing U.S. policies, this trend had significant indigenous roots. Additionally, in some quarters there was a renewed awareness after 1969 that the Peking regime was a constant and real factor with which a *modus vivendi* had to be reached.

On the regional level, perhaps the most significant shift was the enuncia-
tion of the Nixon Doctrine by the U.S. President while in Guam in mid-1969.
No matter how unclear its precise meaning, the Nixon Doctrine, when coupled
with the beginnings of American withdrawal from Indochina, seemed to augur a
greatly reduced American presence in the region. This has had an impact on all
area states, not only those closely allied to the United States. In addition, the
rapidly expanding Japanese economic footholds have fostered changes, particularly in trade, aid, and investment patterns. While the declining American role is
in the interests of the Soviet Union and China, neither country's leaders wish to
see the resulting power vacuum filled by Japan.

There have of course also been external changes of such overwhelming
significance in world politics that Southeast Asia could hardly escape their
impact. The CPR's withdrawal inward and initial isolation after the Indonesian
debacle left the USSR with an open field and greater opportunities to advance
its interests. Subsequently, the turmoil and excesses of the Cultural Revolution
in China between 1966 and 1968 increased the insecurity of many of Peking's
neighbors and inclined them to search more actively for security-granting
relationships with outside powers. Beginning in 1969, however, this picture
began to change. In March of that year, the Soviets and Chinese engaged in a
bloody clash along their border. Tensions between the two escalated to a
dangerous high, triggering fear of a full-scale war and a possible Soviet preemptive nuclear strike. Moreover, Chinese apprehensions were heightened not
only by the threatening Soviet buildup along their mutual border during 1968,
but also by the Soviet-led invasion of Czechoslovakia, which was quickly
justified by the menacing Brezhnev Doctrine of "limited sovereignty" with its
potentially broad application to any socialist state.

All of this provided a substantial impetus to China's reappearance in
international politics. What seemed gradually to materialize was a more
moderate and more pragmatic Chinese foreign policy, less identified with
militant ideology and the spread of violent revolution and more interested in
traditional state-to-state relations. The anti-Soviet emotionalism of the Cultural
Revolution and the border clashes encouraged the Soviets to step up efforts to
"contain" China. Peking's emergence from its international isolation in 1969
only gave Moscow added incentive to try to limit the CPR's influence. Perhaps
the most significant development of all was the indication of a transformation
in Sino-American relations, which gained plausibility soon after Richard Nixon
came to office in the United States, and reached fruition with his visit to China
in early 1972. The evolution of this development further convinced the Soviets
of the utter necessity of consolidating their position vis-à-vis both Peking and
Washington and of seeking strenuously to limit the influence of both powers.
The record of Soviet behavior since 1969 reveals intense efforts in this direction concerning China, the United States, and also Japan. This accelerated
Soviet involvement was to find fruition dramatically in South Asia—with
the change in Moscow's regional posture leading to the Soviet-Indian treaty
of 1971 and Soviet support for India in the Bangladesh conflict—but
Southeast Asia was also to be an important arena for new Soviet
initiatives.

RECENT SOVIET POLICIES IN COUNTRIES
OF SOUTHEAST ASIA

The Southeast Asian states exhibit great diversity in their political and economic systems, levels of economic development, relations with each other and relations with external powers. For this reason, the most promising analytical path would seem to be to examine each "target" country individually in light of the themes we are exploring: changing Soviet policies, the nature of Sino-Soviet competition, and the factors that have caused these policy changes and made for different Soviet approaches to different countries. A certain pattern emerges in dealing separately with each state. Indonesia and Burma stand out as the parameters of Soviet and Chinese policies and accomplishments: they are the respective arenas in which Moscow and Peking have been investing perhaps their most significant efforts while confronted with relatively little competition from the other. Malaysia and Singapore (treated together since they share so many of the aspects under consideration) rank lower than Indonesia and Burma in emphasis given by the two powers, but both Moscow and Peking are actively involved. These two states as well as the states of Indochina can be analyzed as the arenas of the most direct competition. Lastly, the Philippines and Thailand will be seen as arenas of the least competition and movement.

Indonesia

The USSR's relations with Indonesia[2] in the post-*Gestapu* years and prior to 1969 fall into two periods. Until mid-1968, the Kremlin's new leaders had not allowed the anti-PKI (Partai Komunis Indonesia) "terror" in Indonesia to torpedo relations, but had approached Indonesia cautiously, hardly anxious to be effusive toward the country while it seemed to be exchanging a pro-Peking stance for a pro-Washington one. The Soviets issued protestations with little conviction about the treatment of Indonesian "progressives" and warned the country of the dangers of Western "neocolonialism." As Indonesian Foreign Minister Adam Malik charged quite accurately, the Soviets adopted a "hesitant wait-and-see attitude toward Indonesia." In mid-1968, relations between the USSR and Indonesia worsened substantially. Apparently regarding as a failure their compromise attempt to foster closer relations while slowing down Jakarta's internal anticommunism and external pro-West sentiments, Soviet leaders adopted a harder line. For the next year the Indonesian regime was consistently branded as fascist by the Soviets and encouragement and hopes were expressed for the revival of a Moscow-oriented Communist Party in Indonesia. The upsurge of Soviet interest in a new PKI followed immediately on the heels of the crushing in East Java of a Chinese-supported underground PKI. Violent and bitter exchanges between Moscow and Peking as to which was the rightful beacon for the Indonesian revolution followed through the spring of 1969.

In mid-1969, however, when it appeared that Moscow had strained relations with Jakarta to no gain, Soviet policy began to shift once more, this time
back in the pre-1968 direction. As long as the Soviets were not faced with
Chinese competition in postcoup Indonesia, they felt they could be more
detached and cooler with regard to the new Indonesian government, and try
meanwhile to gain control over what was left of the Indonesian communist
movement. There was little risk that Peking would try to undercut the Kremlin
by halting its denunciation of the Suharto regime and improving relations with
it. But by mid-1969, the Soviets realized that the hard line toward Jakarta was
not working. Their attempt to gain control over Indonesian communism had
come to nothing; the Moscow-oriented PKI remained small and ineffectual. In
addition, the Sino-Soviet border clashes had occurred in the meantime and a
more pragmatic China had begun to emerge from its previous isolation to
assume a more active international role. Although there were no dramatic
Chinese overtures toward Jakarta, Chinese enthusiasm for the Indonesian
communists had noticeably cooled by late 1968. Moscow sensed that Peking's
new moderation might soon alter the equation.

Symbolic of this change in Soviet policy in 1969 was the dispatch of a
new ambassador to Jakarta in August, accompanied by assurances that the
Soviet Union stood for noninterference in the internal affairs of other states
(an obvious swipe at Peking). In corroboration of these assurances Moscow's
idea of a new PKI was played down, although not totally ignored.[3] Also
signaling changing Soviet policies was the arrival in Jakarta in September of a
fifteen-man delegation to discuss another rescheduling of Indonesia's debt.
Even though no agreement was signed after a month of talks—indicating that
there still would be no return to the Khrushchev era of "give-aways"—
Moscow's willingness to discuss the issue that Indonesia had been trying to raise
virtually since signing the last agreement, showed that the USSR's shifting
attitude might be reflected in material changes. Indeed, after a fruitless visit to
Moscow by Foreign Minister Malik in February 1970, the Soviets finally agreed
in August of that year to another rescheduling with terms comparing closely to
those granted by Indonesia's western creditors.

Moscow has followed these gestures of 1969 and 1970 with gradual moves
toward a resumption of economic aid and cooperation. Malik returned from
Moscow in August 1970 saying that the Soviets had agreed in principle to
extend economic aid to Indonesia—which may be the USSR's way of signifying
explicit interest in a *quid pro quo*, an interest that has been characteristic of
the current leadership's view of the Third World. In July 1971, Moscow and
Jakarta signed an agreement to study the feasibility of resuming work on two
major Soviet aid projects: the steel mill at Tjilegon (West Java), and the
superphosphate plant at Tjilatjap (Central Java). In August a large technical
team from the USSR arrived in Indonesia to undertake the study. Moscow was
also partly responsible for the increase in trade between the two countries.
Total volume was higher in 1969 and 1970 than in 1968 and Soviet imports of
Indonesian rubber increased in 1970 amid claims that Soviet purchases in 1971
would be three times greater than those of 1970. In May 1972 the two sides
exchanged a list of export goods in an effort to increase trade.

Moscow's gradual and cautious approach has been matched by the
Suharto regime's own hesitation in its dealings with the Soviet Union. Jakarta

has not yet decided whether the USSR will take part in finishing the Tjilegon and Tjilatjap plants. In connection with military aid, Indonesian commentary has criticized Soviet training programs, spare parts supplies, and financial terms. The chief of the Air Force Operations Command asserted in late 1970 that Indonesia would buy no more military hardware of any kind from the USSR. In April 1971, when the Soviets offered Jakarta $4-5 million worth of spare parts on credit—rather than cash only—the chief of staff of the Indonesian Navy, Admiral Sudomo, rejected the offer. Shortly thereafter, General Panggabean, deputy commander-in-chief of the Armed Forces, also revealed a Soviet offer of military aid, on which thus far no action has been taken.

Moscow's analyses of Indonesia's internal and external affairs after mid-1969 provided further indication of a conciliatory if still qualified Soviet attitude toward the country. Although skeptical of the July 1971 general elections and critical of the ban on communist participation in them, for example, the Kremlin's tone was moderate. Moreover, contrasting sharply with the Chinese press, which allowed the Peking-resident PKI leader Jusuf Adjitorop, a regular forum in which he attacked the "general election farce" of the "fascist military rulers" and their "imperialist masters," Soviet commentators warmed considerably after the election, and the Soviet ambassador congratulated Golkar (the government's electoral apparatus) on its victory as a triumph for democracy and the people of Indonesia. The USSR's view of Jakarta's foreign policy also softened during 1970 and 1971, and the tone and content of its comments marked a return to the pre-1968 position. For example, only "certain political quarters," rather than the Suharto regime itself, were accused of trying to get the country "to renounce the traditional policy of nonalignment" and to avoid normalization with socialist countries.[4]

What heartened Moscow was the increasing discussion of foreign policies within Indonesia in the latter half of 1971, spawned by changes in American economic policies in August, by the U.S. Senate's attempt to curtail foreign aid in October, and by Indonesia's positions (affirmative on the defeated U.S. resolution and an abstention on the successful Albanian one) on the votes concerning communist China's admission to the United Nations. Indonesian complaints of subordination to the United States were enthusiastically highlighted by Moscow. The panic in Indonesia caused by the U.S. policy changes was "graphic evidence of Indonesia's dependence on the United States and the West in general," wrote A. Yuriev in *New Times* in December 1971:

> These developments showed that those quarters in Indonesia are right who see a serious danger in one-sided orientation of the country's foreign ties, in its renunciation of an independent line in foreign relations. . . .
>
> Indonesians with their deep-seated traditions of struggle for national sovereignty and dignity are naturally annoyed and embittered by the fact that the West treats the republic as a second- or third-rate country. These moods tend to erode the positions of the rather influential pro-Western group in Jakarta which is doing its utmost to prevent Indonesia from pursuing an independent policy in its economic and political relations with other countries.

Yuriev concluded:

> There is a growing awareness in Indonesian political circles that
> having weakened its links with the socialist and Third World coun-
> tries in recent years, the republic is in danger of finding itself isolated
> on the world arena. . . .

Two months later, Moscow must have been pleased when the influential
Jakarta daily, *Pedoman* (thought to be closely associated with Adam Malik and
the Foreign Ministry), advocated raising relations with the USSR, especially in
light of U.S. President Nixon's visit to China.

A disquieting aspect of the Indonesian foreign policy discussion for the
Soviets, however, was that it broached the idea of restoring relations with
Peking. Although it was the CPR's entry into the UN that accelerated the
discussion in the Indonesian press and softened anti-Chinese positions per-
ceptibly, there had been signs in 1969 and 1970 of Indonesian initiatives
toward Peking. During 1971 Malik dealt with the Rumanians and Yugoslavs as
intermediaries and talked with representatives of both countries both in
Indonesia and during a visit to Eastern Europe. In July, however, he revealed
that the CPR had not shown the good will he had been anticipating and that
Peking would have to stop trying to subvert the Suharto Government through
support for guerrillas (especially in Kalimantan), cease support for Indonesian
emigrés in China, and halt Radio Peking's daily beaming of propaganda into
Indonesia, if progress was to be made. Despite some increase in trade—it had
been suspended in 1967-68—Indonesian Trade Minister Sumitro continued
to oppose any trade normalization with China. In Indonesian political circles
and the press, calls for the restoration of relations have been mixed with
criticisms of Chinese policy and questioning of the economic value of ties with
China.[5]

Responsibility for the nonmovement in relations seems also to rest with
Peking. The Chinese leadership, although less enthusiastic about the PKI and
while dropping occasional hints favoring trade normalization, has been unresponsive to reported Indonesian overtures. Still, enough potential exists for a
Sino-Indonesian rapprochement to make Moscow wary. Behind-the-scenes
Soviet diplomatic efforts to keep Indonesia from "the consequences of a return
of the Chinese to Indonesia" have been reported. Undoubtedly, the Soviets
have tried to use the resumption of aid as a bargaining lever in this regard. They
have also sought to link the American and Chinese threats to Indonesia; Yuriev
described the "developing rapprochement between Washington and Peking" as
being carried out "behind the backs of the Southeast Asian countries." Finally,
the Kremlin has attempted to prevent any improvement in Sino-Indonesian
relations by exposing the adventurism that Peking advocates for Indonesian
communism.

Burma

In stark contrast to the Indonesian picture, the situation in Burma is one
of significantly changing Chinese policies and improving Sino-Burmese relations

overshadowing lesser Soviet efforts. While Soviet relations with Rangoon are far more positive than Peking's with Jakarta, Soviet efforts in Burma's direction seem to have gained little for Moscow. This arena has been dominated (relative to other external major powers) by the CPR and the Chinese have restored a close relationship with Prime Minister Ne Win.

The USSR did seek to capitalize on Sino-Burmese difficulties during China's Cultural Revolution. The Kremlin seized on the 1967 crisis in relations between Rangoon and Peking to blame the "Mao Tse-tun group" for its provocation and to commend the Burmese government's energetic measures in restoring normal conditions. Premier Kosygin is reported to have sent Ne Win a message pledging "full support and sympathy for Burma in its troubles with China" and to have stepped into the "void" by offering the Burmese military and economic support.[6] Beginning in the latter part of 1969, however, China's approach to Burma gradually lessened in hostility. The subsequent improvement in relations was crowned with Ne Win's visit to the CPR in August 1971 and the revival of Chinese aid. Moscow's room for maneuver in the face of this new relationship seems to be restricted. While concentrating their efforts in Southeast Asia on states where Peking's stock is lower than it is in Burma—and the Sino-Burmese relationship has continued to warm into 1974—the Soviets still have not given up on Burma. Moscow has drawn Rangoon's attention to clandestine radio broadcasts from within China, which call for the overthrow of Ne Win's regime, and has also contended that the Chinese are engaged in training insurgents in Burma. In addition, the Soviets loudly attacked U Nu's campaign against Ne Win and have dispatched high level leaders to visit Burma (President Podgorny in October 1971 and Culture Minister Furtseva in February 1972). Moscow has consistently endorsed and praised Burma's new constitution, its internal progress, and its foreign policy stance of peaceful coexistence.[7] Finally, the Soviet leadership has stressed the growth of Soviet-Burmese trade and economic and technical cooperation. Despite these Soviet assertions and other efforts, however, the Soviet aid program appears to have all but dried up with the failure of a farm mechanization project the Russians had sponsored. Desperately in need of foreign loans if the Burmese road to socialism is to be salvaged, Rangoon still is only seeking 100,000 sterling from the Soviet Union as compared with 2.5 million and 9.4 million from the United States and Japan, respectively. Recently, the Soviets have seen the Rangoon government turn down a Russian offer to build an oil refinery and "forget" to invite Moscow to tender a bid (while inviting China and others) for a feasibility study on a project first studied by Soviet experts. A pervasive frustration with its limited role in Burma and with Sino-Burmese friendship—as well as the growth in Japanese-Burmese relations—is clearly evident in the Soviet approach.

Malaysia and Singapore

Moscow had equivocated in its support for Sukarno's anti-Malaysia campaign, so it was not surprising that the Soviets were quick to applaud the end to *konfrontasi* in 1966 and the restoration of Indonesian relations with both Malaysia and Singapore.

Singapore's expulsion from the Malaysian Federation in August 1965 had enabled Moscow to initiate changes in relations with Singapore more rapidly than with Malaysia. Trade delegations were exchanged with Singapore beginning in late 1965 and in late 1966 with Malaysia. The announcement of the withdrawal in the near future of British forces from the area and the perceived threat from a chaotic and revolutionary China dictated a search for new arrangements involving guarantees or balances by both governments. One response was an increased desire in Kuala Lumpur and Singapore to strengthen relations with the Soviet Union and Eastern Europe. Contacts were increased in 1967-69, and diplomatic relations were established between the USSR and both states in 1969.

Further changes came in Malaysian foreign policy with Tun Razak's assumption of the Prime Ministership in mid-1970. While seeking stronger ties with the Eastern bloc and reversing Malaysian policy of support for U.S. involvement in Vietnam—both of which Moscow saluted enthusiastically— Razak also expressed a willingness to enter into a dialogue with China. Singapore's concern for its security and its vulnerability heightened throughout 1970 and 1971 as it too sought to adjust, if somewhat more slowly, to the changing power balance in Asia. Although changes in relations with China have (as of early 1974) not led to the establishment of diplomatic relations between Peking and the two states, Moscow has reacted energetically to that perceived danger. On the most sensitive issues, communist insurgency and racialism, the Soviets have indicated their nonsupport and nonsympathy for the Malaysian Communist Party and toward Chinese efforts "To stir up trouble . . . by encouraging pro-Peking elements to drive a wedge between the Overseas Chinese and the Malays."[8] Perhaps the greatest Soviet emphasis is on trade and aid. Not only does Moscow have a trade agreement with both Malaysia and Singapore, but so do a number of its East European allies. It has made strenuous efforts to convince the two states of the advantages of doing more business with the USSR. The Soviets held a large-scale trade fair in Kuala Lumpur in late 1970 and a substantial machine tools exhibition in Singapore in early 1971. *Pravda* (13 April 1971) hailed the latter as "the first opportunity . . . representatives of business circles and industrial enterprises in this part of Asia have had to become broadly familiar with products of the Soviet machine tool industry." The Soviet paper went on to applaud the growth of Soviet-Singapore trade, the increasing diversity of items besides rubber on the trading list, and the fact that it was Soviet ships that did the carrying. An agreement for ship repair and servicing facilities has also led to an increasing number of Soviet ships calling at Singapore. On the subject of aid, Soviet Ambassador Kuznetsov stated in a speech over Radio Kuala Lumpur that the USSR was ready to cooperate with Malaysia in technical projects, industrial ventures, and the training of scientific and technical personnel, and was prepared to supply the country with nuclear power stations, cement factories, and many other enterprises.

But trade climbed slowly and Malaysia especially was unresponsive to Soviet offers of technical assistance.[9] The USSR's balance of trade with both states was heavily unfavorable. Thus, the Soviets' main efforts were to improve their own exports and develop the Southeast Asian countries as markets for

Soviet goods rather than merely suppliers of raw materials. In this connection, Peking's efforts to increase its trade with Malaysia and Singapore compounded Moscow's problems. To diplomats and traders in the area it appeared that one of the main incentives for the Chinese trade mission to Malaysia in August 1971 was to deprive the USSR of a potential market. Peking is at an advantage in that its trade balance with Malaysia and Singapore is favorable and thus it can appear eager to buy more goods from these two states, which already provide substantial markets for Chinese exports.

Perhaps the most direct challenge the Chinese have issued to the Soviets, in the interest of better relations with Malaysia and Singapore, was their offer in 1971-72 of ships to ply routes between Singapore/Malaysia and Europe and the Middle East. This was in response to pleas from the Southeast Asian states concerning the unfair rates and regulations imposed by the Far Eastern Freight Conference, and enabled the Chinese to catch up to the Soviets, who had made a similar offer in 1968. Peking's willingness to engage in direct competition with Moscow was apparent. Moscow's response has been the continuation of past efforts of building closer relations with Malaysia and Singapore.

Indochina

The war in Indochina involving the direct involvement of the United States singled out this area of Southeast Asia as far as the Soviet Union was concerned. The problems it has presented them are, if not unique, greatly different in degree from those presented elsewhere in the region.

The USSR has historically been confronted with a dilemma in dealing with the Democratic Republic of (North) Vietnam and the conflict in South Vietnam. On the one hand, Moscow has sought to prove that the USSR is more concerned and can do more about the revolutionary struggle of a fellow communist state than Peking. To this end it has given Hanoi extensive material and propaganda support. Public opinion benefits and the draining of U.S. power in a peripheral area are also in the USSR's interest. On the other hand, the Soviets have also been increasingly anxious through the 1960s for détente with the United States. Moreover, they have been increasingly wary of the possibilities of the escalation of local conflicts. These dangers counsel restraint, caution, and a reduced Soviet involvement. This dilemma has continuously provided the framework for Soviet policies in Indochina. Thus, although the Brezhnev-Kosygin leadership took the significant step of shifting the relative emphasis of the two extremes by reversing Khrushchev's disengagement and dramatically increasing Soviet support for North Vietnam beginning in 1965, Moscow still hedged and sought the proper opportunities to indicate subtly its desire for a negotiated settlement. The difficulty achieving such an ambiguous position clearly illustrated one further aspect of the problem of Indochina for the Russians: the extreme limitations of their influence. (Of course, this is also characteristic of Soviet relations with all the other Southeast Asian states.)

The changing relationships and alignments since 1969 have produced certain changes in Soviet policy. All have been, however, within this above framework. One aspect of the Soviet response has been the continuation of substantial Soviet military and economic aid. As a primary means of seeking influence, this assistance grew yearly through 1972.[10] Second, Moscow has stepped up its anti-Chinese efforts in Hanoi's direction. The Soviets attempted to capitalize on North Vietnam's uneasiness in the face of the beginnings of the U.S.-China détente. Podgorny's visit in October 1971, after Nixon's announcement but before the President's actual visit to Peking, is probably the most significant of many examples[11] of this Soviet approach. At the same time, Moscow was extremely sensitive to reassuring Hanoi that improving U.S.-*Soviet* relations would not be detrimental to Vietnamese interests. (Three high-ranking Soviet officials were dispatched to North Vietnam to reaffirm Soviet support within days of U.S. Presidential Adviser Henry Kissinger's secret visit to Moscow in April 1972.) Finally, there was evidence in 1971 and 1972 of an increased disenchantment on Moscow's part with the war and the risks involved. The Kremlin's fundamental position (one that it has held all along) was made clear in May 1972 when President Nixon's actions of mining and blockading North Vietnam's harbors just prior to his visit to the Soviet Union forced the Soviet leadership to make an unpleasant, if not unpredictable, decision. Although they denounced the American moves, the Russians did welcome Nixon to Moscow and the summit was carried out successfully. The Soviets issued an almost audible sigh of relief with the signing of "The Agreement on Ending the War and Restoring Peace in Vietnam" in January 1973. The Russians have hailed the agreement as a "glorious victory" for the Vietnamese people. They have also expressed confidence in U.S. trustworthiness and made clear to the Vietnamese that since Soviet prestige is also tied to the accord it ought not to be violated. The Soviets have further seized on the opportunity to assert that the historic victory was largely due to "the all-round fraternal assistance of the Soviet Union and other socialist countries. . . ."[12] Thus, Moscow continues to seek to capitalize on its aid (a significant trump card vis-à-vis China) while hoping fervently that the relative peace will last and they will, in fact, be extricated from their dilemma.

Soviet policies and fortunes in both Cambodia (Khmer Republic) and Laos have been intricately interwoven with developments in the Vietnam War. Moscow's increased attention to the former in 1968 and 1969—particularly in terms of military aid, visits and educational programs—probably directed against Chinese influence, was undermined by the overthrow of Prince Sihanouk in March 1970 and the emergence of a military regime increasingly allied with the United States. Although Moscow's stake in Cambodia is very small, as is the case in Laos, the Soviets had to respond in some manner. Basically, they tried a version of the dual policy that had been working adequately in Laos (the maintenance of friendly relations with the neutralist Royal Lao Government, headed by Souvanna Phouma, and material and propaganda support for the Lao Patriotic Front and Pathet Lao). In the Cambodian case, this led to the continued recognition of the new regime of Lon Nol in Phnom Penh—that is, support for the regime in power—while rather qualified support was also expressed for Sihanouk's newly established National

United Front. Clearly, one of the problems for Moscow was that Sihanouk had taken up residence in Peking and seemed increasingly tied to the Chinese. Moscow's rather uncomfortable position here gradually became more difficult after the American incursion into Cambodia and the accelerated cooperation between the Lon Nol regime and the United States against North Vietnam. Although Moscow's ambassador to Phnom Penh was withdrawn, diplomatic relations were maintained. The Soviet and the Czechoslovakian governments in August 1970 even defended the Lon Nol government's embassy in Prague against Sihanouk supporters. Moscow's attempts to offset this position by calling for the neutrality of the Cambodian government and by offers of military assistance to Sihanouk were rejected by the exiled Prince (among others). In fact, one of the most interestingly perceptive analyses of Soviet policy in Indochina was delivered by Sihanouk himself (in his typical, candid fashion) in an interview in December 1971:

> We no longer expect anything from the Russians. We are fighting side by side with socialist Vietnamese and left-oriented Laotians, who are both helped and recognised by the USSR. We too had hoped that Moscow would treat us accordingly. However, the Russians turned us down. Recently, they offered to give us military help and to recognise us as a Front. We simply said "No." We told them that we want to be recognised as a government per se. This is the only thing we want from them, and this is the one thing the Russians refuse us. They want to give us aid, but the Chinese already give us all we need. We have more aid than we can use. We only need one type of aid, and that is to be recognised as the legal government of Cambodia, but this the Russians refuse. . . .
>
> I think the Russians consider themselves white, and they do not want yellow people to become too strong. It would be difficult for the USSR not to help North Vietnam, which belongs to the socialist family of nations. But I have seen what the Russians give the North Vietnamese. I have seen the jet planes, the radars, the missiles. None of this equipment is up to date. In terms of both quantity and quality, the Russians have not given Hanoi a quarter of what they have given the Egyptians. Why? Because the Russians don't want Hanoi to win. They will give the Vietnamese just enough to keep them from losing the war but not enough to enable them to win it. Speaking as an Asian, I feel that the Russians want to keep Asians in a state of subservience. There is, in the Russian mind, a neurotic fear of an imaginary "yellow peril" embodied by China. By hindering the Indochinese, the Russians are aiming at China. The Americans are also motivated by this same fear of China. Their intervention in Vietnam is aimed at China. They kill the Vietnamese because they are afraid of the Chinese. As for the Soviets, they do the same thing: they refuse to help the Cambodians because they are afraid of China. Ultimately, both the Americans and the Russians are motivated by a common racism, a common fear of a "yellow peril" embodied by China.[13]

Nevertheless, the Soviets still sought to sit on the fence in Cambodia. It was not until two factors came together that the Kremlin felt compelled, in October 1973, to withdraw its recognition from Lon Nol and extend it to Sihanouk and his government-in-exile. First, there were the increasing gains during that year for insurgent forces in Cambodia. Lon Nol clearly looked less like a winning horse (and the Soviets quite consistently in Southeast Asia and elsewhere have chosen to support the likely winner). Second, Sihanouk attended the non-aligned summit conference in Algiers in September where he was well received *and* where he denounced Soviet policy in Cambodia.[14] Given its long record of efforts in the nonaligned world, Moscow could hardly rest easy in the face of Sihanouk's performance and reception. This, in addition to the perceived changing balance of forces within Cambodia, seemed to leave the Soviets little choice but to recognize the Sihanouk regime.

In retrospect, it would seem that the Russians would have preferred not to be involved in Cambodia or Laos. Both states are of great significance to North Vietnam, however, and influence in North Vietnam *is* a significant goal of Soviet policy. Moreover, much of the motivation for that goal is China, if not Soviet fear of China as Sihanouk has asserted, then certainly Soviet competition with and hostility toward the CPR.

The Philippines

The Philippines and Thailand have been less significant arenas of competitive Soviet and Chinese efforts. Not only does Manila not have diplomatic ties with Peking (outside of Indochina only Rangoon has diplomatic relations with Peking; Jakarta's are in suspension), but it is unusual in being without Soviet diplomatic representation. Recent developments, however, indicate that this may not long be the case. Soviet-Philippine relations have progressed some distance, and there has also been considerable movement between the CPR and the Philippines. It is likely, therefore, that competition between Moscow and Peking vis-à-vis Manila will increase.

The keynote of Philippine foreign policy, of course, has been that country's relationship with the United States. The close ties between the two, which Moscow (and Peking) see symbolized in Manila's membership in the Southeast Asia Treaty Organization (or Manila Pact) and in its assistance to the American effort in Vietnam, have until recently prevented any forward motion in relations with the communist world. Since the beginning of the period under consideration, however, Filipino nationalism has become stronger and the effort to establish a distinct national identity more pervasive and articulated. Much of this new nationalism has been reflected in an increasing assertion of independence from the United States. The added factor of an American withdrawal from Asia, as foreshadowed in the Nixon Doctrine, has accelerated processes of self-examination and self-assertion that were already under way. As early as his State of the Nation message in January 1967, President Marcos was predicting a reduction of the U.S. military commitment in Asia. Philippine defense and foreign policy would have to "undergo a complete change," he said, particularly with regard to a "more flexible approach vis-à-vis the main powers" in Asia and "consideration of regional defense arrangements. . . ." Significantly, he also pointed to the need to view the Soviet Union and Eastern Europe with an "open mind" and "the urgent need to strive toward a *modus vivendi*" with communist China.

Further American steps toward disengagement confirmed the accuracy of Marcos' perception. While China during its Cultural Revolution largely ignored such signs of change in the Philippines' foreign policy, the Soviet Union was far more responsive. In late 1966, the first Soviet journalist had visited the Philippines and, thereafter, Soviet-Philippine cultural exchanges increased. In April 1968, Manila went a step farther when it approved a project for establishing trade relations with the socialist countries. Nevertheless, the Philippines leadership was so cautious in its response to various Soviet gestures, which were in themselves still far from effusive, that little progress was made until the end of 1970. In November of that year, faced with an increasingly critical decline of the American financial commitment to his country, Marcos sent a three-man inspection team to the Soviet Union. The purpose of the mission was to explore Miscow's willingness to deliver long-term aid for development. Stories in the Philippine press quoted the Soviets as being ready to undertake loans to Manila. The head of the Southeast Asian Department of the Union of Soviet Societies for Friendship and Cultural Relations with Foreign Countries, visiting in the Philippines at the time, asserted that the USSR was ready to give economic aid to the Philippines if necessary, "but the issue must first be negotiated." According to one report, this official said that Moscow was fully prepared to exchange ambassadors and was merely waiting for the Philippines government to make up its mind.

Obviously Philippine caution and reticence toward the socialist countries—fostered by still strong domestic anticommunism, international uncertainties about the communist threat, and perhaps U.S. pressure as well—was the crucial stumbling block. Moscow's wooing has been evident. The Soviets have been careful to assure Manila of their noninterference in Philippine affairs and thus have been by inference critical of the "leftist" and "adventurist" tendencies in Philippine communism and the Maoist New People's Army.[15] They have warmly received Philippine emissaries such as Alejandro Melchor, the cabinet's executive secretary and have sent them home generally enthusiastic about Soviet sincerity, Soviet offers, and the benefits of ties with Moscow. Melchor, for example, returned strongly recommending the establishment of diplomatic as well as trade relations.

As Marcos began to acknowledge that ties with the Soviet Union were "only a matter of time" and in the "national interest" (especially in order to diversify trade), and that, as an "independent country," the Philippines could not ignore "the sixth of the world which is Socialist," Soviet emissaries to Manila reiterated that development loans to the Philippines would be forthcoming as soon as Marcos would request them.[16] Moscow continued to advertise that trade ties with the USSR would enable the Philippines to loosen the "iron grip of the foreign monopolies." Unless Manila sought economic cooperation with the USSR in order to promote its national independence and economic development, wrote a Soviet official from the Philippine capital, it might only exchange U.S. economic (and therefore political) domination for that of the Japanese. Yet, strong arguments persisted concerning the doubtful economic benefits of trade with the Soviet bloc, warning that the Philippines could not afford to give communism an entering wedge and hope to avoid Soviet pressures.

Clearly an additional incentive—beyond reducing the U.S. role—to the Kremlin was the gradually emerging Chinese interest in some sort of normalization of relations with the Philippines. Although mixed with old hostilities, the tentative Chinese approaches helped to lead to an acceleration of activity between Moscow (and Eastern Europe) and Manila beginning in 1972. In early January Marcos announced the establishment of diplomatic relations with Yugoslavia and Rumania. Defending himself against charges by the Manila *Times* that this was too cautious a move, since it did not involve the USSR or the CPR and only called for nonresidential ambassadors, he asserted that this was only the first step in the improvement of relations with all communist countries. He went on to say that he hoped full diplomatic relations would be established with the Soviet Union before his term of office ended in December 1973. In March Marcos' wife journeyed to the USSR, where she was most warmly received by the Soviet leaders. On her return, she reported that Premier Kosygin had promised "any and all forms of assistance" to the Philippines and that diplomatic ties had been a subject of discussion. In the fall of 1973, Marcos established diplomatic relations with Czechoslovakia, East Germany, Hungary, and Poland amid continued assertions that the same would soon be accomplished with the USSR and China.

Thailand

Thailand has been the least significant arena to date of Sino-Soviet competition. Like the Philippines, it is a member of SEATO and has been deeply involved in the American war effort in Indochina. In addition, it has been faced with its own serious insurgency problem supported and supplied by China and North Vietnam. For these reasons, it has been the slowest of all the countries in our survey to adjust to the changing power configuration in Southeast Asia and the world. As then Foreign Minister Thanat Khoman stated in 1969, despite changes in U.S. and Chinese foreign policy, Thailand does not want to "live with the crocodile" (the Soviet Union) just to "avoid a tiger" (China).[17] Since the Thais have given little intimation of seeking new and stronger relationships with the two communist powers, neither Moscow nor Peking seems to have invested substantial efforts in this country. Nevertheless, there has been some movement since 1965 and it seems likely to continue in the 1970s.

Thailand's historical attitude of "bending with the wind" is best served by keeping options open. This has been the case respecting the USSR, with which Bangkok has had diplomatic relations since 1947. A modest cultural exchange program has continued and grown slightly since 1965. Talks held with Moscow about a trade agreement during the 1960s were renewed in 1969, and in

December 1970 an agreement was finally signed. Trade agreements with Bulgaria and Rumania were signed in early 1969. However, in the words of one analyst:

> Thai trade with the Soviet Union and Eastern Europe has in the past been quite small (representing less than 1 percent of total Thai exports), and the potential for expansion is limited. Such trade will not significantly promote the major economic policy objective of diversifying trade and reducing Thai dependence on Japan.[18]

An agreement was also reached that grants the Soviet national airline, Aeroflot, landing rights in Bangkok.

In the face of tentative gestures toward Peking by Bangkok (despite some degree of continued Chinese support for Thai guerrillas) and increasing strains in U.S.-Thai relations, the USSR might be expected to be undertaking extensive new initiatives toward Thailand. There is no evidence of these, however. Whether this is because of a negative Thai response—Thai foreign policy has in fact been rather dormant over the past few years—or just a concentration of effort in Southeast Asian states other than Thailand (and Burma) is unclear. Nevertheless, Moscow is certainly concerned about the U.S. role and any future Chinese role in Thailand.

THE USSR AND THE REGION

The regional and international changes have presented Southeast Asian states and external powers with an entirely new and still evolving situation. The configuration of world power is shifting as Sino-Soviet hostility has increased, as the United States has begun a disengagement from Asia, as China is a more active and cooperative international actor, and as the new Sino-American rapprochement develops. Moscow's policies have adjusted to these changes since 1965—especially since 1969—and the USSR has become increasingly active in the region. Both the Soviet Union and China seem once again to be embarking on an ambitious campaign to woo the countries of Southeast Asia. As has been seen, there have been widely varying responses from the different Southeast Asian countries to these changes in regional and world politics and to Russian (and Chinese) overtures.

In an attempt to construct a pattern from this variegated record, it seems that much of the motivation for Soviet efforts in Southeast Asia since 1969 has been provided by Moscow's rivalry with China, especially in Indonesia, Malaysia and Singapore, as well as Indochina. Moreover, changes in Soviet policy toward Indonesia since 1969 indicate a reaction to the new Chinese posture. Yet, China's role as an integral part of Asia has in many ways made it easier for her to affect Southeast Asian policies even while doing little of a concrete nature. As a prime example, even though China's reentry into world affairs in 1969 resulted in no new initiatives in Southeast Asia until late 1970 (and none of any significance until 1971), there was an immediate effort in most Southeast Asian capitals to deal in some way with the changed so-called China factor. Despite the USSR's insistent claims to be an Asian power and thus local states' likely ally against the Chinese threat, Southeast Asians have remained unconvinced, and thus Moscow has never had the benefit of the endemic influence belonging to China. As a result, the Soviets' strenuous efforts since 1965 have left them only marginally ahead of the Chinese, who did not become serious rivals until late 1970. In the face of this frustration, the Soviets remain convinced that they can do more for the countries of Southeast Asia economically, technically, and financially, and in offering security, to offset the United States, than China can. Nevertheless, the technical and economic assistance that Indonesia, Burma, and Singapore have taken from Moscow has been slight, and military assistance has been next to nothing. Also, China is a more important trading partner for at least Burma, Malaysia, Singapore, and the Philippines. Peking seems to have made significant progress in the region through small-scale shipping and trade deals and, moreover, may have successfully defused the overseas Chinese issue since Chou En-lai's statement to Ne Win in August 1971. (Chou said that overseas Chinese "should obey the laws of the countries in which they reside" and that Peking opposed the concept of dual nationality and exploitation by overseas Chinese capitalists and moneylenders. Chou reportedly made the same statement to a Philippine emissary in early 1972.)

Given, then, only this slight return on its investment, perhaps the most Moscow can realistically hope for is to be considered a main guarantor of the region's neutralization, security, and economic development. The increased visibility of the Soviet navy and merchant fleet, particularly with the granting by Singapore in 1970 of berthing facilities for Soviet use, is at least in part intended to present a strategic and psychological (as well as economic) counterweight to the United States and the West. Toward this end the USSR has also sought to raise its trade turnover with states in the region and has been playing an increasingly active role in the Economic Commission for Asia and the Far East.[19] Moreover, Moscow has launched its most intriguing initiative in the form of a proposal for an Asian collective security system designed "to make Asia a continent of peace and cooperation." First put forth by Leonid Brezhnev on 7 June 1969, in his address to the Moscow International Meeting of Communist and Workers' Parties (see the Appendix for Brezhnev's statement and related documents), this idea has been reiterated frequently by various Soviet leaders and commentators but has been elaborated upon only marginally.[20] No Southeast Asian state has shown itself anxious to support the Russians on the proposal. The armed forces' daily in Jakarta, *Angkatan Bersendjata* (14 October 1969), summed up the perception of many in the region when it stated: "We in Indonesia believe that regional cooperation for prosperity is better than a defense system. We think that no Southeast Asian country is eager to join the Soviet defense system. The invitation is unwelcome." Although this collective security approach would seem to fit in well with the calls of the Association of Southeast Asian Nations (ASEAN) for the neutralization of the region, to be guaranteed by the major powers, Moscow was unresponsive to and generally skeptical of the latter idea. The ASEAN declaration for neutralization and noninterference by foreign powers, in

November 1971, was greeted by *Pravda* as denoting a "far from easy" task. The Communist Party of the Soviet Union (CPSU) daily asserted that several steps had to be taken to clear the atmosphere first: the ending of U.S. "aggression" in Indochina, of China's "hegemonic aspirations," and contradictions among Southeast Asian countries (Manila was the most skeptical, Bangkok and Singapore moderately so), and the removal of foreign military bases and foreign troops from the area.

Since mid-1972, however, the Soviets seem to have warmed slightly in their views of both ASEAN and the neutralization theme.[21] It is not clear if this is a response to the partial ending of the war in Indochina or other regional changes. It may well indicate Moscow's willingness to establish collective security via whatever route proves necessary. Recent Soviet commentary, for example, has cited the Soviet treaties with India and Iraq as foundations for an Asian collective security system. One aspect that does stand out in the Soviet approach, and one which is a chief obstacle to Moscow's obtaining greater support for the proposal, is its anti-Chinese nature. Whether or not the Soviets envision an actual defense system, they clearly are directing their efforts to countering China's hegemonic aspirations, as mentioned by *Pravda*. Efforts to sponsor such a system spring from Moscow's primary concern with China's more active posture internationally and with its desire to be the champion of the medium and small countries of the Third World.

Despite Moscow's denials, Soviet actions imply that the Asian collective security idea as well as Soviet efforts in the individual countries of the area are primarily directed against the Chinese. Moscow is certainly not interested in an ASEAN-sponsored neutralization that could well be either a smokescreen for continued U.S. control and influence (Soviet doubts about ASEAN have been especially related to supposed U.S. influence in the organization), or a vacuum from which the USSR is excluded but the CPR, because of its location and ambitions, is not. Moscow's vigorous attempts to establish a heightened presence in individual states and in the region as a whole are indeed intended to make it natural and necessary that the USSR be included in any future security system or agreement.[22] The Soviets have approached this goal through state interests and policy rather than through ideological analysis, local Communist Parties, or guerrilla movements. Moreover, this Soviet goal has in action been defined in terms of opposition to China, Moscow's greatest perceived threat. The crucial problem for the Soviets, then, has been revealed throughout this chapter: while certain countries seek protection against this Chinese "threat" (most notably Indonesia), even more are groping for some way to establish peaceful coexistence with their powerful neighbor. All the states of the region are seeking to widen their foreign policy options. Yet not one of these states, not even those persuaded of the danger of Chinese subversion or aggression, is interested in becoming a battleground for Sino-Soviet competition. The headline of a dispatch from Rangoon could be applied equally well to all countries of the region: "Big-Power Duel Worries Burma: Rangoon Fears Involvement in Soviet-Chinese Rivalry."[23] Nevertheless, the next few years seem likely to witness an increase in Sino-Soviet competition in Southeast Asia as the United States reduces its military presence and as the Soviet Union seeks to fill that vacuum and contain an increasingly assertive China.

NOTES

1. R. A. Yellon provides an excellent discussion of changing Soviet policies in the Third World in his paper, "Shifts in Soviet Policies Toward Developing Areas 1964-1968," in *Soviet Policy in Developing Countries*, W. Raymond Duncan, ed. (Waltham, Mass.: Ginn-Blaisdell, 1970), pp. 225-286.

2. Soviet policy toward Indonesia between 1965 and late 1970 is covered in detail in Robert C. Horn, "Soviet-Indonesian Relations Since 1965," *Survey*, 15, no. 1 (Winter 1971): 216-232.

3. Indonesian accusations that the Soviets were engaged in subversion and attempts to revive the PKI continued into 1972. See, for example, A. U., "Indonesia: Reactionary Propaganda Figments," *World Marxist Review*, June 1970, pp. 91-93; *Nusantara*, 14 June 1971; *Angkatan Baru*, 18 October 1971; and *Chas*, 5th week of January, 2nd week of April, and 1st week of May 1972.

4. I. Antonov, "Against Indonesia's National Interests," *New Times*, 7 October 1970, pp. 25-26.

5. For a discussion of Indonesian foreign policy perspectives, see this author's "Indonesia's Response to Changing Big Power Alignments," *Pacific Affairs*, 46, no. 4 (Winter 1973-74): 515-533.

6. Peter Boog, "The People's War," *Far Eastern Economic Review*, 16 November 1967, p. 323. According to Boog, "a top-level seven-man economic mission" arrived in Rangoon shortly after Kosygin's message and spent over a month there discussing "the possibility of Soviet aid to help stabilize the Burmese economy. . . ."

7. Recent Soviet assessments of Burmese developments can be found in A. Ledovsky, "Burma on the Road of Progressive Development," *International Affairs*, March 1973, pp. 45-47; and A. Malov, "Burma's Progress," *New Times*, 1974, no. 1, pp. 14-15.

8. For example, refer to Radio Moscow, 3 March 1971.

9. It is perhaps indicative of Tun Razak's desire not to offend China that he has spurned Soviet aid offers but has signed a technical assistance agreement with Rumania, the current communist maverick. For a recent examination of Soviet failures in trade and technical assistance, see *Far Eastern Economic Review*, 8 July 1972. The Malaysians have also expressed dissatisfaction with China in the trade area, according to United Press International, 2 May 1972.

10. See Douglas Pike, "North Vietnam in the Year 1972," *Asian Survey*, 13, no. 1 (January 1973): 56.

11. A valuable discussion can be found in Gene Gregory, "Moscow Awaits a Windfall," *Far Eastern Economic Review*, 19 February 1972, p. 16.

12. For a typical commentary at the time of the signing of the agreement, see L. Ivkov, "Vietnam's Victory: Lessons and Prospects," *New Times*, no. 6 (February 1973): 406. A more recent discussion in the same vein is A. Sergeyev, "Along the Path to Genuine Peace in Indochina," *International Affairs*, March 1973, pp. 18-25.

13. From an interview with Sihanouk by Alessandro Casella, in *Far Eastern Economic Review*, 25 December 1971, pp. 19-21.

14. See the Los Angeles *Times*, 8 September 1973.

15. See *World Marxist Review*, December 1970. Moscow did react positively, however, to reports in 1969 that Marcos was considering legalizing the Communist Party. Radio Moscow, in English to South Asia, 8 December 1969.

16. Los Angeles *Times*, 25 January 1971, and Bernardino Ronquillo, "Shy but Greedy," *Far Eastern Economic Review*, 20 March 1971, p. 28.

17. Quoted in Astri Suhrke, "Smaller-Nation Diplomacy: Thailand's Current Dilemmas," *Asian Survey*, May 1971: 438. For an overview of relations between the USSR and Thailand, see Paul R. Shirk, "Thai-Soviet Relations," ibid., September 1969: 682-693.

18. Suhrke, op. cit., p. 437.

19. See, for example, Frances Starner, "Selling Security Soviet-Style," *Far Eastern Economic Review*, 8 April 1972, pp. 72-74. The Soviets have been far more interested in the UN-related ECAFE, where their vote is equal to any other, than in the Asian Development Bank (which they have not joined), where voting weight is based on financial contributions. See, M. Lavrichenko, "Colonialist Plans and the Asian Development Bank," *International Affairs*, February 1972.

20. Useful analysis of the proposal and Asian reactions to it can be found in Peter Howard, "A System of Collective Security," *Mizan*, 11, no. 4 (July-August 1969): 199-204; Hemen Ray, "Soviet Diplomacy in Asia," *Problems of Communism*, 19, no. 2 (March-April 1970): 46-49; and Alexander O. Ghebhardt, "The Soviet System of Collective Security in Asia," *Asian Survey*, 13, no. 12 (December 1973): 1075-1091. Recent Soviet discussions are in Brezhnev's address to the World Congress of Peace Forces in October 1973, in *New Times*, no. 44 (November 1973), p. 8; and V. Kudryavtsev, "Problems of Collective Security in Asia," *International Affairs*, December 1973, pp. 94-98.

21. For example, see V. Pavlovsky, "Collective Security: The Way to Peace in Asia," *International Affairs*, July 1972, pp. 23-27, 69.

22. A current development that reflects on a number of Soviet goals in the region has been the Indonesian and Malaysian claim that the Straits of Malacca is not an international waterway. The Soviets have argued against this and even circulated a roving ambassador through the area in March 1972 to get support for internationalizing the Straits. For commentary, see *Asia Research Bulletin*, December 1971, p. 523, and *Far Eastern Economic Review*, 15 April 1972, pp. 18-19.

23. Tillman Durdin in the New York *Times*, 9 February 1972.

THE CHINESE
PERSPECTIVE
Alain-Gerard Marsot

"In international relations, there can be no eternal friends, nor can there be eternal enemies. The only thing eternal is the national interest." The accuracy of Lord Palmerston's cynical remark was once again reaffirmed when, on 15 July 1971, simultaneous communiqués were issued in Washington and Peking, announcing that President Nixon had been invited to visit China. This coup de theatre had been well stage-managed by Mr. Kissinger, the mastermind behind Mr. Nixon's foreign policy. Coming from a president who had started his political career under the banner of anticommunism, this move constituted a major surprise to many, especially those who still considered communism in general, and China in particular, as the arch-enemy that U.S. troops were battling in Vietnam through the interposed North Vietnamese. But while it is a paradox of politics that it is often easier for a conservative politician to initiate progressive measures—and vice versa—and while the proximity of the 1972 presidential elections was probably not unrelated to Mr. Nixon's bold moves in foreign policy, a rapprochement between the United States and China was logical, necessary, and long overdue.

The war in Vietnam had progressively made clear to many Americans that in spite of Chinese (and Russian) aid, the Vietnamese were fighting a war of their own and were not pawns of either the USSR or even China—a fact that should have been obvious by the time of the French Indochina war. But, more important, global politics had changed. The cold war had practically ended, with the disappearance of most of its principal actors. It had lost its essential raison d'être, in proportion to its protagonists increasing knowledge of each other, and discovering that they had much to gain through cooperation and understanding, and a lot to lose through a violent, possibly terminal, conflict. The progressive realization of that situation made a détente possible, and sought after. That a practical compromise could be reached between the protagonists of the former cold war did not, however, exclude the possibility of confrontations between them. But when a confrontation did occur, objectives and achievements remained limited, not so much because of the threat of a nuclear holocaust, which already prevailed in the heyday of the cold war, but because of a new game of nations, in many ways similar to that of the nineteenth century. In that game, someone's gains are nearly always someone else's losses, with the potentially dangerous implication that the loser might seek compensation elsewhere, in which case it therefore appeared counter-productive to make doubtful gains, and more astute politically to accept some losses to prevent such a danger.

But what makes the game flexible, and often unpredictable, is the participation of more players. While in military terms the world balance of power is still a two-way affair and likely to remain so for some time, in political terms there has been an evolution toward multipolarity. An important factor in the emergence of a multipolar structure has been the development of the Sino-Soviet dispute, which has shattered, probably forever, the monolithic character—often more apparent than real—of the former communist bloc. Whether or not the dispute ever gets peacefully resolved, China will in all likelihood retain a large measure of independence and autonomy from the Soviet Union, allowing her to play her own game, according to her perceived interests and capabilities. The Sino-Soviet dispute caused China many grave problems that still persist, notably on its borders with the Soviet Union, but it also created new possibilities and opportunities for her, which otherwise might not have materialized.

The emergence of a multipolar structure can be accompanied, on the part of the new poles of power, by the possession of nuclear armament. But it need not necessarily be so, for the very existence of that multipolar structure somewhat lessens the importance of nuclear armament. Among the new centers, Europe is still in the throes of its difficult birth, but two others, Japan and China, are fast emerging as major players in the game of nations. Japan has developed at an amazing speed into a major economic power, although it is hampered by its political and military weakness. China under a strong regime, because of its landmass, its huge population, its historical traditions, aspires to play a major role in world affairs, possibly one of political hegemony in Asia and ideological hegemony within the socialist world, or even within part of the so-called Third World.

In its approach to world affairs, China has followed a path somewhat parallel to that of the United States, where dogmatism and ideological con-siderations progressively gave way to pragmatism and national interests. In that case, the Sino-Soviet dispute has acted as a catalyst. This is not to say that pragmatism was previously absent from the determination of Chinese foreign policy, or that dogmatism is bound to disappear. But, for a long time, there was a close solidarity between China's domestic and external policy, with the result that foreign policy was not allowed to endanger or jeopardize domestic politi-cal and ideological unity, or the rapid buildup of the economy. This has become less and less true since the late sixties with the development of the Sino-Soviet dispute, and the more recent emergence of a new balance of power in Asia. Now, with changing domestic and external conditions, there is both room and necessity for a relative autonomy in Chinese foreign policy vis-à-vis internal developments.

If there is an area in the world where this new balance of power is, therefore, fully apparent and where the new game of nations shows its full significance, it is Asia and most of all Southeast Asia. In Europe, on the American continent, in Africa, and the Middle East, a modicum of equilibrium has been reached, and if a situation of confrontation arises it essentially involves the two superpowers: the United States and the USSR. But in East and Southeast Asia, the new balance of power shows its full significance because of the conjunction of two factors:

1. It is an area where nearly all major powers are present or have direct interests, whether they be China, Japan, India, the United States, or the USSR. Western European nations, which used to control most of the area, are no longer an important factor there, but may still retain some interests. Asia, and especially Southeast Asia, has been the major area of violent and ceaseless conflicts since the end of World War II. For the past thirty years, the sound of firearms has abated in the region hardly a day. But even should violent fighting stop or sizably diminish, the area will remain a center of the highest diplomatic interest. What we are in fact witnessing is possibly a displacement toward the Pacific and Southeast Asia of the center of world diplomacy.

2. Southeast Asia is an area rich in resources, easily accessible, and considerably fragmented. These "Balkans of Asia" are often seen as a natural power vacuum, and seem to attract interference and intervention on the part of major powers near and far.

Of all the major powers, it is China that may be in the best strategic position to play a lasting role in Southeast Asia. This is due first, to her geographic proximity, second, to her traditional consideration of Southeast Asia as a historical sphere of influence, and lastly to her special assets in the region such as the overseas Chinese communities and the national communist parties. Therefore, when one considers the new balance of power in Southeast Asia, it is imperative to study China's perspective in relation to the area, in terms of China's foreign policy objectives and capabilities. This will be illustrated by a rapid survey of the stages of China's foreign policy and tactics in Southeast Asia, ending with a tentative appraisal of the possible lines of evolution.

CHINA'S INTERESTS IN SOUTHEAST ASIA

In the course of history, the foreign policy of nations has been essentially inspired by considerations of national interest. Throughout the nineteenth century and the first half of the twentieth, nationalism was a major force, a dynamic element in the national and international history of most nations.

But the advent in 1917 in Russia of a political regime inspired by a powerful ideology, the multiplication across the world of communist parties, and the more recent establishment of a communist regime in China have complicated international politics by adding ideological considerations to national ones in foreign policy motivations.

In the developed countries of the western world one notices, however, the progressive disappearance of ideologies, or at least their lessening ability to mobilize minds and energies. But in the countries of the Third World, where dissatisfaction and need are the rule, the influence of ideologies has remained potent. In some of these countries, communist regimes have assumed power following revolutionary struggles inspired by Marxist ideology. But while ideology has continued to inspire their domestic and external policy, it has not eliminated considerations of national interest. Ideological and national objectives have, therefore, become inextricably intertwined in the determination of the foreign policy of those states, especially in the case of the most powerful among them: China.

Ideological Objectives

The first of these objectives derives from the truly "messianic" spirit of communist doctrine. It consists in the spreading of world revolution and its principles. The Chinese Revolution is seen as part of the world proletarian and socialist revolution. It is a moment in a historical process that is taking place presently within the Afro-Asian world and that follows the decline and fall of the old colonial order, the crumbling of the nineteenth century international order centered around Europe, and the evolution of a bloc of antiimperialist nations, newly independent and liberated from western domination. Imperialism being considered as the final stage of moribund capitalism, colonial and semicolonial countries are of special importance in the revolutionary struggle against capitalist countries. The Chinese experience shows the validity of the Maoist strategy as a revolutionary model for these countries, especially in Asia, while underlining the inadequacy of traditional methods in those countries.[1]

This experience in China's eyes justifies her role and influence in the vanguard of the world revolutionary movement, particularly within underdeveloped countries, although the Chinese believe, and repeatedly affirm that the revolutionary process should adapt itself to local conditions in each specific country.

Therefore, China claims a sort of moral leadership in the direction of the antiimperialist crusade in Asia, so that Chou En-lai could say: "When China speaks, she speaks for Asia." Not content with leading the antiimperialist crusade in Asia, China has recently arrogated to itself the leadership of world communism. As a matter of fact, from the beginning of the Sino-Soviet dispute, it has become more and more obvious that China was aspiring to become the second metropolis of world communism, and to supplant the Soviet Union in this role. China considers herself the guardian of orthodoxy and her leaders display greater revolutionary zeal than Soviet leaders.[2] It appears that she has succeeded in Asia, where most communist parties lean toward Peking rather than Moscow.[3]

Finally, China provides the countries of the Third World, and in particular those of Southeast Asia, with a strongly appealing model of development.[4] That appeal was somewhat tarnished after the excesses of the "Great Leap Forward" and the Cultural Revolution, but there has been a resurgence of interest in that model and in China's domestic achievements in the wake of the post-Cultural Revolution relaxation and China's relative opening to the outside world. Among the reasons for the attractiveness of the Chinese model is the similarity of conditions within China and the majority of the Asian states. It seems to be a system readily adaptable to poor, underdeveloped countries, mainly populated by peasants, and to one-time colonies. Russia, which was never colonized, began its revolution and its development in more propitious circumstances. In the eyes of the Asiatic peoples, therefore, there seems to be a contradiction between two models of communism: one, the Soviet, representing in some measure a communism of the rich, and the other, the Chinese, representing a communism of the poor. It is this last one that appears to be the most accessible, the more so in Southeast Asia since the Chinese model is nearer in time and space, and also the most desirable because of its rapid rate of growth compared to that of the Soviets, and even more rapid compared to western methods. China can, therefore, use the appeal of her model to remove the former colonial countries of Southeast Asia from the sphere of western influence, thus creating favorable conditions for ultimately bringing those countries within China's orbit. However, that objective is at most a long-range one, as in the short term China is probably neither willing nor able to take charge of underdeveloped countries such as those of Southeast Asia. This would quickly become an unbearable burden on China's limited resources, and furthermore entail risks of foreign intervention. But here, ideological objectives and considerations overlap national objectives.

National Objectives

It is generally believed that in its ascendant period, a large state tries at first to define and defend its borders, then to surround itself with buffer states providing real security, and finally to exercise hegemony over the region to which it belongs.[5] The first phase, therefore, includes the territorial unification of the country. The importance of that objective is underlined by the unhesitating way in which China in 1959 invaded Tibet and crushed the resistance of its inhabitants, in spite of unfavorable reactions abroad. China, however, considers Tibet an integral part of the Chinese territory, a view shared by the Nationalists in Taiwan. And had it not been for the interposition of the U.S. Seventh Fleet after the outbreak of fighting in Korea in June 1950, the Chinese communists would have attacked Taiwan, likewise considered as Chinese territory by both sides. Under the influence of this idea pieces of territory are claimed by China on her borders, generating numerous incidents, and in one case leading to limited warfare with India. There, national imperatives apparently took precedence over the desire to maintain good relations with neighboring countries. But, in point of fact, equitable border settlements were concluded by China with both Pakistan and Burma. The border dispute with India was motivated by considerations other than simple territorial ones.

This national objective directly proceeds from Chinese tradition concerning territory and the delimitation of borders established by powerful ancient dynasties. According to that tradition China was *the* civilized world. Territory conquered by civilization should not be returned to the barbarians, and if it has been lost it should be recovered at the first opportunity.[6]

From the very beginning, the Chinese communist leaders considered their country as one of the great world powers, which should consequently exercise the prerogatives of a great power. That involved being party to the solution of major international issues, above all in Asia, but also outside that continent. It is within this context that China demanded admission into the United Nations and the explusion of Taiwan as the spokesman for China—a goal finally achieved in the fall of 1971.

The second phase, after domestic and external consolidation, in the achievement by a nation of great power status, includes the constitution of a series of buffer states, preferably kept in a state of vassalage, or in modern parlance satellites. Less well-provided than the Soviet Union, China has only two buffer-states, which are not even satellites: North Korea and North Vietnam. Imperial China used to exercise, more or less nominally, rights of suzerainty over peripheral states, especially in Southeast Asia. However, that relationship stood in lieu of diplomatic recognition and was often requested from, rather than imposed by China, as a form of legitimization. New Southeast Asian rulers would beg for Chinese "seals of investiture," in order to reinforce their legitimacy. That type of relationship is hardly appropriate in modern times, particularly vis-à-vis a communist state. For the time being, China seems satisfied when such peripheral countries follow a neutralist line, since she is confident that eventually they will join an Asian socialist camp headed by China. Even though China has, loudly at times, encouraged revolutionary movements and subversion in countries that were neutralist, like Burma, or western-oriented, like Thailand, these encouragements have rarely been more than verbal. The reason is partly fear of American intervention and partly the desire to project the image of a faithful revolutionary power—in contrast with the USSR, which has never hesitated, in China for example, to abandon communist movements when it found it expedient to support the governments that persecuted them.

Whatever the substance of Chinese pronouncements in relation to revolutionary movements in Asia, they constitute a potential threat that can be used to keep governments in line and leave Peking's options open. Thus China began making verbal pronouncements in 1964-65 in favor of a Thai Communist Party, until then fairly insignificant, and supporting communist insurgency in north and northeast Thailand, at the time when Thailand started participating in the Vietnam War and allowing the U.S. Air Force to bomb North Vietnam and Laos from airfields on her territory.[7]

In the hierarchy and timing of foreign policy objectives, those of the third phase have both been present early on and important. They consist of establishing China's political and ideological hegemony in Southeast Asia. This region is considered by the Chinese communist leaders as China's normal sphere of influence, gathering under the leadership of China a series of nations having interests in common that should be pursued without the intervention of non-Asian nations. The area constitutes a Chinese conception of an Asian Monroe Doctrine. To implement this conception, the Chinese insist on recalling the historical friendship existing between China and the other Asian countries, and they emphasize relations between peoples—assumed traditionally to have been friendly—as opposed to relations between governments, that may have been subject to fluctuations. But in this friendly relationship with the peoples of Asia, there is, on the part of China, a protective side and a feeling of superiority, which is the consequence of tradition. The Chinese, even the revolutionary ones, are conscious of the excellence of their cultural heritage, be it in letters or sciences, and of the unique quality of their language, history, literature, philosophy, or fine arts.[8] They also regard their own model of development as a valid example for the underdeveloped countries of Asia, while remaining skeptical as to its partial adoption by those countries, short of a total revolutionary transformation.[9]

Other essential considerations inspire China's policy in Asia. For a long period, there was the desire to extend her sphere of influence on the one hand at the expense of the United States and other western nations, and on the other hand to prevent Japan from becoming again a strong political and military power, able to contest China's representation and leadership of Asian affairs. In spite of many frictions that have set India to China against each other and are likely to continue, China, no doubt through experience, considers Japan as potentially much more troublesome than India.

Until the late fifties, the Soviet Union appeared to have limited ambitions in Southeast Asia, being content to leave to China the care of communist interests in the region. From the beginning of the sixties, with the development of the Sino-Soviet dispute and then the escalation of war in the Indochinese peninsula, Soviet interest increased in Southeast Asia. One can wonder whether Soviet interest in the region is genuine and of a long-range nature, or essentially aimed at securing bargaining points in relation to both the United States and China, possibly in order to outflank the latter country and divert her attention from the key area of contention between them—their common border. But in either case, China views an increased Soviet presence in Southeast Asia with a jaundiced eye, to the point that since U.S. involvement is declining, she might wish to see disengagement delayed, if only not to create greater opportunities for the Russians.[10]

Here we notice an added reason for a Sino-American rapprochement, as well as an example of how gains and tactics by one power (the USSR) might turn out to be counterproductive by pushing China toward the United States. This is a clear result of the new balance of power, which has completely modified the previous triangular relationship and created an eminently fluid situation in Southeast Asia. During the cold war period, there was a clear-cut distinction between the communist bloc and the western bloc, so that, for Southeast Asian nations to choose a side, mostly the western one, was necessary if not imposed, and once the choice was made there was little possibility of any sort of relationship with the other bloc. The neutralist, nonaligned path, though attempted in some instances, was extremely uncomfortable and generated perils from all sides. This situation no longer prevails, which allows China (and also the USSR naturally) and several Southeast Asian countries the possibility of initiating rapprochement and relations with each other, whether diplomatic, economic, or cultural. The new balance of power has enhanced China's capabilities of action in Southeast Asia, through the increased or renewed potential of some instruments, such as diplomacy, commerce and aid, and cultural action, while other special instruments such as the Chinese communities and the communist parties of Southeast Asia always remain available.

CHINA'S INSTRUMENTALITIES IN SOUTHEAST ASIA

A country's power and influence are measured by several yardsticks: its population, its area, the richness of its civilization, its economic potential, its military might, and last by its organization. China has always been one of the largest countries in the world, and also the most populated. Her civilization is one of the most ancient and most brilliant, the Chinese race is intelligent and conscious of its unity, and Chinese resources are abundant and diversified. But throughout her history, because of her very size, China has been continuously subjected to centrifugal forces imperiling her political unity, and her inhabitants' individualism constantly hindered any organizing effort. However, whenever China was unified and organized under a strong sovereign, it showed a potential for imperialism and expansion.

In the nineteenth century, governed by a weak and despised dynasty, China, after being subjected to the western impact, had really become the sick man of the Far East. The nationalist regime, which had succeeded the Manchu dynasty, had come up against the same problems as its predecessors, compounded by war and foreign invasion. Finally, it had sunk into anarchy and corruption and broke up under the communist armies' repeated blows. The ultimate victory of the latter has brought a fundamental change in China's stature and capabilities.

In 1949, a strong regime was set up in China, under the leadership of an intelligent and long-united team, which undertook to unify and organize the country in all domains: political, social, and economic; to rise above underdevelopment; and to return China to what they considered her rightful place in the concert of nations. While the work that remains to be done is enormous, and while some past failures were costly, the results achieved are significant and the country has come a long way. As of now, because of her organization, human masses, and military potential (which is now nuclear) China has reached great power status and her influence can only increase in international politics. That fact was at last acknowledged in 1971 by communist China's admission into the United Nations and permanent membership in the Security Council.

China's influence is most felt in Southeast Asia, where her massiveness and proximity have often appeared to neighboring governments to pose a threat of either direct or indirect subversion, that is support in material or men of the volunteer type, to local insurrectionists. In fact, in the few cases of direct Chinese military intervention, since 1949—in Korea, Tibet, and the Straits of

Taiwan—China considered her vital interests to be threatened, a view shared by many outside observers. Border incidents, even those with India in 1962, were of a limited character and, according to some studies, were precipitated by China's opponents.

The support accorded by the Chinese communists to the rebellions that developed in several Southeast Asian countries after the take-over of the mainland in 1949 was essentially moral, and the support to the Vietminh during the French Indochina war consisted of armaments, not men. During the American Indochina war, however, there were more than 50,000 Chinese soldiers in North Vietnam for road and rail repair work in 1965-68, at the time of the U.S. air war. But this constituted assistance to an embattled allied government, not to an insurrectionist group.

On the whole, there is no evidence that China intends to practice a policy of open aggression in Southeast Asia, partly through the fear of American intervention and partly because she does not as yet possess the logistical capabilities (navy and offensive army) necessary for such ventures—not to mention the fact that it would be contrary to her official and proclaimed policy of nonaggression. As to indirect aggression, that is subversion, the record shows that it is practiced with a lot of circumspection. China considers that neutralism and nonalignment are a necessary stage, after decolonization and before entering the communist system. It is characteristic that she threatened to intervene in Laos in 1960-61 following a right-wing coup and a setback of neutralism in that country, and was instrumental in the reconvening of the Geneva Conference to reestablish a neutral Laos.[11]

But clearly the existence of a threat of indirect aggression has contributed until 1970 to the adoption of a neutralist, nonaligned policy, by some countries such as Burma or Cambodia, lest they provoked their powerful neighbor. China's behavior toward Thailand from 1964-65, as mentioned earlier, clearly shows that it is no idle threat. With the new balance of power, now that the United States has decided to diminish its presence in the area, the pressure will be greater than ever for the countries of Southeast Asia to go in the direction of neutralism, or at least to find some accommodation with China. There are many signs that show an evolution in that direction.

China's policy in Southeast Asia takes different forms. There are, first of all, political and diplomatic measures that generally fit within the traditional framework of the external policy of a great power, and which can end, if need be, in the utilization of armed force. Next, there are economic measures, in the shape of trade, or aid and assistance, but political considerations play an extremely important part in determining China's external economic policy. Lastly, cultural measures join the diplomatic and economic ones to create or reinforce ties between China and the various countries she is interested in influencing.

Besides these policies, which have the nature of traditional instrumentalities, there are measures of an indirect, or at least less direct nature, which China carries out by means of the Chinese communities and the communist parties in Southeast Asia. However, the distinction between those policy instruments is not clear cut, as both the overseas Chinese and the communist parties can be, and have been, used in a direct fashion.

Regular Policy Instruments

In mainland China central organization, controlled by the Communist Party, direct the action of diplomatic and consular posts and that of the New China News Agency bureaus, which are in charge of developing contacts with native circles, either directly or through "Friendship with China" Associations, and also with the overseas Chinese. These are supplemented by numerous Chinese missions (commercial, cultural, technical, athletic, trade unions, and so on) that travel throughout the world. At the government level, there is the Ministry for Foreign Affairs, the Ministry for Foreign Trade, as well as three commissions: Economic Relations and Cultrual Relations with foreign countries, and the Commission of Overseas Chinese Affairs. Various other committees and organizations help in the dissemination abroad of Chinese information and propaganda.

But the essential organization coordinating China's action abroad is naturally the Ministry for Foreign Affairs. Poor in career diplomats at the beginning, China exerted efforts to train foreign service officials. Constitutionally, the conduct of foreign affairs is in the hands of the President of the Republic and the Council of State (Government). Although Mao does not seem to be particularly interested in foreign affairs, until his demise President Liu Shao-Ch'i, was active in this field. Currently, the Prime Minister Chou En-lai appears to play a predominant role in the domain of foreign affairs, where he has always played a key part and is considered a master.

In Southeast Asia, Chinese embassies were established at one time in only five countries: North Vietnam, Burma, Laos, Cambodia, and Indonesia. After Sukarno's era, diplomatic relations were suspended with Indonesia, and altogether severed with Cambodia after Sihanouk's overthrow. However, with China's entrance into the U.N. and the new situation in Southeast Asia, it is to be expected that diplomatic relations, or at least extensive commercial contacts, will develop between China and several other Southeast Asian countries. Such contacts have already been established with Malaysia, Singapore, and Thailand.

Economic action, in the form of trade or programs of aid, is considered by China as an important instrument of foreign policy, especially vis-à-vis underdeveloped countries. But while political motivations are paramount in China's economic actions, economic considerations are by no means absent. The goals are first to increase China's prestige by establishing her presence on the international markets, and in some cases by granting aid; secondly, to encourage as many countries as possible to practice a policy of nonalignment towards western nations and to loosen their ties with the West; then, especially in Southeast Asia, to bring those countries ultimately within China's economic and then political sphere of influence.[1][2]

The success of such a policy depends, as far as China is concerned, on respect for the national integrity of these countries, and on nonintervention in their domestic affairs, according to the five principles of peaceful coexistence

defined in 1954.* China's purpose would be defeated through political intervention, military infiltration, or economic pressure. The Chinese, on the whole,
have adopted a cooperative attitude and are even generous in terms of aid, but
sometimes, for example with Japan, they have not hesitated to use economic
pressure to secure political results—which might make these countries think
twice in the future, before establishing steady economic relations with China.

China's economic policy in Southeast Asia has taken the directions of
both trade and aid. At the beginning of the communist regime, Chinese foreign
trade was heavily leaning to the side of the Soviet bloc. From 1952 and
especially in 1955, with her new policy of peaceful coexistence in the spirit of
Bandung, China tried to restore and develop economic relations with noncommunist countries, particularly in Asia (Japan and Southeast Asia). By the
beginning of 1955, trade relations had been established with 60 countries.
Traditionally, Chinese trade has mostly consisted of an exchange of raw
materials for manufactured goods. China has tried, as much as possible, to
transform her exports into semifinished goods. From 1958, she began exporting manufactured goods to Southeast Asia, particularly to Hong Kong,
Singapore, and Indonesia. These goods were sold at low prices and were made
competitive with Hong Kong and Japanese products, partly for political reasons
and partly because of China's need for foreign exchange,[13] at a time when she
was importing equipment from Western Europe. This policy of massive exports
to Southeast Asia slowed down in the aftermath of the "Great Leap Forward"
(1958-62).

The countries of Southeast Asia, generally less industrialized than China,
constitute natural markets for Chinese manufactured goods—added to the fact
that their resident Chinese (the overseas Chinese) favor food, medicines and
other specialties from China. In return, those countries can provide indispensable tropical products, such as rubber. But China's trade did not develop
equally in all the Southeast Asian countries for political reasons, especially
when those countries were anticommunist and western oriented. Apart from
North Vietnam, China has expanded her commercial relations with Burma from
1955, exchanging equipment goods and services for Burmese rice, of which she
really had no need at the time. That clearly showed a political calculation. The
Chinese volume of trade with Burma diminished after reaching a high of 57.8
million dollars in 1961, and by 1971 it was only 14.2 million dollars (exports:
12.6; imports: 1.6).

China's long-time volume of trade with Malaya and Singapore, consider-
able because of the important Chinese communities there, declined after the
Korean war due to the embargo on strategic goods such as rubber to China.
However, China continued to export textiles and manufactured goods to
Malaya-Singapore. The volume of trade reached a peak in 1960, but later
diminished due to restrictions on the part of the Malay government, which was

---

*These principles are: (1) mutual respect for each other's territorial integrity and
sovereignty, (2) nonagression, (3) noninterference in each other's internal affairs, (4)
equality and mutual benefit, (5) peaceful coexistence.

afraid of China's growing economic presence. It started increasing again in the late sixties and by 1971 Singapore and Malaysia had become respectively the first and second major trading partners of China in Southeast Asia, with the Chinese volume of trade with Singapore reaching 148.1 million dollars (exports: 132.9; imports: 15.2), and with Malaysia 62.1 million dollars (exports: 44.7; imports: 17.4).

With Indonesia, trade also increased during the same period, reaching a peak in 1959 with a total volume of 114.3 million dollars. It also consisted of an exchange of Chinese manufactured goods for Indonesian raw materials (copra, sugar, rubber) and agricultural products. But trade relations considerably diminished after the coup of 1965. By 1971, the Sino-Indonesian volume of trade had gone down to 36.2 million dollars (Chinese exports: 31.2; Chinese imports: 5.0).[14]

With the other countries of the area, China's trade has long been inconsequential, and is practically nonexistent with the Philippines and South Vietnam. With Thailand, it was more important than was officially apparent, since goods from China were coming in large quantities via Hong Kong, until the Thai government clamped down on them.

These fluctuations in China's volume of trade with only a few countries of Southeast Asia show a potential for growth of that trade in the region when circumstances are favorable. But for the present, China's volume of trade with Southeast Asia is still small, amounting to about 261.8 million dollars in 1971, out of a total of about 4,250 million, or approximately 6.16 percent of China's total volume of trade.[15]

The second aspect of China's economic action in Southeast Asia is of much more significance than her commercial policy. China's policy of aid to several countries of the area is particularly striking because of China's own development problems.

Four years after its advent to power, the Chinese communist regime began granting aid to small communist countries, such as North Vietnam, and then, after 1956 to noncommunist countries of Southeast Asia such as Cambodia, Indonesia, and Burma. Aid took the form of technical assistance, credits, loans, and outright grants. The principal beneficiary of Chinese aid in Southeast Asia has been North Vietnam, which received technical assistance, military equipment during the two Indochina wars, various grants in money, and loans for industrial construction and reconstruction. Until 1965, Chinese aid to North Vietnam was more important than Soviet aid, reaching a total of 367.8 million dollars. With the U.S. bombing of North Vietnam and the escalation of the war, Soviet aid, especially military, increased sizeably in relation to China's. And while, throughout the conflict China observed a cautious attitude, the reason might also have been that the North Vietnamese were wary of too great a Chinese influence in their country.

Three other neutralist countries (at the time) in Southeast Asia have benefited at some stage from China's generosity and assistance: Burma, Indonesia, and Cambodia. Of these three, Cambodia under Sihanouk was most favored, because of its attachment to neutralism in the heart of the SEATO-covered area, and also probably because China's limited capabilities could have a maximum impact in a small country. Cambodia was given a grant of money to be used for the construction of several factories and for various works of an economic and social nature, for a total amount of 92 million dollars.[16] Burma was granted several loans, at low interest or without interest, for the construction of several factories and the purchase of equipment, for a total of 84 million dollars. Indonesia was likewise granted credits, some of them on a long-term basis, for various purchases and the construction of textile factories, for a total of 105 million dollars.[17]

In general, Chinese aid programs favor light industry, aiming at making the receiving countries less dependent on agriculture and more independent industrially of the more developed countries. (One might note that such a policy could ultimately deprive China of markets for its own manufactured goods.) Light industry requires less investment and brings about quicker results. Compared to western, or even Soviet aid, Chinese loans and grants are small—though large in the context of the Chinese budget. But they include generous facilities of reimbursement, unlike many western ones. In any case, Chinese aid is significant for the small countries that receive it. It has enhanced China's prestige, built up political capital, and showed China's will to be present and to occupy a larger place in Asia.

While economic relations between China and the countries of Southeast Asia are somewhat limited by objective reasons, such as supply and demand and China's still limited capabilities at this time, the field of cultural action is much broader and more flexible. Therefore, cultural activities aiming at the promotion of sympathy and interest for the Peking regime have been important characteristics of China's policy in Southeast Asia. The political character of this cultural campaign is underlined by the contrast existing between the treatment of culture at home and abroad. Abroad, the Chinese communists glorify China's ancient and rich cultural heritage and present themselves as its legitimate heirs. On the domestic scene, however, they subject this cultural heritage to a continuous process of adaptation, within the context of their program of total transformation of the Chinese society. That latter tendency was particularly obvious during the Cultural Revolution, to such an extent that it might have jeopardized the long positive effects of the Chinese cultural policy abroad. Cultural activities can serve China's cause in several ways. Through visits, cultural delegations, artistic, sport, and movie festivals, book exhibitions and "friendship weeks," contacts can be established with foreign cultural circles and even large masses of people, attracted by colorful and well publicized shows and other cultural manifestations. In these visits, opera singers, actors, ballet dancers, folklore artists, sportsmen, writers, painters, musicians, and even jugglers and clowns, play their part in developing foreign peoples' feelings of interest and friendship for China. The overall objective, like that of the external economic policy, is to win the goodwill of noncommunist countries, to neutralize their relations with the West, and eventually to draw them toward the Chinese orbit. The immediate aim is to help bring about the establishment of diplomatic relations. These cultural exchanges are naturally two-way, as many Asian visitors—politicians, trade union leaders, writers, artists, scientists—have been invited and have visited China, often reporting enthusiastically about their trip, impressed as they were by China's dynamism and achievements.

In several Southeast Asian countries, the large overseas Chinese communities are particularly susceptible to Chinese cultural action, through the absorption of Chinese communist publications, the use of Chinese textbooks in schools, attendance at Chinese movies, or even trips to the mainland for higher education. However, it is to be noted that Chinese cultural action has sometimes been more successful with the people of countries such as Burma where overseas Chinese were few and did not pose a challenge to the majority. Chinese culture was therefore more palatable.

Chinese publications, books, magazines, and so forth, whether they are directed at the native people or at the overseas Chinese, are not always welcome or even allowed by the various governments of Southeast Asia. In some circumstances, they have to be spread through clandestine means, using those indirect instruments available to China in Southeast Asia such as the overseas Chinese and the communist parties.

Special Policy Instruments: the Overseas Chinese and the Communist Parties

There are approximately 15 million overseas Chinese, who have emigrated throughout the world, but the largest numbers by far are found in the countries of Southeast Asia, where they often constitute the most dynamic element of the economy. In that region, the overseas Chinese are therefore a problem, especially since they are rarely totally assimilated. They feel Chinese, and are very proud of it. They consider China as their mother country and keep for her a feeling of fundamental allegiance, regardless of her political regime. Throughout history, Chinese have emigrated to Southeast Asia, though in small numbers, but most of the Chinese communities in Southeast Asia date from, and were a consequence of western colonization. Western colonization encouraged Chinese immigration to Southeast Asia, made use of it and gave it some measure of protection. Once the countries of the area became independent, the Chinese no longer enjoyed western protection, but became exposed to the resentment of the local peoples and governments, because of their control of the economy and the possibility that they could be used by the Peking communist regime for subversive purposes. The communist insurrection in Malaya (1948-60), not to mention the insurrections in other countries— Indonesia, Burma, Vietnam, and the Philippines—in which the presence of Chinese was not as obvious, was both an example and a warning for the Southeast Asian countries, even though it was neither instigated nor directed by Peking.

Therefore, several Southeast Asian governments undertook to control closely the overseas Chinese, encourage their assimilation, and sometimes drastically limit their grip on the economy. The main goal of most overseas Chinese is to succeed economically and enjoy the fruits of their efforts. For them, ideology and politics are of secondary importance, except in Malaya and Singapore where, because of their numbers, they have become aware of the role they could play. Elsewhere, their small number, wealth, and alien character render them vulnerable and precludes their playing a political role. But as a result of the restrictions, even persecutions they are facing, the Chinese are tempted to find support outside. That support they could find either with the Chinese in Taiwan or on the mainland. With mainland China's growing influence and respectability, it is obvious that the overseas Chinese have been increasingly looking to Peking for assistance, and that tendency will doubtless develop further. However, it has made and will make the overseas Chinese susceptible to being used by Peking as an instrument of its foreign policy in Southeast Asia.

Very early, with the advent of communism in China, the new regime claimed the allegiance of the overseas Chinese and presented itself—like previous regimes—as their defender. Communist China sought the overseas Chinese allegiance for reasons of nationalism and prestige, as a means of further legitimizing the Peking regime, and to deprive Taiwan of such legitimacy. But the search for that allegiance also arose from definite objectives on the part of Peking: to use the Chinese communities as a means of influence and as policy instruments in Southeast Asia. However, this plan came up against a series of theoretical and practical obstacles.

The new Chinese regime was caught between contradictory goals: the protection of its nationals, the desire not to exacerbate the resentment of the new nationalisms in the area, and the development of communism. As a communist state, China recognized the political and economic equality of all races. It was, therefore, difficult for her to claim a special treatment for the overseas Chinese in relation to the native peoples of Southeast Asia, at a time when Chinese communist propaganda was appealing to Asian solidarity in the struggle against foreign imperialists and colonialists, especially in countries where the Chinese minority represented a foreign community, both capitalistic and exploitative according to Marxist conceptions. On the other hand, if the Peking government had assumed in earnest the task of defending the overseas Chinese, it would have been faced with the fact that it did not as yet have the practical means to implement that policy, for example with an adequate navy or air force for punitive expeditions, if necessary.

China has used, and even exploited, the overseas Chinese financial resources through remittances to relatives in China, which were a source of needed foreign currency. But she has also used the Chinese communities as a means of pressure or a bargaining tool vis-à-vis the Southeast Asian government, through proclamations of support or conciliatory moves. China has sometimes considered the overseas Chinese as a means of political influence, able to provide information on the country of residence, and to help China's cultural and commercial offensives.

The communist regime, therefore, attaches a great importance to the overseas Chinese. It has paid a special attention to the question of their children's education, and in China itself several organizations deal with overseas Chinese affairs, notably the Commission for the Overseas Chinese, which has the rank of a ministry, while thirty seats in the National People's Assembly are reserved to representatives of the overseas Chinese.[18] But the evolution of the past few years clearly shows that Peking has progressively abandoned any effort to make political use of them and is more and more willing to put state-to-state relations ahead of protection of the local Chinese.[19]

To make her influence felt in Southeast Asia, China, as a communist state, can use one other instrument on the local level: the communist movements, whether official or clandestine. Naturally, these parties or movements do not act uniquely as intermediaries, they principally operate on their own account. But they strongly feel the influence of China, the Chinese Communist Party, and the Chinese revolutionary model, and some have representatives in China.

However, in the utilization of the communist movements in the region, China has met from the very beginning two permanent obstacles, to which a third and perhaps a fourth have been added in the past few years.

To begin with, the members of the communist movements in some Southeast Asian countries are mostly recruited from within the Chinese communities. This constitutes a double danger, both for the Chinese community to become identified with a subversive movement—which happened in the Malayan insurgency or in the repression of the communist coup in Indonesia in 1965—and for the communist movement to become identified with a community resented for its economic power and lack of assimilation, which has often been the case elsewhere. The communist parties have attempted to circumvent this obstacle by promoting native leaders and recruiting more from the local population, but they have not so far been very successful in their efforts.

The second obstacle derives partly from the previous one and partly from China's geographic proximity. It is the risk that a local Communist Party will be considered—not entirely without foundation—by the government or people of the country as the instrument of the national interests of China, whose imperialism is feared. That is why, in several parts of Asia, Peking's support to the native communist movements may be received by them as a mixed blessing.

A last obstacle to the full utilization by China of the communist parties of Southeast Asia has developed in the past few years. It is based on the ideological conflict that opposes China to the Soviet Union, and which is translated in Southeast Asia into a struggle for influence with the local communist movements, but also, in political terms, with the local governments. While most communist movements would probably have preferred not to take sides in the dispute and to remain neutral, they have generally, and for obvious reasons of affinity and proximity, bent in the direction of China.

However, there is another factor that further limits China's potential utilization of the communist movements in Southeast Asia, particularly in the Indochinese peninsula, and that is the influence of Vietnamese communism. Apart naturally from North Vietnam and South Vietnam, where the final outcome of the conflict is still undecided more than a year after the U.S. pullout, Vietnamese communism is influential in Laos, Cambodia, and Thailand, and North Vietnamese interests in these countries by no means coincide with China's.

The case of Vietnam is significant and relevant to China's potential use of the communist movements in Southeast Asia. Communism succeeded in North Vietnam not so much because of China's proximity (although that helped), but because the communist movement there, under a very able leadership, identified itself completely with nationalism and the struggle for independence or, later, freedom from "imperialism." Furthermore, overseas Chinese in North

Vietnam were extremely few and did not participate, in an obvious or important fashion, in the nationalist/communist struggle. All of these conditions are lacking, to a greater or lesser degree, in the other countries of the region, in addition to weaknesses of local communist leaderships and organizations—weaknesses well recognized in Peking.[20] This is significant, in terms of both the chances of communist spread and the potential utilization by China of the communist movements in Southeast Asia.

STAGES OF CHINESE FOREIGN POLICY IN SOUTHEAST ASIA

When one studies the stages of China's foreign policy in Southeast Asia and the tactics she has used since 1949, one is struck by two facts: on the one hand, these stages seem to coincide with the stages of China's domestic policy especially during the first ten years; on the other hand, while Chinese foreign policy objectives, both ideological or national, remain constant, their implementation is conducted with varying amounts of forcefulness. An essential character of Chinese foreign policy is, therefore, its flexibility summed up thus by Maoist dialectics used on the domestic scene: two steps forward, one step backward. The West, preoccupied by the vocal excesses of China's nationalist and bellicose proclamations, has often tended to underestimate her tactical flexibility and firm perseverance in progressing from one controlled tension to another, in the pursuit of long-term objectives.[21]

However, corresponding with some approximation to the stages of her domestic policy, one can distinguish several phases in the foreign policy of China since 1949.

1949-53: Self-assertion and Aggression

During the first period, that of the setting up of the communist regime (a preparatory phase on the domestic economic and social scene with the agrarian reform and the progressive socialization of the economy), China displayed abroad a militant and nationalist attitude, typical of most newly successful revolutionary governments, encouraging movements of national liberation and attempting to check U.S. influence in Asia. A decisive moment in this period was China's intervention in Korea, which to a large extent can be considered as a reaction of defense.

China's official foreign policy was marked by an alignment with the Soviet Union. She leaned completely to one side, in the world's division into two blocs following the beginning of the cold war. The communist line at the time was fundamentally hostile to most of the rest of the world, including neutral countries. China closely followed Soviet policy regarding colonial Asia, and toward noncommunist nationalist movements or governments. For Mao, a third way did not exist, a neutralist position such as Nehru's was to be condemned, since it objectively served imperialist interests.

That is why the Chinese leaders encouraged communist rebellions every-where, convinced that revolutions were going to spread throughout Asia following their example. Following a communist conference held in Calcutta from December 1947 to March 1948, communist-led revolts broke out or regained activity in India, Burma, Malaya, Indochina, Indonesia, and the Philippines, and the Chinese communists proclaimed their support of these various armed rebellions. But only in Vietnam did China directly support revolution.

From the very beginning of this period, therefore, China's tactics in Southeast Asia were based upon the support, at least moral, of insurrectionist communist movements, as the only revolutionary forces. They placed emphasis on military strength and subversion. For the Chinese, inde-pendence and social reforms were meaningless unless they were achieved under antiimperialist and, if possible, communist controlled governments. In June 1950, however, China established diplomatic relations with the govern-ments of Burma and Indonesia, probably considered as antiimperialist, as well as with the Vietminh.

But the results of that "hard" policy were not encouraging. Most of the communist revolts were repressed by the national governments, except in Vietnam, and the cold war had reinforced the western nations in their determination to resist communist military efforts in Asia as well as in Europe. Besides, China was beginning to gain the sympathies of nationalist Asia, as a symbol of a formerly oppressed Asian country that had recovered power and prestige. She was progressively realizing that a neutralist bloc, composed of countries desirous of peace, but outside of the alliance system, could in fact be directed against the West. That bloc could be used by China as an instrument, allowing her to play an essential role on the world scene, provided, however, that she played the role of a spokesman and leader, not of the communist countries, but of countries formerly colonized or oppressed.

Therefore, signs of a change of tactics on the part of the communist nations and especially of China could be felt by the middle of 1951, when negotiations began in Korea. In 1952, an international economic conference held in Moscow showed a willingness on the part of the communist countries to engage in trade relations with noncommunist countries. In Southeast Asia, the communist parties tended to substitute political action for armed insurrection. Even Stalin, before his death, mentioned the possibility of establishing peaceful coexistence and economic competition between the capitalist and the com-munist blocs. In October 1952, at the conference, "Peace in Asia and the Pacific" held in Peking, the Chinese proclaimed their adherence to the new line of peaceful coexistence between countries of different economic and social systems, advocated a halt of fighting in the various countries of Southeast Asia, and showed their desire to take up the leadership of the nations of Asia, with an emphasis on common interests. These tendencies further developed after Stalin's death, and one may consider that this first period in communist China's foreign policy ended with the armistice in Korea of July 1953—at a time when, on the domestic scene, the Chinese were launching their ambitious first five-year plan.

1953-57: The Era of Peaceful Coexistence

This second phase in China's foreign policy was to last from approximately the middle of 1953 to the end of 1957. It corresponded, on the domestic scene, to the first five-year plan. On the external scene, Chinese foreign policy was dominated by the subtle and flexible personality of Mr. Chou En-lai, her prime minister and foreign minister.

While fighting had ceased in Korea, it was continuing in Indochina, where the Chinese were providing the Vietminh with increased military supplies at a time when the Americans were doing the same thing for the French and the threat existed of still greater military escalation. Because of that threat, and the general war weariness on the part of most parties concerned (exacerbated for the French by their defeat at Dien Bien Phu), the Geneva Conference, which had opened earlier in April 1954, succeeded in bringing to an end the first Indochina war. At that conference, China played a crucial role in helping work out an acceptable arrangement, to the extent of pressuring the Vietminh into concessions they were convinced they did not have to make.

The Geneva Conference marked a milestone in the development of China's foreign policy. The Chinese leaders then began to realize fully the possibilities of an active foreign policy and of relations between governments. From then on, Chou En-lai started a diplomatic campaign of contacts and seduction, to broaden and reinforce China's influence, particularly with the nonaligned countries of South and Southeast Asia.

The method was simple. It consisted in minimizing China's communist or revolutionary character and emphasizing good neighborliness and sympathy with the aspirations of the Asian nations to remain aloof from power struggles and alliances involving the major powers. In so doing, China hoped to conciliate forces much larger than just the communist parties of Asia.[22] This was an attitude that appealed to the anticolonialist and antiwestern feelings of many Asians, and their common desire to tackle pressing internal problems with a common approach.

The first step in that direction was the signing of a commercial agreement with India in April 1954, which mentioned for the first time the five principles of peaceful coexistence as a common basis. These principles were reiterated by Chou En-lai a few months later during a visit to New Delhi and later Rangoon, and then he expressed the hope, in a speech given in China in September 1954, that the same principles could apply to relations with Indonesia, Cambodia, Laos, and other Asian countries. The overseas Chinese were exhorted to abide by the laws and customs of their resident countries. The Chinese government hoped they would not be discriminated against and declared it was willing to settle the question of their nationality with the local governments on a bilateral basis.

Until then, all previous Chinese governments had considered that the overseas Chinese and their descendants had retained Chinese nationality. This position was revised, as a significant concession destined to remove the most serious obstacle to China's popularity in Southeast Asia: her identification with the generally unpopular overseas Chinese.[23]

They could be sacrificed in the interest of the antiwestern front. For, by calling upon Asian solidarity and neutralism, China was attempting to weaken the anticommunist coalition set up by the United States in 1954 through the Southeast Asia Treaty Organization (SEATO), and she presented the organization as an effort to reestablish western control in Southeast Asia under the cover of a struggle against subversion. China declared itself in full agreement with the important Asian countries (India, Burma, and Indonesia), which had refused to take part in the Manila Conference from which SEATO developed, in order to preserve their independence and freedom of action.

While peace had been reestablished in Korea and Indochina through mutual concessions on the part of both camps, China maintained an aggressive posture towards Taiwan, marked in 1954-55 by a propaganda campaign and the shelling of coastal islands held by the nationalists. However, while disapproving the use of force, there were many Asian states that recognized the validity of China's claim over Taiwan and its dependencies and welcomed Chou's call to the United States to negotiate the Taiwan and offshore islands questions. That crisis abated by the spring of 1955 and China's policy of détente manifested itself clearly through her participation in two conferences held in April 1955, one in New Delhi and the other in Bandung, Indonesia. The latter was the famous first conference of the Afro-Asian group, convened by several South and Southeast Asian countries.

At this meeting of the "Estates-General of the Third World"[24] from which representatives from both the western nations and the Soviet Union were excluded, China, in the person of Chou En-lai, played a key role, together with Nehru of India.

The Bandung Conference had been conceived partly as an answer to SEATO, and partly as an effort to bring together those nations, many of which were former colonies, that had in common both a heritage of dependence and vital problems of development in an unstable international context. Through brilliant personal diplomacy, Chou En-lai succeeded in making many contacts, winning friendships and working toward presenting an image of China as an essentially conciliatory and peaceful country. While advocating a complete end of colonization, western exploitation, and the policy of military alliances, bases and confrontation, he affirmed China's policy of cooperation and nonintervention in the affairs of other nations, peaceful coexistence, and a desire to establish normal relations on that basis with all countries, including the United States. Thereafter, contacts were made with the Americans in Geneva, and then in Warsaw. As a token of goodwill, China signed an agreement with Indonesia on the status of the overseas Chinese there.

For several years, the invocation of the spirit of Bandung became one of the *leitmotifs* of Chinese diplomacy abroad. This was the great period of cultural and economic diplomacy, and exchanges of visits between Chinese and Asian personalities. Several border problems were solved amicably (with Burma), and China began making loans or grants to several Southeast Asian countries (Burma and Cambodia). Relations were excellent with Indonesia, and in August 1957 China recognized the Federation of Malaya. Informal contacts were even made with conservative prowest regimes such as those of Thailand and the Philippines.

But this period of détente and goodwill in international relations came to an end toward 1957. China's foreign policy toward Asia hardened, even though her propaganda repeated the same principles of peaceful coexistence. That hardening corresponded fairly well to the initiation on the domestic scene of the Great Leap Forward and the people's communes.

1958-68: A Chaotic Decade

It is somewhat difficult to delineate the recent phases of a major country's foreign policy, when some facts or shifts of policy have not yet taken on their full significance and when one lacks enough perspective to determine clearly the precise location of major watersheds. This is especially true in a country as secretive and isolated from the rest of the world as China. A few years ago one could distinguish in China's history during the troubled decade that began in 1958 and lasted until 1968-69, three phases that corresponded on the domestic scene to the Great Leap Forward (1958-61), the following period of relaxation (1962-65), and then a new upheaval with the Cultural Revolution (1965-68). As in the previous phases, these periods in Chinese domestic history could somewhat be paralleled with phases in foreign policy. With some distance in time and the clear beginning of a new phase in China's domestic and foreign policy by 1969, it now appears preferable to consider the period from 1958 to 1968-69 as one phase, going from one upheaval on the internal scene to another. During that period, Chinese foreign policy was dominated by the progressive development of the Sino-Soviet dispute, and affected by internal events. Its application in many areas, particularly in Southeast Asia, was marked by a large amount of pragmatism and frequent erratic moves.

The policy of peaceful coexistence had produced positive results for China, but maybe not the goals she envisaged, such as the liberation of Taiwan. The hardening that took place from the end of 1957 was probably related to a series of complex developments both on the domestic and international scene. It apparently began with Mao's speech of November 1957 stating that the east wind now prevailed over the west wind. This corresponded to a reassessment by Mao of the balance of power in the world, which seemed to have tilted toward the socialist camp in the wake of Soviet technological advances, such as the launching of Sputnik and the possession of intercontinental ballistic missiles. Meanwhile, Europe, after Suez, and especially the United States in the last Eisenhower years, seemed to be lagging behind and on the verge of an economic recession. That situation could have presented opportunities for the Socialist bloc, but on the other hand, there also had been a dangerous relaxation in the bloc with Khrushchev's de-Stalinization speech (February 1956), the events in Poland (summer 1956), the Hungarian revolt (autumn 1956), and in China itself the Hundred Flowers episode (1956-1957), which had necessitated a harsh campaign of rectification. All those developments pointed toward a tightening both on the domestic and international fronts, made possible by the placement in key posts of men who were partisans of radical measures, and soon made necessary by the launching of the Great Leap Forward and the beginning of the people's communes.

For several years, Southeast Asia would play a backstage role on the scene of China's foreign policy. Internally, Chinese energies were mobilized for the great leap, and then occupied by the recovery from its excesses. Externally, the trouble spots were the straits of Taiwan in the summer of 1958, the Tibetan revolt and its repression in the spring of 1959, and the first signs of Sino-Indian differences over their border. The major enemy remained the United States, while China was becoming uneasy about the Soviet Union's attempts to relax tensions with the United States. With Southeast Asia, relations remained at first peaceful and then fluctuated in response to local events in 1959, such as the crisis in Laos and the repression of the overseas Chinese in Indonesia. By 1960, frictions had disappeared and friendly relations continued with Burma, Cambodia, and even Laos and Indonesia, marked by visits and economic agreements. China attended the Geneva conference on Laos in May 1961, indicating a greater interest in that country. The limited war with India took place in 1962. But while China's policy in Southeast Asia remained pragmatic, her overall general line was increasingly defensive with the development of the Sino-Soviet dispute, which was progressively adding a major threat and a major enemy in addition to the United States. It created, on the part of China, a justifiable feeling of encirclement and increased isolation. That feeling had two main consequences. On the one hand, there was the necessity for China to become self-reliant and develop defensive capabilities, leading, among other things, to nuclear armament. On the other, there was the necessity to break the encirclement and come out of isolation, which manifested itself in several ways. First, by attempts to limit or keep out foreign influences from the chosen Chinese zone of influence, Southeast Asia. Those influences were mainly American, but also, increasingly included Soviet ideological and political ideas. That is why the president of the Chinese Republic, Liu Shao-ch'i, visited several Southeast Asian countries in 1963 (Indonesia, Burma, Cambodia, and North Vietnam) following a visit in the area by the Soviet minister for defense. Second, in 1964 there were Chinese overtures toward Western European and African countries.

By the end of 1964, two events greatly affected Chinese foreign policy: the escalation of the conflict in Vietnam, with increased American intervention by 1965, and the explosion of the first Chinese atom bomb in 1964, followed by others in 1965 and 1966 and finally a thermonuclear experiment in 1967. Paradoxically, these two events, while enhancing China's prestige in Asia, increased even further China's defensive posture, by making her vulnerable to a preemptive attack on the part of either the United States, or even more, as years went by, on the part of the Soviet Union. Therefore, China chose to pursue a very prudent external policy, indulging only in verbal violence. The year 1965 saw major setbacks for Chinese influence in Africa and above all in Indonesia, with the coup leading to the savage repression of the communists— and incidentally of many overseas Chinese—in that country. These tendencies were further accentuated in 1966, when the beginning of the Cultural Revolution in China virtually brought Chinese diplomacy to a halt with the recall to China of practically all Chinese ambassadors.

Throughout the Cultural Revolution, China appeared to have no clear guidelines in her foreign policy, which was affected by such internal events as

Red Guard demonstrations against foreign embassies and diplomats in Peking, as well as Red Guard disruption of the Foreign Ministry in 1967. These developments on the Chinese domestic scene were received rather unfavorably abroad, and various countries in Southeast Asia were irritated by demonstrations on the part of young overseas Chinese in favor of Mao's personality cult. Those in Burma and Cambodia, for example, strained those countries' relations with China and even led to apologies to Cambodia on the part of Chou En-lai.

But the turmoil generated by the Cultural Revolution finally came to an end by 1968-69. After a hiatus of nearly four years, Chinese foreign policy again became active and could take initiatives rather than simply react to events. A fourth phase in China's foreign policy, therefore, began in 1969, and was marked by striking developments and changes.

1969-74: Normalization and the Emergence of a New Balance of Power

The formal end of the Cultural Revolution took place at the time of the Ninth Congress of the Chinese Communist Party in April 1969. The Congress opened a period of relaxation on the domestic scene, allowing for recuperation and reorganization of the country and rebuilding of the Communist Party. It also allowed Chou En-lai, the main architect of Chinese foreign policy, to return to that field, after a period when he had had to devote all his energies to internal developments. Within two years, major changes were to occur in China's foreign policy. But if a relaxation on the domestic scene had made an active Chinese foreign policy again possible, external events had made initiative and dynamism necessary, if not indispensable for China. In point of fact, those external events may actually have brought about—or at least contributed to—the end of the Cultural Revolution and the consequent domestic relaxation.

In March and August 1969, violent armed clashes occurred between Russian and Chinese troops on the Ussuri River. The Sino-Soviet dispute, once almost exclusively verbal, had become bloody, with the threat of further escalation looming large. The possession of a fledgling nuclear armament by China made her even more vulnerable to a Soviet preemptive strike, which was talked about not only in China but also in the USSR. It was, therefore, more imperative than ever for China to come out of her isolation, recover and increase her respectability on the international scene, and most of all prevent the collusion of the two superpowers against her—if possible by pitting one against the other for her self-preservation. This was the traditional principle of "using one barbarian to control another."[25]

Throughout that fourth phase, these various approaches, which were interdependent, were used simultaneously by China. While limited contacts had already been made with the United States during the two preceding years, a momentum developed from December 1970, when Mao told American writer Edgar Snow he was ready to receive President Nixon, to the visit to China of American ping-pong players, the lifting of several U.S. restrictions against that country, and the July 1971 visit by Mr. Kissinger to Peking that led to Mr. Nixon's announcement of a future trip to China. Washington was now ready to define a new China policy, but above all eager to extricate itself from Vietnam. China, which had always been very prudent in relation to the Vietnam War, giving the North Vietnamese greater verbal than material support, further diminished its material support, leaving a heavier burden in that respect to the Soviet Union,[26] with the concomitant risk of jeopardizing the détente between the two superpowers. With the Paris peace treaty of 1973 and the U.S. troop pullout, one of the major causes of friction between China and the United States was apparently removed. (Who by then remembered that U.S. buildup in Vietnam was originally aimed at halting the spread of Chinese communism in Southeast Asia?)

But even before that, the second bone of contention—U.S. support of and treaty with Taiwan—had been somewhat bypassed, when China entered the U.N. and the Security Council in October 1971 and Taiwan was expelled. The Nixon visit proceeded on schedule in February 1972, followed, in September by that of the Japanese Premier Tanaka. The latter visit was accompanied by the end of the state of war and establishment of diplomatic relations between the two countries.

By the time of the Tenth Party Congress in August 1973, Chinese foreign policy had achieved all the major objectives, some of them long-standing, others more recent, which had become imperative at the beginning of this fourth phase. She had come out of her isolation and acquired international respectability and major power status in the U.N. She had mended fences with a former archenemy, one of the two superpowers, the United States, and established with it promising, if still somewhat limited, relations. Because of all that, the major threat she was facing on her northern borders from the Soviet Union had been diminished, if not permanently suppressed, as the United States had let the USSR know that it would not tolerate a preemptive strike against China.

While all these brilliant successes may have been essentially pursued for reasons of self-preservation, their consequences go far beyond lessening the Soviet threat to China. They have given China a front seat on the world's stage, and made her a key element in a new balance of power, which is progressively emerging in the Pacific area and especially in Southeast Asia. Now that the conflicts in Indochina have lost, if not their violence, at least much of their capacity to involve directly the major powers, and while the United States seems willing to observe a lower profile in the area, a flexible situation has been created there, presenting opportunities for various influences to compete, and for various alignments and realignments to take place. There is no doubt that China both wishes, and is now in a position to play an essential role in Southeast Asia. However, her perspective and attitude vis-à-vis the area, in the light of the objectives and instrumentalities previously defined, and in view of past practices, will in the coming years also depend upon a series of factors that remain to be determined.

CHINA'S PERSPECTIVE IN THE NEW BALANCE
OF POWER IN SOUTHEAST ASIA

Developments during the fourth phase of China's foreign policy seemed to point toward a greater autonomy than before of the country's foreign policy in relation to internal developments, at the same time that national interests appeared to take precedence over ideological interests and objectives. In that respect, the most striking examples would be the rapprochement between China and the United States and China's support of Pakistan in the Bangladesh war. The circumstances, which are making the major powers willing to practice a balance-of-power policy in Southeast Asia,[27] seem further to guarantee an evolution of Chinese foreign policy in the direction of still greater emphasis on national interests and greater autonomy in relation to domestic policy. However, that tendency might be reversed and certain internal developments in China could, presumably, strongly affect her foreign policy.

Mao's theory of the permanent revolution requires, from time to time, shakeups, sometimes violent, of the Chinese society in order to keep the people on their toes and the revolutionary spirit alive. By 1974, China seemed to be overdue for such an upheaval and the campaign that began at the end of 1973 against Confucius and Lin Piao might just be the beginning of such an upheaval. There are signs that the overtures toward the West might have gone too far for some, to the point of endangering ideological purity without markedly benefiting Chinese security, and an adverse reaction could significantly affect the course of present Chinese foreign policy.

Closely related to the question of the permanent revolution and of China's attitude in foreign policy is the problem of Mao's succession. His death could mean the end of, or a lesser emphasis on, the idea of permanent revolution, but could also mean a reversal of the relaxation with the United States and less attention to revolutionary movements.[28] The opposite, although unlikely, should not be excluded. Also at the present highly unlikely, but by no means to be excluded, is the possibility of a rapprochement between China and the USSR.

Personality problems played a large role in the development of the Sino-Soviet dispute, and a change of leadership in one or both countries could radically change their attitude toward each other, and consequently the balance of power in Southeast Asia. After all, if China could effect a rapprochement with the United States, her former ideological and national archenemy, presumably she could go back to a former friend. At the present time, however, areas of friction are of such magnitude that they seem to preclude more than a limited relaxation of tensions between the two.

At a time when the United States appears to be disengaging progressively from Southeast Asia and when, on the contrary, the Soviet Union is trying to expand its influence there, China's efforts are likely to be directed mainly at stopping the Soviet Union in its containment of China policy. But it should never be forgotten that in spite of the U.S.-China rapprochement, it is still essential for China to diminish American influence in Southeast Asia, and that the rapprochement is, first of all, a tactical move and may only be temporary, lasting long enough to permit readjustments favorable to China.

Excluding a rapprochement with the USSR, China's attitude toward that country with respect to Southeast Asia, therefore, appears clearly defined for several years to come. As for India, in spite of that country's present close relations with the USSR, China does not perceive her as a threat in the Southeast Asian area, because of India's limited capabilities there. The most complex and uncertain types of relationships between China and other major powers in Southeast Asia can be expected to involve both the United States and Japan.

What makes China's relations with the United States and Japan complex and uncertain is the interaction and sometimes opposition of political and economic factors. It is well established that Southeast Asia is an area rich in natural resources, a fact which never left the major powers indifferent. But the Arab-Israeli war of October 1973 and the ensuing oil embargo have given the existing and potential oil-rich areas—in the coastal waters of Indonesia, Indo-china, and China, for example—an increased importance. The question is whether that importance is temporary or long-lasting, in relation to such factors as the potential renewal of the embargo, the stabilization of oil production in the Middle East in the face of increased world demand, and the search for alternative sources of energy. Accordingly, U.S. economic as well as political interests in the area may increase. Japan's economic interests are also important, long-standing, and can only increase in Southeast Asia because the region is seen by her as a source of raw materials and markets—also leading to competition with China. China could benefit from U.S. technical knowledge, and there has even been mention of joint U.S.-Chinese explorations for oil off the China coast, as China's own need for oil is likely to increase with her growing industrialization to the point she will no longer be self-sufficient in oil. But economic cooperation between the two countries on a large scale is probably unrealistic, given the blatant disparities between them, especially in terms of economic level of advancement, ideologies, and heritage. Furthermore, China would not want to become overly dependent on a superpower, the United States, for political reasons, and her past experience with the USSR was certainly a lesson. Far greater appear to be the prospects for Sino-Japanese cooperation. Economically, China needs Japan far more than Japan needs China.

In spite of recent and bitter antagonisms, Japan is much closer to China geographically and mentally than any other major power. She could provide China with capital and expertise and find there the huge market of which the nineteenth century Europeans dreamed. In Southeast Asia, Japan is at present strong economically, but weak politically. The Southeast Asians have not forgotten the Japanese occupation of World War II, and are wary of Japanese economic colonialism and its chances of again developing into political imperialism, as shown in the anti-Japanese demonstrations that took place in Thailand and Indonesia in 1973. Under these circimstances, it would be to China's advantage to work out a compromise with Japan in Southeast Asia in terms of economic interests, keeping the superpowers out with an Asia for the Asians approach, and progressively detaching Japan from the U.S. alliance. But in so doing, care has to be taken not to make Japan feel insecure, and consequently drive the Japanese to full-scale remilitarization, possibly at the nuclear level. So long as that last eventuality does not exist, China can expect, by continuing to observe a moderate and peaceful stance, to become the politically dominant power in Southeast Asia.

As important as any other consideration is China's attitude toward the countries of Southeast Asia themselves, in the framework of the new balance of power. We have seen previously what were China's interests and objectives in Southeast Asia, what sort of instrumentalities she could use, and her record up to the present time. But the emergence of a balance of power in Southeast Asia, with its flexibility and possibilities for realignments between the major powers involved, has also created new possibilities of flexibility for the Southeast Asian nations themselves.[29] Most Southeast Asian countries are acutely aware that the new situation can only enhance China's influence in the area and several governments, such as Thailand's, are rapidly taking steps to improve their relations with their giant neighbor, and there have been contacts even between the Philippines and China. There are also growing prospects for the establishment of official relations between China and Malaysia and Singapore.

In asserting her influence, China is going to proceed with caution, taking the government to government approach, using the traditional channels of official diplomacy, developing trade and aid (the aid program to Burma has been resumed), and deemphasizing the subversive use of either the overseas Chinese or even the communist parties.[30] Thus, Sihanouk complained bitterly of Chinese lack of support for the communist insurrection in Cambodia.[31] However, Chinese support of subversive activities could always be revived should the need arise, since China's ideological objectives are not likely to disappear, and such support—or the threat of it—can also serve China's national interests. In that respect, the significance of the renewal of communist activities in Burma and Malaysia is somewhat unclear[32] and might simply demonstrate independence on the part of local communist insurrectionists.

As long as Mr. Chou En-lai, or someone following his line, remains in charge of determining China's foreign policy, it is reasonable to expect China to play a major role—if not *the* major one—in Southeast Asia, within the framework of the new balance of power.

NOTES

1. A. M. Halpern, "The foreign policy uses of the Chinese revolutionary model," *China Quarterly* (July 1961): 2. See too: Robert C. North, *The foreign relations of China* (Belmont, California: Dickenson, 1969), p. 60.

2. A. Doak Barnett, *Communist China and Asia, A challenge to American policy* (New York: Praeger Publishers, 1960), p. 68.

3. Robert A. Scalapino, "Moscow, Peking and the communist parties of Asia," *Foreign Affairs* (January 1963): 323.

4. Cf. Alain G. Marsot, "L'influence de la Chine Populare en Asie du Sud-Est." Unpublished dissertation, Paris University, 1964.

5. Robert A. Scalapino, "Traditions and transitions in the Asian policy of Communist China," in Edward F. Szczepanik ed., *Symposium on economic and social problems of the Far East* (Hong Kong: Hong Kong University Press, 1963), p. 266. See too: Ishwer C. Ohja, *Chinese foreign policy in an age of transition: the diplomacy of cultural despair*, 2nd ed. (Boston: Beacon Press, 1969), pp. 49-50.

6. C. P. Fitzgerald, "The Chinese view of foreign relations," *The World Today* (London: Chatham House, January 1963), p. 10. See too: Gavin Boyd, "China," in Wayne Wilcox, Leo E. Rose, Gavin Boyd, eds., *Asia and the international system* (Cambridge, Mass.: Winthrop Publishers, 1972), p. 27.

7. Cf. Melvin Gurtov, *China and Southeast Asia—The politics of survival: A study of foreign policy interactions* (Lexington, Mass.: D. C. Heath, 1971), p. 22.

8. H. A. Steiner, "Ideology versus interest in China's foreign policy," in Szczepanik, ed., op. cit., p. 249.

9. Cf. Werner Klatt, ed., *The Chinese model* (Hong Kong: Hong Kong University Press, 1965), especially G. F. Hudson, "The Chinese model and the developing countries," pp. 205 ff.

10. Cf. Frank G. Langdon, "China's policy in Southeast Asia," in Mark W. Zacher and R. Stepehen Milne, eds., *Conflict and stability in Southeast Asia* (New York: Doubleday, Anchor Books, 1974), p. 294.

11. North, op. cit., p. 95. See too: Harold J. Hinton, *Communist China in world politics* (London: MacMillan, 1966), pp. 343 ff.

12. Yuan Li-wu, "The weapon of trade," *Problems of Communism* (January 1960): 31.

13. T. J. Hughes and D. E. T. Luard, *The economic development of Communist China, 1949-1958* (London: Oxford University Press, 1959), p. 127.

14. "Communist states and developing countries: Aid and trade in 1972," Department of State, Bureau of Public Affairs, News Release, August 1973.

15. Ibid. See too: "Issues in United States foreign policy," Department of State, General foreign policy series 264, Publication 8665, August 1972.

16. Cf. Alain G. Marsot, "China's aid to Cambodia," *Pacific Affairs*, vol. 42, no. 2 (Summer 1969): 189 ff.

17. Department of State, "Communist states and developing countries," op. cit.

18. Cf. Alain G. Marsot, "La Chine Populaire et les communautés Chinoises du Sud-Est Asiatique," *Revue Juridique et Politique Indépendance et Coopération*, Paris, April 1964, pp. 179 ff.

19. See Stephen Fitzgerald, *China and the Overseas Chinese* (Cambridge, Mass.: Cambridge University Press, 1972), p. 185 ss.

20. Melvin Gurtov, "China's policies in Southeast Asia: three studies," *Studies in comparative Communism*, vol. 3, nos. 3-4 (July 1970), 13 ff.

21. Tibor Mende, *La Chine et son ombre* (Paris: Le Seuil, 1960), p. 290.

22. Guy Wint, "The first decade, China and Asia," *The China Quarterly* (January 1960): 64.

23. J. H. Brimmel, *Communism in Southeast Asia, A political analysis* (London: Oxford University Press, 1959), p. 288. See too: Harold J. Hinton, *Communist China in World Politics* (London: MacMillan, 1966), p. 402.

24. Julien Cheverny, *Eloge du Colonialisme* (Paris: Julliard, 1961), p. 92.

25. John Bryan Starr, *Ideology and Culture, An Introduction to the dialectic of contemporary Chinese Politics* (New York: Harper and Row, 1973), p. 241.

26. Thomas W. Robinson, "The view from Peking: China's policies towards the United States, the Soviet Union and Japan," *Pacific Affairs*, vol. 45, no. 3 (Fall 1972): 333 ff.

27. Gurtov, op. cit., chapter 1. Also: Howard Wriggins, "The Asian state system in the 1970's," in Wilcox et al., op. cit., pp. 350 ff.

28. Thomas W. Robinson, "Future domestic and foreign policy choices for mainland China" *Journal of International Affairs*, vol. 26, no. 2 (1972), p. 192.

29. Wriggins, in Wilcox, op. cit. Also see below: Chapter 7: "The View From Southeast Asia in the Seventies."

30. Jean-Claude Pomonti, "Pekin a assoupli son attitude a l'egard des regimes anti-communistes d'Extreme-Orient," *Le Monde*, 9 May 1973. See too: Robert S. Elegant, "China's new stance on rebellions," Los Angeles *Times*, 20 January 1974.

31. Sihanouk's interview to *Le Monde*, 27 October 1973.

32. Catherine Lamour, "Les forces du P.C. prochinois marquent des points dans les regions shans, strategiquement importantes," *Le Monde*, 10 January 1974. Also: Jacques Decornoy, "Malaisie: Le renouveau de l'insurrection communiste est sensible dans l'ouest du pays," *Le Monde*, 16 March 1974.

CHAPTER

5

JAPAN AND THE
SOUTHEAST ASIAN
CONFIGURATION
Alvin D. Coox

Japan's postwar relationship to Southeast Asia is colored by the fact that she was the one defeated country among the great powers interested in the area. Whereas the United States, China, the Soviet Union, and even India have clashed repeatedly on the battlefield against one or more of the others since 1945, or have (with the exception of India) become militarily involved in Indochina, Japan has remained on the sidelines, essentially disarmed, long unnoticed, and making money. No uniformed Japanese soldiers have been seen in the region for almost 30 years, and even occasional United Nations' appeals for peacekeeping teams have been rejected for constitutional reasons. This is a far cry from the situation in 1941, when Japanese Imperial General Headquarters could plan to overrun the Philippines, Guam, Hong Kong, Malaya, Burma, Java, Sumatra, the Celebes, Borneo, and Timor within 150 days.

Economically, however, have-not Japan can neither live without nor, as recent events suggest, can she live *with* the countries of insular and continental Southeast Asia. Through the Malacca Strait, Japan receives 85 percent of her crude oil, 42 percent of her copper, and over 17 percent of her iron ore. From Indonesian waters comes 13 percent of her lead, 31 percent of her bauxite; and from Australia, 19 percent of her iron, over 13 percent of her lead, and 38 percent of her bauxite.[1] Despite feverish Japanese attempts at diversification of sources, the geopolitical facts of life have remained immutable.

Today Japan is the main trading partner of every Southeast Asian nation. Her total trade with this part of the world approaches the level of commerce with Western Europe and exceeds the trade with Northeastern Asia. In 1973, for the first time in a decade, Japanese exports to Southeast Asia exceeded sales to the United States. During recent years, trade with Japan has accounted for the following percentages of Southeast Asian countries' imports: Thailand, 32.2 percent, the Philippines, 31 percent; South Vietnam, 28.8 percent; Indonesia, 20.9 percent; Singapore, 11.1 percent, Malaysia, 7.8 percent; and the whole area, 22.8 percent.[2]

Having learned, to her agony, the essentially uneconomic quality of attempted military solutions to insoluble problems, Japan has turned with remarkable success to private overseas investment, which is expected to total $26 billion by 1980 (about three percent of the GNP), flowing outward at the rate of some $3.5 billion per year. In the nineteen years through 1969, Southeast and South Asia have attracted 43.5 percent of Japanese investment projects and 22.5 percent of investment volume on an approval basis. Indonesia drew 32 percent of Japan's Asian investments; Thailand, 13 percent; Malaysia; 6 percent; and Singapore, 4 percent. As of early 1973, cumulative Japanese private investments, in millions of U.S. dollars and distributed among securities, loans, real estate, direct investment, and overseas branches, totalled $473 million in Indonesia, $129 million in Thailand, $88 million in the Philippines, $86 million in Brunei, $90 million in Singapore, and $76 million in Malaysia.[3]

Apart from utilizing more abundant and cheaper labor while penetrating markets for industrial products, Japanese business has concentrated on developing natural resources, a category which has been accounting for over 35 percent of Japanese investments; manufacturing totals about 27 percent and commerce 12 percent.[4] Even before the spurt in investment and trading activity, the Japanese government had adopted a policy of arranging reparation agreements with aggrieved but recognized nations of Southeast Asia. The trouble was, according to critics, that the benefits were not diffused and that greedy contractors felt "there was no business like reparations business"—a refrain that more recently has been applied to the "aid business."

Nevertheless, the scars of World War II run deep in Southeast Asia, or are at least uncovered easily when desired, even by those who were not yet born when the war ended. Episodes of erstwhile military inhumanity can still inflame the public, from the retold stories of the bridge over the River Kwai, to the Bataan death march, to the dread dungeons of Singapore. Even the gentle folk of rice-rich Annam remember the grim winter of 1943-44, when the Japanese occupiers wantonly destroyed thousands of tons of precious rice and caused the deaths of an alleged 2 million noncombatants.

JAPAN'S IMAGE IN SOUTHEAST ASIA

Japan's present search for a peaceable balance in Southeast Asia has been retarded and complicated by a number of Japanese behavioral phenomena— some important, some whimsical—which give rise to cumulative local images of a so-called Ugly Japanese, a hyperaggressive businessman, or ill-mannered and ostentatious tourist. The Thais, according to Japanese in Bangkok, object to the following practices:[5]

The Japanese compare Thailand to the USA and Europe, ignoring the fact that Thailand is an Asian country. They are kind at first but not for long. When they give us something or do us a favor, they expect gratitude long afterwards. They say we are lazy, but don't they overdo things? They always keep busy and always say, "Fast! Fast!"—even on the golf course. They often work overtime, even on Sunday.

They speak ill of each other to us, but don't get angry when foreigners speak ill of their own prime minister. They tend to form a closed community, and there are too many of them (about 6,000) in Thailand. They drink heavily every day, sing loudly in restaurants and bars, and eat too fast. They keep holding office meetings, and they like to talk about their jobs even while socializing. They don't try to make friends with us or learn our language; they urge us to master Japanese in their offices. They make excessive profits in business and trade.

A foreign visitor at the President Hotel in Jakarta, owned and operated by Japan Air Lines, detected symbolic evidence of Japanese heavy-handedness in the rooms themselves. Insofar as he could discern, "Every item in the room— bed, bath, carpets, even light bulbs and ashtrays—was made in Japan. Not even batik curtains. The only thing Indonesian about the room was a reproduction of a Balinese painting on the wall—and it wouldn't surprise me if that was printed in Japan."[6]

Part of the problem derives from the fact that Japan's relations with Southeast Asian countries began on a crude, person-to-person, not international basis. In the Meiji period (1868-1912), the preponderance of Japanese who went to the region were female prostitutes. There was also a certain number of door-to-door peddlers, shopkeepers, and fortune hunters (many with a misfit or criminal background in Japan), as well as overworked coolies who died in droves. Japanese military victories over "white" powers in the Russo-Japanese War and World War I enhanced Japanese prestige and, in turn, stimulated Japanese romanticizing of Southeast Asia.

Japanese interest in the region declined in the 1930s during the worldwide Depression; attention turned to Manchuria, China, and Mongolia. Concern with Southeast Asia was rekindled by the Japanese official policy of a Greater East Asia Coprosperity Sphere in general, and of an acute energy crisis in particular, in about the years 1940-41. At the beginning of the Pacific War, the Japanese military forces conquered all of the important European and Asian possessions in Southeast Asia with impressive ease. Espousing "Asia for the Asiatics," Nippon then sponsored ostensibly sovereign client states under the nominal leadership of nationals, who gained considerable on-the-job training for the responsibilities of postwar independence in the process.

Japan's defeat in 1945 was followed by a long but undesired hiatus in Japanese attention to Southeast Asia—a trend reversed in the 1950s and 1960s by the exigencies of the Allied Occupation of Japan, the ideological cold war, and the pair of hot wars in Korea and Vietnam, which brought all of Japan's neighbors plus the United States into collision. From the limited wars Japan profited greatly in the economic sense, since the markets on the Chinese mainland had been closed to Japanese interests.[7]

In part, the Japanese have been suffering from the fact that they are torn in two directions themselves. On the one hand they regard themselves as

Westernized and non-Asian by virtue of their technology, politics, and power. Ichiro Kawasaki, a veteran diplomat, goes so far as to characterize the Japanese as obsessed by worship of the West, with the result that the Foreign Ministry cannot alone conduct a foreign policy that emphasizes Asia, and certainly not Southeast Asia.[8] On the other hand the Japanese naturally think of themselves as Asian because of their geography, heritage, language, and customs. It has taken a long time for the Japanese to realize that the wartime verbiage about Asian "community" represented little more than propaganda, and that they were woefully ignorant concerning Southeast Asia. Impatient, frustrated, and sometimes arrogant, certain Japanese technicians have come home saying that the Southeast Asian countries are not 50 or 100 but 200 or 300 years behind Japan.

The cultural and intellectual problems have been compounded by Japanese tariff and quota policies, which contributed to an excessively favorable (or at least highly visible) balance of trade; by hidden strings in reality imposed on loans and controls on indigenous companies; and by a lack of coordination and communication between corporate headquarters and local men-on-the-spot. In competition with American enterprises, the Japanese generally paid Asian employees at a drastically inferior scale, while taking lavish care of their own directors and managers in terms of salaries, bonuses, allowances, transportation, and housing. As for emphasis in business, the Americans tended to focus upon items of heavy industry, but the Japanese centered their efforts on consumer goods, which often compete with local industry. It was also not unknown, reportedly, for some Japanese traders to deal with corrupt local officials and to operate outside regular channels.

Mochtar Lubis, editor and publisher of the daily *Indonesia Raya*, has observed that Japan's economic development has left the rest of Asia far behind, thus giving Nippon the unenviable reputation of a neocolonial power. If the growing gap between the economies of Southeast Asia and of Japan become unbridgeable, international relationships could be distorted and would probably create perpetual tensions. Strain has already appeared because of the Japanese tendency to regard Southeast Asia primarily as a source of raw materials for industry and as a market for finished products. Lubis has explained how the Indonesian government has had to act to protect native entrepreneurs, after it was found that Japanese firms "were in control of the whole process of extracting raw material from Indonesia, transporting [it] to Japan, the processing of the raw material in Japan into semi-finished or finished products, again in the transportation of these processed products back to Indonesia, and Japanese firms also represented the Japanese manufacturers in Indonesia." Although such a phenomenon was by no means confined to the Japanese, the tendency to dominate the entire process of extraction, transportation, manufacturing, and trade was regarded by the Indonesians as "An absolute expression of the tremendous economic power now developed by Japan, and [it] is frightening many people in Asia."[9]

A Thai observer reflects similar concerns in his country, while comparing the methods of the competing great powers. "The British were too slow," asserts Pritoon Sayswang, "at adapting to the situation in a Thai setting—they thought they were in Singapore or Malaysia. The United States always proposes big projects and wants to do everything. . . . We delayed the projects for so long that the Americans became frustrated and went home." The Japanese, Dr. Sayswang notes, began by sending experts, "followed by one or two men who came pretending not to know anything." The Japanese supplied the capital and took in Thai partners; local businessmen did the rest. Thereupon the Japanese entered all available economic sectors, took over businesses, moved from import substitution to textiles and, needing larger partners, eventually combined with the Americans in a petrochemical complex. Sayswang worries lest these developments exacerbate the situation in Thailand even further: "When business gets this big it will no longer be JETRO (Japan External Trade Organization) but . . . the [Japanese] embassy who will play the major role. And this will be intolerable."[10]

A cartoon in a Bangkok newspaper in 1974 shows a Thai swordsman battling many enemies—the Central Intelligence Agency, profiteering and hoarding, and Japanese economic domination. Similarly, in the Philippines, President Ferdinand Marcos told an American interviewer in the spring of 1974: "The bankers—they are the no-risk fellows—have come here in hordes. Some companies have come in too fast, particularly Japanese. Let's admit it, the Japanese have outstripped the Americans. They are our biggest trading partner. If they increase any more, we'll be completely dependent on them."

CONSEQUENCES OF TANAKA'S VISIT
TO SOUTHEAST ASIA

In a many sided effort to assuage Southeast Asian nations and to restore perspective, while assuring Japan of enhanced access to desperately needed natural resources (especially petroleum and related sectors), Prime Minister Kakuei Tanaka visited the Philippines, Thailand, Singapore, Malaysia, and Indonesia between January 7-17, 1974. The results will not soon be forgotten. Foreign journalists had warned the Japanese not to persist in the "classic man-woman mould—'getting and forgetting' [Japan] vs. 'giving and forgiving. [Southeast Asia].'" In Thailand, where massive boycotts had already occurred, thousands of students demonstrated in the streets of Bangkok, and some pounded on Tanaka's car. The Japanese premier later conversed with a delegation of Thai student leaders, in an attempt to improve his country's image.

In Malaysia there were peaceful demonstrations against Tanaka and the Japanese, but the prime minister's most harrowing experience took place in Jakarta. There, in the words of the American journalist, Edward Neilan, Japan had "come on the scene with all the subtlety of a train wreck." Japanese neon advertisements dominated the city's skyline; next door to the JAL hotel stood an enormous Japanese-constructed office building (Nusantara, largest building in Jakarta), with a Japanese nightclub on the roof. Across the street were a Japanese bank, the 11-story Japanese embassy, and the Japan Air Lines offices. Only a short time before Tanaka arrived, the Japanese had finally decided to dismantle the 30-foot Toyota sign atop the Nusantara Building.

When Tanaka arrived at the airport, a band of 30 militant demonstrators broke through the security cordon and rushed onto the airstrip to charge the plane. In two days of disastrous rioting that ensued on Jakarta's streets, involving perhaps 100,000 demonstrators in all, 11 people died, 807 vehicles (mainly Japanese cars and motorcycles) were burned, and 144 buildings were damaged. "Go to hell with your aid, Tanaka-*san*," one banner read. At a rally, students called on the prime minister to prevent cutthroat, scheming Japanese companies from entering Indonesia "just to make profits." The rioters tore down the Japanese flag at the embassy, broke window panes, attacked stores dealing in Japanese goods, chased a Japanese photographer for UPI, and assaulted a busload of Japanese. The largest Toyota dealership was gutted by flames. Armed with billiard sticks, table legs, and bamboo spears, the rioters then looted, burned, and rampaged through Jakarta's Chinatown, where the unpopular Chinese bore the brunt of hostility as Japan's "front men" for ostensibly Indonesian businesses. Premier Tanaka and his daughter had to be flown to the airport by helicopter from the presidential guest house, to avoid new violence.

The commander of the Indonesian armed forces has claimed that proscribed political enemies were involved in a conspiracy to overthrow the Suharto government. Some demonstrators were known to have travelled to Jakarta from as far as 800 miles away. A spokesman for JETRO insisted that Tanaka's visit might merely have "sparked the pent-up complaints of the public, which were not necessarily international." Japanese traders wondered why American and Dutch enterprises, which had invested more heavily in Indonesia than the Japanese, were not attacked. Representatives of C. Itoh & Co. believed that misunderstanding by the Indonesian populace contributed to the riots; whatever evils existed on the Japanese side were conveyed in exaggerated fashion, while the mutual benefits were unknown. "It is the plain truth," argued Japanese sales representatives, "that our Indonesian partners are very happy about our efforts to work in joint ventures, and so is the Indonesian government."[11]

Home at last in Japan, Tanaka sought to pour oil on the troubled waters. He was not too concerned with the demonstrations, he insisted, because many different elements were involved. Tanaka and Foreign Minister Masayoshi Ohira assured the parliament that the Japanese government would meekly heed reasonable criticism, and would search patiently for a solution to the dissatisfaction and objections voiced in developing countries against Japan's economic activities abroad. Ohira asserted that Japan would "rectify what ought to be rectified," and would stress mutual advantage and mutual concession in economics, while striving to deepen comprehension of other countries' "general situation and mentality, including history, culture, and society." The Japanese authorities, Ohira continued, would work to correct trade imbalances, make best use of private investment, and insure the effectiveness of governmental economic assistance to developing countries. In particular, Japan would promote economic and technical aid in such fields as medicine, agriculture, and education to elevate standards of living. In the long run, Chief Cabinet Secretary Susumu Nikaido told the public, the Jakarta riots, although deplorable, would give the Japanese government a "major lesson" in devising and conducting foreign policy, and would not constitute a "minus factor" in reappraising the situation.

With pious resolve, Japanese companies promised to show more consideration for the well-being of the host country and to adjust their activities to local economic needs. They would set aside funds, they said, to improve their hosts' lot, by establishing clinics and schools and by subsidizing native employees with housing allowances and nightschool tuition. Cynics remarked that increased wages were not included in the promises.

Prime Minister Tanaka sought to demonstrate more concrete effects of his trip at the governmental level. A "youth ship," for example, is being routed to Southeast Asia, although unkind critics claim that the Japanese complement always consists of carefully chosen "gilded youth" who adhere to the incumbent Liberal-Democratic Party; these critics doubt that the inclusion of Southeast Asian young people will improve matters. More importantly, it has been decided in Tokyo to appoint a new cabinet minister in charge of overseas economic cooperation and to create a Corporation for Economic Cooperation to coordinate private business activities. Improvement in the quality of Japanese aid and the deepening of neighborly relations with Southeast Asia, Tanaka stressed, are essential to the maintenance of permanent peace in that region. The Japanese government has announced that, in extending economic assistance, emphasis would temporarily be accorded to making aid available to the least developed countries. Assistance extended through international organizations, however, would continue. Ultimately, Japan would contribute one-third of the funds for the Asian Development Bank (ADB). In 1972 Japan contributed over $2 billion in bilateral economic assistance abroad, of which 28.4 percent went to Southeast Asia. The same year, governmental economic assistance by Japan totalled $478 million, 61.9 percent of which was destined for Southeast Asia.[1][2]

Domestic evidence of Tanaka's reactions to his Southeast Asian tour is thought to be the sudden resignation in February 1974 of the Vice-Minister for Foreign Affairs, Shinsaku Hogen. Among the criticisms that had been made of alleged diplomatic ineptness, the Foreign Ministry—and Hogen in particular—were blamed for failure to predict the scale of anti-Japanese demonstrations during the premier's trip to Southeast Asia in January. Secretary Nikaido admitted that the Jakarta disturbances, although anticipated generally, were far worse than expected.

Japanese commentators insist that Tanaka's explanations are shallow. For example: "Our neighbors hope that we will wear sandals and take a meal with them at the same table. We have to turn a misfortune into a blessing. Japanese businessmen are not gods, after all." Some assert that the Japanese government is not sufficiently contrite about the country's responsibility for and behavior in the Pacific War. Tanaka is especially criticized for trying to impress newsmen with the "benevolent" nature of the Imperial Japanese Army occupation of Asian lands. He had argued that Japanese troops proffered assistance to distressed local areas "in a manner they would never have expected from Western soldiers."

Critical response has emphasized that unless Japan resorts to sincere soul-searching and to self-restraint, she may lose not only the remnants of Southeast Asian amity but even the oil of the Indies. The Japan Socialist Party (JSP) charges that the Jakarta riots indicated that the incumbent Japanese government's foreign policy was based upon big-power chauvinism and an attitude of economic aggression. According to the Japan Communist Party (JCP), the riots showed the angry reaction of the Indonesian people against Japanese government intervention in Indonesian domestic affairs for the benefit of Japanese capitalists.

JAPAN'S DILEMMA

What emerges from the preceding discussion is that Japan, in trying to accommodate every nation in Southeast Asia, large or small, has pleased none. "Lacking experience as colonialists who have come to terms with freedom movements," writes Derek Davies, "and tending to an arrogant impatience with those from rural communities slower than themselves to acquire technical skills, [the Japanese] have borne the brunt of the resentment against the foreign 'exploiter'." Gregory Clark, another observer of the Southeast Asian scene, suggests that "much of the anti-Japanese emotionalism is part and parcel of the kicking and screaming as the rest of the region is dragged into the mid-20th century." In this view, Japan suffers "because it is the most conspicuous modernising force in the area, falling heir to the bitterness which other agents of change have inspired." It often seems, however, that the Japanese view of modernization "does not go beyond their bright, shiny machines," and that the personal element is ignored or ill understood. At a time when Japan might do well to adopt a certain degree of historical amnesia, Prime Minister Tanaka reportedly asked for a larger number of war memorials to Japanese military dead in the Philippines.

It is significant that Tanaka did not even set forth to visit Southeast Asia in 1974 until after (like most recent Japanese premiers) he had first toured the United States, Europe, and the Soviet Union. The trip was the first by a Japanese prime minister to Southeast Asia since "dignified but remote" Eisaku Sato's journey in 1967. Tanaka himself had wanted to eliminate visits to Singapore, Malaysia, and Bangkok, but the Foreign Ministry not only urged that he go in the first place but also pressed him to include all five ASEAN countries.

These facts seem to indicate, the *Asahi Shimbun* editorialized, that "superpowers and advanced nations are given priority in Tanaka's concept of diplomacy. Southeast Asian people are re-assessing Japan's position in the region in sobering terms." Regardless of such strictures, the Japanese have turned vigorously—and understandably—to the Middle East, in a quest for new sources to cope with the insatiable petroleum requirements which underpin the Japanese economy. In face of the overweening energy crisis, textiles, food processing, shrimp raising, and machinery manufacturing ventures in Southeast

Asia pale in importance to Japan. A Japanese company, JAPEX, operates a fifty-fifty enterprise with Union Oil in the promising field offshore from Kalimantan. Official Japanese financing will underwrite the private firms, which by 1980-81 will build the huge Asahan River hydroelectric and aluminum smelting project in Sumatra, the biggest in Asia, entailing $500 million on a 30-year lease.

Japan has tried to walk the tightrope of neutrality amidst divided states and competing national interests in Southeast Asia. Thus, although Ali Murtopo and General Humardani—Suharto's assistants—apparently convinced the Indonesian president of the wisdom of politico-economic triangular links with Japan and Australia, the Japanese government proved to be unresponsive and negative. A knowledgeable Japanese political commentator, Taro Akasaka, believes that the Jakarta riots of January 1974 stemmed from the fact Premier Tanaka had already restored relations with the People's Republic of China. With this in mind, Indonesians feared the consummation of a Sino-Japanese bloc that could dominate all of Asia.

Such apprehensions are often heard, but in practice Japan has endeavored to separate economics from politics and to eschew the resurrection of spheres of influence in the traditional sense. Japanese officials explain that while other countries (such as France) may try to purchase oil and other resources by bartering military arms, Japan will not cease to work through economic cooperation. This is also the view of foreign analysts who judge that the cornerstone of Japanese foreign policy, in Southeast Asia as elsewhere, has been the use of trade as the basic strategy in the search for influence, and as a substitute for direct relations with even those states not as yet officially recognized.

Even North Vietnam has agreed to accept a team of Japanese experts from the government-subsidized Japan Petroleum Corporation to survey undersea oil resources in the Gulf of Tonkin. Through aid programs, Japan would like to promote good relations with both parts of the divided Southeast Asian country. Thus, at a Ministerial Conference for the Economic Development of Southeast Asia, held in Tokyo in October 1973, Foreign Minister Ohira announced that, even before establishment of a system for international cooperation in the reconstruction of Indochina, Japan would provide $50 million in assistance to the Republic of Vietnam to meet immediate needs. The delicate task of balancing opposing aspirations has been facilitated by Hanoi's high hopes of obtaining Japanese economic support for large-scale reconstruction and development projects in the North, as requested for the first time in January 1974. In return, North Vietnam may assure Japan of a steady supply of raw materials such as crude oil. Nevertheless, Keisuke Iwatsu has warned, "Despite their apparent need of Japanese aid, the North Vietnamese are not about to tolerate the pushy inroads which Japanese businesses have been known to make with aid."

Japan's other external strengths, Foreign Minister Ohira has stressed, lie in the fostering of cooperation in energy development in Southeast Asia and elsewhere, the attack on poverty in developing countries, environmental protection, food production, international monetary reform, population control, and oceanographic development. But the inner thinking within the Japanese

Foreign Ministry regarding Southeast Asian problems in particular is typified by the private comments of a senior *Gaimusho* (Foreign Ministry) official in November 1973. The Japanese, he felt strongly, were confronted with a serious contradiction; if they attempted to be more outward-looking, they could be accused of enlarging their influence at the expense of countries requiring cooperation. Yet if the Japanese sought to ease the pressure by reducing levels of aid, there would be accusations of selfishness. While Japan wanted its own people to attain high standards and to enjoy "happy feelings," the official said, it also wanted to help friends abroad savor these aspirations. Japanese cooperation in nation-building was done with "sincere hopes."

The preceding type of commentary has been denounced in some quarters as coy idealism. Nevertheless the distinguished Japanese writer Masaru Ogawa has asked how his countrymen can understand nationalism and patriotism in Southeast Asia "when we Japanese now hold these virtues in disrepute." Ogawa refers not to the militant ultranationalism of the past but to the "need for a sympathetic understanding of and close affinity with the national aspirations of this region." He reminds Japanese that "respect breeds respect, and much must be done to remodel our hearts and minds, if Japan is to gain the trust and confidence of the people of Southeast Asia."[13]

In an effort to become less dependent upon Japan and the other advanced industrial powers, Southeast Asian leaders have spoken bravely of neutralism and regional groupings such as ASEAN, extending even to the building of automobiles through cooperative efforts. Such grandiose schemes cannot survive the fiscal, pricing, and fuel crises which erupted worldwide in 1973. Japan remains the key economically in Southeast Asia, especially since several of the countries in the area possess a healthy trade surplus vis-à-vis Japan, thanks to very high commodity indices. It would, of course, be naive to think that "healthy" Japanese trade and investment are not welcome. The Malaysian government, for instance, in 1974 opened an Investment and Tourist Information Center in Tokyo; 70 Malaysian-Japanese joint venture factories have already been built in Malaysia, and another 75 are under construction. Still, the fragileness of Japan's own processing operations, hampered by reduced supplies of petroleum, coal, and electric power, could cut back the demand for Southeast Asian iron ore, tin, rubber, and timber, and so on, by many millions of tons.

JAPAN AND SOUTHEAST ASIA IN THE 1970s

It is often predicted that Japan, in frustration, will have to rearm in all seriousness, perhaps to the extent of acquiring nuclear weapons, in order to exert greater leverage on the international scene. The Indonesian editor Lubis alluded to the danger obliquely when he asserted that growing Japanese economic interests, coupled with the withdrawal of American forces from the Asian continent, must induce Japan "sooner or later to develop a greater military strength to secure these interests." Less restrained journalists expect a rerun of the 1930s and 1940s, so far as Japanese "militarists" are concerned.

All recent Japanese history refutes such a projection, especially in view of the traumatic pacifism engendered in the Japanese people at large by the experience of Hiroshima and Nagasaki. One must also consign to the realm of journalism the unrealistic prediction that the feeble Japanese Maritime Self-Defense Force will participate in some kind of Indian Ocean naval task force designed to screen the Malacca Strait. Of course, the Japanese comprehend the vulnerability of their sea-lanes. Like the Southeast Asian countries, Japan dreads a new era of great power rivalries, especially between Russia and China, if the United States withdraws from the region too precipitously. Naval commentators have observed that one of the side effects of the war in Vietnam was the huge expansion of Soviet maritime operations in the waters of Southeast Asia. Whereas the appearance of a Russian ship in Singapore was a novelty in 1962, ten years later about 500 vessels used the port. Soviet naval activity in the Indian and Pacific Oceans, involving ICBM firings, has also been noteworthy, causing the Japan Defense Agency to state that the Russians were now achieving the final phase of their global maritime strategy. It is clear that neither Japan nor the Southeast Asian countries regard the Soviet activity as a current security threat, but they do fear that the dilution of western power and influence may attract Russian attention. In the words of an Australian analyst, "And everywhere the Russians go, the Chinese are sure to follow." As Japan knows well, "It is not a question of what makes the lamb love Mary so."[1][4]

Halfway into the 1970s, Japan remains the only great power lacking the military clout to complement or support her economic and financial capabilities. Presumably her national defense against hypothetical foes is assured by the controversial but still effective U.S.-Japanese mutual security pact, which was revised in 1960 and automatically extended in 1970. Toward mainland China, Eisaku Sato's successor as prime minister, Kakuei Tanaka, has moved far to normalize Sino-Japanese relations, at the inevitable expense of the Nationalist Chinese government on Taiwan. Although territorial questions have prevented the consummation of a peace treaty with the Soviet Union, Japan has been dealing effectively with the Russians, again in the economic sphere, particularly with respect to joint development of Siberian resources, a project of not inconsiderable interest to the United States.

Japan, in sum, must live within her limitations and lack of maneuvering space, although she has been emerging gradually from behind the skirts of her erstwhile occupiers, the Americans. The latter's war in Indochina and subsequent forced disengagement, however, elicited mixed reactions in Japan. Intellectuals, students, and the powerful mass media generally criticized the conservative Liberal Democratic regime for docilely taking America's side—for calling the bombings of North Vietnam unavoidable, agreeing that the hostilities represented an invasion by the North and not civil strife, providing offshore logistical and base support for the American war effort; in short, for continuing the cold war policies of the John Foster Dulles era. North Vietnamese virtues were extolled, American cruelties were emphasized—an inevitable blending of sympathies for fellow Asians and resentment of "white" victory in 1945.

As for developments in Veitnam since the 1973 armistice accord in Paris, domestic critics regard Japan as less interested in the rebuilding of the ravaged Indochinese peninsula than in carving out lucrative markets to replace the

French and American ascendancy. The streets and shops of Saigon some feel are but an extension of Tokoy's Ginza shopping area, and this augurs ill for Vietnam's escape from colonialism. In this connection, it may be significant that Japan—which has been so active in innumerable international economic and financial conferences—was not invited to the general meeting on Indochina problems. Many Japanese suspect that it was the North Vietnamese and the Americans—equally distrustful of Japanese long-range intentions in the area— who declined to invite representatives from Tokyo.[15]

Japan may truly be enmeshed in the web of international relations affecting Southeast Asia, but she must confront special specters in the shape of economic nationalism, long memories, vituperation, distrust, and recrimination. Despite their alleged insensitivity and inscrutability, the Japanese do not enjoy being berated as an "economic animal" or "Japan, Inc.," being blamed for corruption, which in Indonesia supposedly comes to 30 percent of that country's Gross National Product, and being told that "Toyota, Mitsui, and Mitsubishi have replaced the *Kempeitai* [the cruel military police of yore]," or hearing that change for the Filipino peso comes in yen nowadays. The previously mentioned *Gaimusho* senior official suggests that the fundamental problem is not one-sided. Amidst whispering campaigns against the Japanese, he finds it hard to forgive those who charge that what the Japanese failed to accomplish during World War II, they are now achieving by means of economic invasion. "Every nation has its rotten apples," the official insists, "but some use these exceptions to generalize about the 'dirty Japanese.' And who is most to blame? If corruption existed in Thailand, were the Japanese involved any more guilty than those on the receiving end?" A Japanese businessman in Bangkok explained the situation, as he saw it, in almost plaintive terms. He had come to realize that Japan was like a little boy who envies his big brother's power. As the small boy grew up, developing his own strength, he retained the mentality of a little boy; he simply did not comprehend his new power, or the effects it had on others. The Japanese, the businessman felt, resemble that little boy: "There is no hostility in the Japanese, only an amazement to realize the reaction we have caused. . . . We do have a deep concern."[16]

In the larger sense, Japan desires no upset in the regional *status quo* in Southeast Asia. She is striving to jettison old concepts of an East-West confrontation, in favor of the idea of a north-south axis involving advanced and underdeveloped areas. Stability, to cautious and pragmatic Japan, means good business, sound monetary reserves, a strong yen, attractive profits, and a hedge against fatal recession. Unresolved contradictions persist. As Hellman suggests, the Americans have tried to push Japan into assuming a larger role on the Asian international scene, while the United States went on dealing with every military conflict. Of late, however, the Americans have eliminated or pared down their military presence in Southeast Asia, at a time when Japanese and American economic and political interests were colliding as often as they coincided. Japan's blissful pursuit of the yen has been disrupted by profound and permanent challenges ranging from monetary tremors to the fuel and commodity crisis and the critical damage dealt by the Vietnam War to the credibility of America's self-proclaimed role as international policeman.

Under the circumstances, Japan would like to think that, for all of their ideological differences and tensions, Russia, the United States, and particularly China (which is closest to Southeast Asia geographically and culturally) share the Japanese desire for balance in the area, from reasons of self-interest and survival, not altruism.[17] For, to express the concept in Asian imagery, "When elephants fight, the grass gets trampled."

NOTES

1. Yuan-li Wu, *Raw Material Supply in a Multipolar World* (New York: National Strategy Information Center, 1973), p. 30. Also see Ryusuke Kiku'iri, "Shigen shokoku: musashi mo ima mo" [A small country's natural resources, then and now], *Bungei-Shunju* (January 1974), pp. 134-149.

2. Owen Harries, in *Prospects in the Pacific*, Richard L. Walker, ed. (Washington, D.C.: HELDREF Publications, 1972), pp. 82-83; Saburo Okita, ibid., p. 168, 171 ff.; *Japan Times Weekly* (*JTW*), 24 November 1973.

3. Japanese Ministry of Finance data.

4. "Genchi Nikkei kigyo no kono genjitsu: shinpojiun" [The facts of Japanese investment enterprises in local regions: A symposium], *Chuo-Koron*, January 1974, pp. 192-211.

5. Based on *Shukan Asahi*, 15 February 1974; *JTW*, 23 February 1974. Also see special issue on the Japanese "Yellow Peril" in typical Thai magazines, *Chuo-Koron* February 1973, pp. 209-69; "Nihonjin wa Ajiya de nani o shite wa naranaika" [What Japanese must not do in Asia], *Chuo-Koron*, January 1974, pp. 132-211.

6. Derek Davies, *Far Eastern Economic Review*, 4 March 1974.

7. Toru Yano, "Kindai Nihon ni okeru nanshin no ronri" [The logic of southward expansion in modern Japan], *Chuo-Koron*, January 1974, pp. 132-157.

8. "Gaiko naki Nihon taishikan no zaijo" [The outrage of the Japanese embassies that have no diplomacy], *Gendai*, March 1974; *Japan Times Weekly*, 9 March 1974.

9. Mochtar Lubis, in Richard Walker, ed., *Prospects in the Pacific* (Washington, D.C.: HELDREF Publications, 1972).

10. *Asia in the World Community*, Prachoom Chomchai and Masahide Shibusawa, eds. (Tokyo: East-West Seminar, 1973), pp. 130-131.

11. For reaction by the Chinese People's Rebublic, see *Peking Review*, 1 February 1974, p. 20.

12. *Japan Report* (*JR*), Special Supplement, 16 February 1974.

13. *Far Eastern Economic Review*, 19 November 1973; *JTW*, 19 January 1974.

14. Denis Warner, "The Whitlam Approach to Asia," *Asian Affairs*, November-December 1973, no. 2, p. 66.

15. Shun'ichi Matsumoto, "Betonamu go no gaiko ni atau" [Giving advice to post-Vietnam diplomacy], *Chuo-Koron*, April 1973, pp. 52-61.

16. Toshio Hara, in *Asia in the World Community*, op. cit., p. 132.

17. See Kazuma Egashira, "Takyo kukajidai no Tonan A-gaiko" [Southeast Asian policy in the multipolar age], *Kokubo*, February 1973, 22, no. 2, pp. 12-29; Hidaka Yoshiki, "Betonamu wahei igo: Nikuson no kake wa seiko suruka" [The post-Veitnam world: Will Nixon's gamble succeed?], *Kokubo*, March 1973, 22, no. 3, pp. 12-23.

CHAPTER

6

INDIA:
A BALANCER
POWER?
D. R. SarDesai

Very few governments will admit that their international behavior and policy are governed by the concepts of power politics and balance of power. To the Third World countries, these represent dirty and dangerous games played by the empire builders of the nineteenth century on a European chessboard with helpless Asians and Africans as pawns. Indian foreign policy pronouncements during the last quarter century, particularly during the Nehru era, reflected the distaste of a former subject people for international power politics.[1] Not all have, however, accepted such Indian disclaimers; some detractors of Indian foreign policy have gone as far as characterizing the policy of nonalignment itself as an exercise in the balance-of-power politics.[2] Further, although the practitioners of Indian diplomacy have, for the most part, frowned upon the relationship between power and politics, they have privately assumed such a connection underlying the policies of all powers. Consequently, whether India likes it or not, she too has played for some time the role of a "balancer" and is likely to emerge in the 1970s either as a constituent or as a balancer in the emerging balance of power in Southeast Asia.

In a sense, a kind of balance was holding in Asia, particularly in Southeast Asia, from 1954 to 1961, in which India played a balancer's role. The subsequent decade saw Indian international posture greatly damaged after its military debacle at China's hands in 1962, even as the Southeast Asian balance was rudely shaken up by one of the bloodiest wars in history. The new policy of détente between the United States and China and between the United States and the Soviet Union might perhaps have brought about a new equation in Southeast Asia in which India would not have figured. However, a whole chain of totally unrelated happenings on the Indian subcontinent during 1971 have introduced an additional dimension to the international politics of the region and have propelled India into what may be characterized as an emerging balance of power in South and Southeast Asia. If the fifties saw India's active involvement in Southeast Asia and the sixties marked a low point for her prestige in the international world, it is likely that during the seventies, India will count increasingly in any plan for settlement of peace or power equation in the region.

INDIA AND THE BALANCE OF POWER, 1950s

Looking at the magnitude and rapidity of recent changes in international alignments, particularly in the Indo-Pacific area, one is reminded of the early fifties when another such major alignment of forces was taking shape. Two wars in Asia—in Korea and in Indochina—had threatened to ignite a global conflagration as the superpowers aided the rival sides in the conflicts. Both situations dislodged India from its position of neutrality and isolation in foreign policy. Geopolitics certainly governed the Indian decision to intervene in these disputes. The greater proximity of Indochina than Korea to the Indian subcontinent caused India proportionately greater concern. In 1954, India and Britain shared apprehension of massive American intervention of the kind proposed by John Foster Dulles, which would have inevitably stepped up Chinese and Russian participation, marking the probable beginning of the Third World War and a nuclear confrontation between the superpowers. Apart from the prospect of "opening a whole bay of gruesome suffering for mankind," as Nehru put it, there was anxiety on India's part to avoid a major war on Asian soil. Nehru espoused at this time a proposal to carve out "an area of peace" in South and Southeast Asia, through neutralization of the region, with guarantees from major powers.

India literally forced itself upon the circle of countries—Britain, France, the United States, USSR, and China—that were determining the fate of Southeast Asia at that time. Indian exertions at the Colombo Conference and in the behind-the-scenes parleys at Geneva, and in half a dozen distant capitals, played an important role in 1954 in deliberations that led to the Geneva settlement on Indochina. Underlying the Geneva agreements was the concept of neutralization of Laos and Cambodia—and by implication a policy of "hands off" in all of Southeast Asia. It was significant that less than three months before the Geneva agreements were signed, another agreement between the two most populous countries (though following two entirely different political and economic ideologies)—India and China—has been arrived at incorporating the five principles, or *Panchasheel*, of peaceful coexistence. India hailed the settlement as a victory and vindication of her *Panchasheel* approach, which had formed, more importantly for India, the basis of a wider agreement for the first time with the People's Republic of China. Through persistent efforts thereafter, notably at Bandung, Nehru secured from China and North Vietnam promises of noninterference in neighboring countries. To Nehru, the Geneva agreements, read in the context of the *Panchasheel* pledges, constituted a nonmilitary defense "system" and an answer to the challenging problem of preventing Chinese and other communist forces from advancing further in Southeast Asia.*

---

*It is significant that the region of Southeast Asia did not receive special attention in Indian foreign policy under Nehru, except as part of his overall concern for maintenance of peace in Asia.

All this, however, was hardly palatable to Washington, which followed during this period John Foster Dulles' perceptions, clouded by fears of communist aggression everywhere. Neutrality, nonalignment, and peaceful coexistence were to remain dirty and immoral words for the U.S. policy until the Camp David talks between Eisenhower and Khrushchev in September 1959, four months after Dulles' death. Dulles' policies of getting the smaller countries of Asia to sign "mutual security" alliances with the United States in order to "contain" communism everywhere would have perhaps created an equilibrium in Asia between China and the United States, even if an uneasy one. But it was India's role that helped the propagation of the policy of peaceful coexistence and the creation of necessary confidence among small, newly-independent nations to counter the American alternative. India worked strenuously to this end during the period from the *Panchasheel* agreement in April, 1954, with China, to the Afro-Asian Conference in Bandung in the following April. The fifties seemed to mark the great success of Indian foreign policy as Indian good offices were both offered and sought after to quench the fires in many troubled areas: Korea, Indochina, Gaza, Congo, Cyprus. The instrument of this policy was nonalignment, which India claimed was different from neutrality inasmuch as the latter predetermined a policy posture while nonalignment would allow for a stand based on the merits of each case.

The policy of nonalignment, however, was more an expression of a country's right to forge its policies independent of outside pressure than a well-formulated doctrine to guide the day-to-day relationship with other countries. Its numerous adherents in the Afro-Asian bloc, particularly in Southeast Asia, found it an alternative to the necessity of aligning with the United States for fear of China. Ideologically too, India's successful democratic experiment provided a viable political alternative to the communist Chinese way of life, which had allowed only a momentary blooming of the Hundred Flowers. Leaders like U Nu, Sukarno, Sihanouk, and Souvanna Phouma shared in the impressive fallout of the policy of nonalignment all the way from Bandung to Belgrade. New Delhi became a logical destination or a stopover for many of these statesmen for consulting with Nehru on their way to and from the Western capitals.

In all, the Indian role in the second half of the fifties seemed to be that of a "balancer" in an equilibrium of power that continued almost until the end of the decade.[3] Yet this was not India's goal or ideal solution for the region. As mentioned above, India's aim was to create an "area of peace" through neutralization of Southeast Asia, and through respect for the independence and territorial integrity of each country, whereby no external power, neither the United States nor China, would be able to intrude in the region. India failed in this objective. She lacked the capability to impose her will; she was unable to persuade the Southeast Asian countries to follow the course advocated by her. But the United States also failed to realize its goals. America was able to secure the support of no more than two Southeast Asian states—Thailand and the Philippines—to join SEATO, designed to counter external communist subversion, which meant "containing" China. On India's part, China and the possible onward march of communism in Southeast Asia had been contained not through military alliances but through the peaceful alternative of

Panchasheel, which formed the common basis of the Sino-Indian relationship and of the Geneva agreements. The position of India as chairman of tthe tripartite International Control Commissions in Laos, Cambodia, and Vietnam, with the crucial veto on "all questions of deadlock" enabled it to reinforce some of the verbal assurances given by China through Indian intermediaries to the western powers at Geneva, essentially reflecting the five principles of peaceful coexistence.

Panchasheel was presented by India during that period as a panacea for the political ills of a power-dominated world and as an alternative to the policy of alliances. In the fifties the Southeast Asian governments accepted either the membership or protection of the U.S.-dominated SEATO or the Sino-Indian alternative. The Indian position, at the Geneva Conferences of 1954 and 1961, at the Bandung and Belgrade Conferences of 1955 and 1961, and above all as chairman of the International Control Commissions, in dealing with governments following differing ideologies in Indochina, the ICC (Canada and Poland being the two other members), and with the cochairmen of the Geneva Conference (Britain and the Soviet Union) was more than that of a disinterested catalyst, peacemaker, mediator, or negotiator. A closer look at the classified Indian documentation of the period reveals an Indian awareness of a balance of power in Southeast Asia that would not allow a single power to dominate the region. India's "tilting" in her crucial role during the period could have upset the balance; in that sense, India acted as a balancer.

Such a pattern of power lasted only as long as China followed the global policy of the Soviet Union—and India—namely that of peaceful coexistence. Toward the end of the fifties and certainly by 1962, Nehru's dream of transforming Asia into "an area of peace" was dissipated. The thawing of U.S.-Soviet relations marked by Premier Khrushchev's Camp David talks with President Eisenhower in 1959, and the estrangement between the two communist giants crystallizing about the same time, disturbed the power equilibrium of the fifties in Southeast Asia. Its outward manifestations were the Chinese encouragement of renewed hostilities in Laos and Vietnam and the beginnings of Sino-Indian skirmishes on India's northern borders with Tibet.

INDIA AND THE BALANCE OF POWER, 1960s

Hostilities on a major scale in October-November, 1962 in the Himalayan heights contributed to dislodging the Indian foreign policy from its pontifical pedestal of *Panchasheel*, ruptured the Sino-Soviet friendship, and revealed to the world the makings of an altogether new power equation in South and Southeast Asia. Nehru confessed his policies were out of touch with the realities of the world, and China disclosed in March, 1963 that her dispute with India marked the beginning of the real rift with the Soviet Union.[4] Nehru characterized the Sino-Indian dispute as part of China's global policy of "wars of national liberation." The Soviet position of neutrality between India and China in October-November 1962, and later the Soviet support of India by fulfilling the MIG arms deal brought certain diplomatic compulsions to bear upon Indian foreign policy. Further, both the Soviet Union and the United States pressed India not to abandon her nonalignment policy, virtually making India one of the areas of agreement in their common opposition to mainland China. In a larger and longer perspective, looking back at the sixties, it is possible to say that in a sense, "India contributed to the U.S.-Soviet détente, for it was in South Asia that the China policies of the two superpowers converged in the 1961-71 decade, making tacit cooperation between them possible in selected set of circumstances in this area."[5]

India's lack of prominence in the sixties in Southeast Asian affairs was in stark contrast with her earlier role. In addition to her dismal debacle on the battlefront with China, downgrading her image of a major power on the diplomatic front as well, there were at least three other factors that eliminated her from the coterie of powers that determined Southeast Asia's fortunes. These were first: China's emergence as a nuclear power, which augmented India's dependence on the superpowers for protection and correspondingly decreased India's diplomatic leverage among the smaller nations in Southeast Asia. The latter now stood in renewed awe of China's military might and political motivation as Lin Piao proclaimed his doctrine of the "wars of national liberation." And although India did put the Chinese role in the Himalayas in the same context of "national liberation," she was hardly in a position to help the Southeast Asian nations to combat communist subversion in their countries. On the other hand, India did not link Chinese behavior in India's border states with the Chinese support of communists in the Vietnamese conflict, which was seen in purely nationalistic terms.

Second, the absence of a charismatic leader like Nehru took its toll. He had given India up to 1962 an international position far out of proportion to her military or economic strength. In the remaining years of his premiership following the Sino-Indian war, Nehru was a broken man. His successor was Lal Bahadur Shastri. Shastri's short-lived twenty month premiership was not marked by any international initiatives except his dramatic leadership in the Indo-Pakistan conflict toward the end of his career. Shastri's successor, Indira Gandhi, even more inward-looking than Shastri, played a low-key role even in domestic politics. Until her dramatic initiatives in 1969 in splitting the Congress Party leadership, Indian foreign policy practically took a holiday during this entire period. It was not until early 1971 that she took some initiatives of note.

Third, the changing contours of the international scene allowing for a multipolar world in place of the old bipolar situation, seemed to question the value and even the viability of the concept of nonalignment. Although India did not abandon her policy of nonalignment, the latter had lost most of its former strength, morale, and initiative in the sixties.

In sum, during the sixties, the powers that mattered in Southeast Asian international politics were the United States, China, and the Soviet Union. Toward the end of the decade, quiet diplomacy on the part of the United States toward a bifocal détente both with the USSR and China would be predicated on the best solution for a breakthrough in the military stalemate in Vietnam. India seemed hardly to matter. Yet, in her capacity as the chairman of the moribund International Control Commission and as a large country, still enjoying some measure of leadership in the largely defunct group of nonaligned nations, and as a country on good terms with the Soviet Union, she was compelled to take a position—particularly in regard to the Vietnamese conflict. In the late sixties, with the flames of the Vietnam War touching the conscience of mankind everywhere, India made peace proposals that largely reverted to her earlier framework for peace in Southeast Asia: strict adherence to the Geneva agreements of 1954; stoppage of bombings of North Vietnam, as a prelude to complete cessation of hostilities in Vietnam; and military neutralization of Indochina, including Laos and Cambodia. Both Shastri and Indira Gandhi insisted that a military solution to the conflict was not possible and, therefore, a political settlement would have to be worked out. This should be done, in the words of Foreign Minister Swaran Singh, at a "Geneva-type conference, a conference which would pick up from the point at which the last conference ended its labors, so that we could find out where the parties have slipped back."[6] India consistently advanced this view at the conferences of nonaligned nations, Commonwealth conferences, and in its special appeals to the belligerents concerned. But such pronouncements did not amount to a policy nor did they give India a position of influence in the new balance of power that would emerge in Southeast Asia.

It is conceivable that the new equilibrium of power that came about in the wake of the Washington-Peking détente and the defusing of the Vietnam conflict might have kept India completely out. As it was, the Nixon Administration did not appreciate Indian statements critical of the U.S. position in Vietnam, and had made it perfectly clear that in any new peace-keeping agency that would succeed the International Control Commissions, India would not be included. Neither would India be invited to a Geneva-type conference when one would be convened. This was also to be expected in view of the Sino-Indian relationship and American efforts to strike a detente with China through Pakistan's mediation. In 1954, John Foster Dulles had staked his personal prestige in keeping India out of the Geneva Conference, threatening to bring in Taiwan if India were invited as a regular member. India had gate-crashed at that time, through active diplomacy on the periphery, particularly playing the middleman's role between China and the West. If in the 1970s, India is counted among the constituents of the new power equation in Southeast Asia, it will be largely due to the fortuitous circumstances of conflict on the India subcontinent during 1971, the Indo-Soviet Treaty of Friendship and Cooperation, and Russian attempts to tie up the security questions in the Indian Ocean area including South and Southeast Asia.

INDIA'S POLICY SINCE DECEMBER 1971

Writing in *Foreign Affairs* in mid-1971, Hedley Bull listed some new factors limiting the U.S. military capabilities in the 1970s, compelling her to accept a new balance of power in Asia. These included the growing presence of Russian naval power in the Indian and Pacific Oceans, the parity between the Soviet Union and the United States in strategic nuclear weaponry, the development of missiles in China, and the rise of Japan as an economic giant with potential for military and political leadership in the region.[7] If the article had been published six months later, Bull would perhaps have included another limiting factor: the 14-day war with Pakistan in December, 1971, leading to a spectacular Indian victory and the end of the trauma and tragedy for the 75 million people of the new nation of Bangladesh. In contrast to a decade earlier, in 1972 India emerged with a new face, vibrant and victorious, self-confident yet sober, adept both in diplomacy and in the use of limited force, manifesting a renewed capability for leadership of the peoples of the subcontinent and beyond.

It was clear that the magnitude of the series of events in the Indian subcontinent during 1971 was not adequately realized by Peking and Washington until the conclusion of the Indo-Pakistan War in December, 1971. It seems that during the secret negotiations concerning the future of Asia in the aftermath of peace in Vietnam, neither the United States nor China had allowed for such a radical shift of power in India's favor resulting from the birth of a new nation on the Indian subcontinent. The balance in South Asia was construed independently of Southeast or East Asia. For the first time in a decade, in mid-1971, the United States administration indicated the end of the U.S.-USSR understanding over India. Instead, when Henry Kissinger returned from his first trip to Peking, the Indian Ambassador to Washington was clearly told that in the event of a war with China, India should not expect any assistance from the United States.[8] What was implied was that if a war broke out between India and Pakistan as had happened in 1965, and China served an ultimatum to India, the latter should expect neither diplomatic nor military assist from the United States. India's isolation was complete. Washington had chosen to "tilt" against India. During the brief war between India and Pakistan, the United States did not remain neutral between the two as in 1965. The United States dispatched the nuclear-powered aircraft carrier U.S. Enterprise, and a task force of destroyers and amphibious ships from the Seventh Fleet to the Bay of Bengal ostensibly to evacuate U.S. civilians from the theater of conflict.[9] It also extended the responsibility of the Seventh Fleet from the Pacific to the Indian Ocean. Both acts damaged the Indo-American relationship still further and enhanced the importance of the Indian defiance of U.S. diplomatic and military offensives.

The conclusion of the 14-day war, the complete defeat of Pakistan's armed forces both in the East and the West, the popular clamor against Yahya Khan, and the birth of Bangladesh, seem to have convinced Washington of its miscalculations. Quick steps were taken to remedy the situation: The U.S. Consulate-General in Dacca was retained to be elevated to embassy level after the recognition of Bangladesh on 21 March 1971. More significantly in regard to the new balance of power, India's status was recognized by the President of the United States in his message to the Congress on 9 February 1972:

> If India has an interest in maintaining balanced relationships with all major Powers, we are prepared to respond constructively. Of interest to us also will be the posture that South Asia's most powerful country now adopts towards its neighbors on the sub-continent.[10]

It was perhaps realized in Washington and Peking that the Sino-U.S. détente in Southeast Asia did not adequately meet the question of Sino-Indian, Indo-Pakistan, and above all, Indo-Soviet aspirations in South and Southeast Asia. The new balance of power would have to accommodate these factors.

Apart from these considerations, it is questionable whether a balance of power can be established in a segment of the world by major powers, if one or more of the latter is interested in using the countries of the "balanced" region for working out a balance of power on the global level. During the 1960s both superpowers seemed agreed on two points in regard to ordering affairs on the Indian subcontinent: first, to give support to India in case of Sino-Indian conflagration and to help India to retain the posture of nonalignment, and second, after 1965, to treat India and Pakistan evenly in the interests of peace. There was one difference of emphasis, however. The United States had for long accepted the Pakistani plea for parity of status with India; the Soviet Union, on the other hand, had always accepted India's claims for a superior status, based on her size, resources, and a longer border to defend. In 1965, the war between India and Pakistan was resolved by the two superpowers in an exemplary fashion, moving jointly through the United Nations to secure a cease-fire before China had any opportunity to make mischief. However, after Premier Kosygin's successful mediatory role at Tashkent between the two rivals of the Indian subcontinent in January, 1966, the United States recognized Soviet primacy in the Indian subcontinent. The new U.S.-Chinese détente in 1971 altered these understandings between the two superpowers. The détente also created for the Soviet Union the need to find new allies on China's periphery to "contain" China at best, or to create an additional defensive frontier for China, which would have the merit of diverting some of the Chinese forces from the Sino-Soviet borders. In 1971, the Soviet and Indian needs for allies to combat their isolation created by the Washington-Peking-sponsored new equilibrium of power, brought them closer in a formal 20-year Treaty of Friendship and Cooperation.

It was, however, the Soviet protective umbrella, not its actual aid, that was a major factor in the Indian resolve to intervene militarily in East Pakistan. Actual Soviet help was more moral than material. As Wayne Wilcox observes: "While some credit for the Indian success was owed to Moscow, most close observers realized that the Soviets had followed, not led, the Indians, and that whatever status the Russians had attained in the subcontinent was a consequence of Indian policy."[11]

The Russian decision to sign the treaty with India, it must be noted, was an outcome of one of the major decisions of the 24th Party Congress in March, 1971. It was to build a "new policy consequent upon China's troop buildup or take measures to strengthen its position in both East and South Asia by improving relations with Japan and India."[12] Thereupon, the Soviet Union made a conscious choice between India and Pakistan in 1971, although in the last two years, Soviet diplomacy has reestablished a large part of its former position at Islamabad. Yet, the fact of the August 1971 treaty between India and the Soviet Union, reinforced by reciprocal visits of top-ranking politicians of both countries, by delegations from the armed forces, economic planning units, and others indicates a closer collaboration, which might create a common platform of foreign policy aims in many areas including the redrawing of the balance of power in South and Southeast Asia. Pertinent to this argument is one of the numerous observations made in the aftermath of the 14-day-war, which sums up the new Indo-Soviet relationship in the Southeast Asian context.

> India and Russia now become invaluable to each other in that both can exert pressures on China from different points of the compass. It would be surprising if the next decade did not see an extension of Indian influence to the east into Southeast Asia, and especially Burma. After Vietnam there can be neither expectation nor desire for American involvement on land in Asia. In the future, the powers of consequence in the Asian hinterland will be Russia, India and China. The powers of consequence on the periphery will be India, Britain and the five-power amalgam in Malaysia and Singapore.[13]

Nevertheless, since the birth of Bangladesh, the Soviet need for Indian friendship seems to have increased rather than the other way around. This is perhaps because there is a greater Soviet interest than before in the Indian Ocean and Southeast Asian regions where Indian cooperation would undoubtedly be an asset. The new phase of Indo-Soviet relationship has successfully denied the viability of a separate balance of power for Southeast Asia and will very likely underline the need to bring India into the picture and to integrate the South and Southeast Asian balance.

Soviet interests and policy aims in Southeast Asia have been discussed in a separate chapter of this volume. Where India figures most importantly from the Soviet point of view is in two areas: first, increased Soviet interest and activity in the Indian Ocean and, second, in creating a structure of regional security in Asia, particularly in South and Southeast Asia as envisaged by the so-called Brezhnev Doctrine. India views the Soviet activity in the Indian Ocean as well as Soviet security proposals from a considerably different standpoint although there is some possibility of common ground for joint action.

Until 1970, India had no reason to be unduly wary of Soviet presence in the Indian Ocean area. For one thing, the total Soviet presence amounted to less than the British or French presence[14] and was perhaps intended merely to build up—as in the Eastern Mediterranean, the Norwegian Sea, and in the Pacific—the capability to counter Polaris or Poseidon submarines and aircraft carriers that could launch strikes against Russia.[15] And though India is suspicious of any foreign power, including the Soviets, seeking dominance of the Indian Ocean, reports of U.S. acquisition of a base on Diego Garcia Island from Britain in 1966, only 1,200 miles from the Indian shores, in an effort to fill the vacuum created by the projected withdrawal of Britain from East of Suez, drew a strong Indian reaction. In contrast, the Soviet Union had proposed in December 1964, that the Indian Ocean be regarded as a free zone—a proposal not acceptable to the western powers. In September, 1970, when the nonaligned nations met in Lusaka, Russia spurred the countries of the Indian Ocean littoral into opposing the escalation of the naval presence of outside powers. Since 1971, however, Russian interest in the neutralization of the Indian Ocean has not been forthcoming. In the same period, India has consistently espoused Sri Lanka's proposal for the complete neutralization of the ocean, a proposal made in the United Nations and repeated by the premiers of India and Sri Lanka in Colombo in April 1973, and in New Delhi in January 1974. The proposal calls upon all the powers of the world to keep the Indian Ocean as a "zone of peace free from military contests."

Soviet interest in the Indian Ocean may have increased in the wake of certain possibilities of reduction of U.S. presence in Southeast Asia. It is also tied in with a keener desire to contain China, which may have its own plans to extend its naval operations in Southeast Asia, if the takeover of Paracel Islands in January 1974 is any indication.

Brezhnev's suggestion of June 1969, for a collective security system in Asia, designed to turn the latter into a "continent of peace and cooperation" has never been elaborated upon in any precise terms.[16] No Asian country, including India, has to date responded favorably to the idea, which is regarded by all as a revival of John Foster Dulles' anti-Chinese phalanx with only the commanding officer changing. Unlike Dulles, however, Brezhnev has not staked his prestige on the "system" and has made it possible for the South and Southeast Asian countries politely to raise questions and to prevaricate on its membership. In theory, even China can be a member of Brezhnev's proposed security system, and indeed, since the proposal is of Soviet inspiration, Russia cannot be excluded from it. Although it has shades of similarity with the Nixon Doctrine (it was announced a month before the Nixon Doctrine), it differs in some essentials. First, Russian national interest is genuinely involved in the security system concerning Asia, not only because Russia is an Asian country but because conflict with China makes it imperative for it to devise ways of weakening the adversary. Second, underlying the Nixon Doctrine is an attempt at graceful withdrawal from Asia despite some dissenting opinions. The Russians seem to be rather eager to take the place both of Britain and the United States[17] in the East, thereby increasing their presence in most Asian countries that are situated in China's backyard.[18] Indian cooperation would be helpful to the Soviet Union in structuring any anti-Chinese policy apart from the mere logistical advantages of access to the Southeast Asian region. Moscow has been trying in the last two years to break the Washington-Peking-Tokyo triangle. If it does not succeed, India's importance to the Soviet Union in stabilizing the Washington-Peking-Tokyo balance of power in Asia would even be greater. It would appear, therefore, that despite India's reluctance to play a major role in Southeast Asia, she will be involved in the region, even if indirectly, as a balancer of power.

India has been politely lukewarm to the Brezhnev proposal, though Moscow interpreted the August 1971 Treaty of Friendship and Cooperation as the most significant step in the impending structure of collective security system in Asia. Instead, India has warmly applauded the Association of Southeast Asian Nations' call for the neutralization of the region to be guaranteed by the major powers. Such appeals were at first criticized by the Soviet Union as impractical and have of late been rather ignored. Again, New Delhi seems to be eager to mend its fences with Washington, and given a chance with Peking as well. And in regard to the Indian Ocean, India seems to be thinking that mere words of protest may not free the region from military buildup by major powers of the East or the West. India has stepped up its construction of the Andaman Islands base and has veered to the acceptance of sea-based deterrent forces as an important asset for an Indian Ocean policy.[19] Thus, both because of Soviet needs for including India in the former's plans for a new security system and for balancing the Washington-Peking-Tokyo triangle, as well as Indian exertions to keep the South and Southeast Asian region free from big-power influence through neutralization or through an active Indian role in the Indian Ocean, India is likely to be playing an important role in the balance of power emerging in Southeast Asia.

As already mentioned in Chapter 1, the kind of balance of power shaping up in Southeast Asia or Asia will not be of the classical nineteenth century European type, where the major powers observed restraint and did not make efforts to become predominant in Europe. If there is any desire at all on the part of major powers not to be singly predominant it is because of the Vietnam experience. India does not have any imperial ambitions in Southeast Asia. Neither historically nor in the present has India shown any expansionist tendencies. For example, the Indian occupation troops were withdrawn from Bangladesh within two months of Pakistan's defeat. Indian military capabilities are considerable. Despite having the fourth largest army in the world, an air force with proven striking abilities, a large ammunition production base that can be geared to military production, however, India lacks and will be lacking in the 1970s the surplus strength and the will to assert any territorial role beyond the subcontinent.

Looking at the balance-of-power proposition slightly differently, India's own stand for the last 20 years since the first Geneva Conference on Indochina in 1954 to have Asia free of big-power domination comes closest to what the major powers seem to be wanting at present in Southeast Asia. In the peculiar situation of power equilibrium in Southeast Asia, where no one power would be allowed to become predominant, India could be regarded as a balancer power. In fact, there will be a need for such a role and none of the four major powers—China, the United States, USSR, Japan—is likely to be acceptable to the other three. True, India's credibility in the present times as a mediator or negotiator is nowhere equal to what it was in the fifties. Yet, given India's reluctance to play second fiddle to the Soviet Union by becoming a lynchpin of the Soviet-sponsored security system in Asia, and India's continued desire to promote neutralization of the region and turn it into an "area of peace," it is conceivable that she will encourage efforts by China and the United States to wean her away from too close a relationship with the Soviet Union. Such a role might even have another functional dimension. In the absence of big-power domination, there is a likelihood of more localized conflicts. It is conceivable that a medium-range power like India, larger than any in South and Southeast Asia, could play the role of a mediator or a balancer in the regional balance of power where no single Southeast Asian country would be allowed to dominate its neighbors.

NOTES

1. For a recent statement see Indira Gandhi, "India and the World," *Foreign Affairs* 51, no. 1 (October 1972): 76.

2. See Ton That Thien, *India and South East Asia 1947-1960* (Geneva: Librairie Droz, 1963).

3. For a study of Indian policy in the context of superpower rivalry in Southeast Asia, see this author's *Indian Foreign Policy in Cambodia, Laos and Vietnam, 1947-1964* (Berkeley: University of California Press, 1968).

4. *Peking Review*, no. 9, 1 March 1963, p. 10.

5. Leo Rose, "India," in Wayne Wilcox, Leo Rose, Gavin Boyd, eds., *Asia and the International System* (Cambridge, Mass.: Winthrop Publishers, 1972), p. 91.

6. See Swaran Singh's statement of 22 December 1964 in *India News*, 25 December 1964; Government of India's note of 8 February 1965, in *Indiagram*, same date; and Swaran Singh's statement before the Indian Parliament in *Foreign Affairs Record* 9, no. 3 (March 1965): 40-41. For a detailed treatment of the Indian attitude toward the Vietnam conflict in the sixties, see this author's article, "South Asia and the Vietnam War," *United Asia* 20, no. 4 (July-August 1968): 210-217.

7. Hedley Bull, "The New Balance of Power in Asia and the Pacific," *Foreign Affairs* 49, no. 4 (July 1971): 671.

8. Kuldip Nayar, *India, The Critical Years* (Delhi: Vikas Publications, 1971), p. 267.

9. *Time*, 27 December 1971, p. 30.

10. *Asian Recorder* 18, no. 14 (April 1-7, 1972): 10699.

11. Wayne Wilcox, *The Emergence of Bangla Desh* (Washington, D.C.: American Enterprise Institute for Public Policy Research, 1973), p. 54.

12. Norton T. Dodge, ed., *Analysis of the USSR's 24th Party Congress and 9th Five Year Plan* (Mechanicsville, Maryland: The editor, 1971).

13. Patrick Cosgrave, "Indian Victory and After," *The Spectator*, reproduced in the *Times of India*, 31 December 1971.

14. T. B. Millar, "Soviet Policies South and East of Suez," *Foreign Affairs* 49, no. 1 (October 1970): 73.

15. For a detailed discussion see Michael McGuire, "The Background to Soviet Naval Development," *The World Today* 27, no. 3 (March 1971): 100; also Geoffrey Jukes, "The Soviet Union and the Indian Ocean," *Survival* 13, no. 11 (November 1971).

16. Text of the Brezhnev Doctrine in *International Affairs* (July 1960): 3-21.

17. Alexander O. Ghebhardt, "The Soviet System of Collective Security of Asia," *Asian Survey* 13, no. 12 (December 1973): 1076.

18. Robert H. Donaldson, "India: the Soviet Stake in Stability," *Asian Survey* 12, no. 6 (June 1972): 481.

19. L. Sondhi, "India and Nuclear China," *Pacific Community* 4, no. 2 (January 1973): 269.

7

THE VIEW FROM SOUTHEAST ASIA IN THE 1970s
The Editors

The hallmark of statesmanship in Southeast Asia has been the ability to recognize and act upon changes in the power relationships of the major states. This is as true today as it was in ancient times, when the political theorist Kautilya, in his *Arthashastra*, advised kings of the proper way to conduct relations with their neighbors.[1] In modern times, whenever one or more of the major powers has shifted its degree of commitment in the region or the character of its relationship to another of the region's major powers, Southeast Asian governments have had to make policy changes of their own. The evolution of a more balanced relationship among the four major powers in the 1970s—"balanced" in that there is a shared interest in détente and normalization, a heightened concern about avoiding direct confrontations, and, with particular respect to Southeast Asia, an acceptance of the principle of access for all and a sphere of influence for none—confronts the region's governments with new demands for foreign policy adjustments.

Viewed historically, the imposition by foreign powers of a "system" to regulate the region's international politics is hardly new. The Chinese tribute system (from the Han dynasty, 206 B.C. to 221 A.D., to the latter half of the nineteenth century), Western colonialism, and Japan's New Order and Co-Prosperity Sphere during World War II had a similar function. To understand how the so-called balance-of-power system has been perceived and responded to in Southeast Asia, it is important to look at international relations there across time and space. For all the differences in their foreign policies, the region's states have much in common when we examine the determinants of policy-making.

THE CONTEXT OF SOUTHEAST ASIA'S
INTERNATIONAL RELATIONS

Political fragility is one common feature of these societies. Leadership and policy-making are dominated by elites, and the political process revolves about personalities and power brokers. There is little institutionalization of authority; jockeying for power is a political constant, and changes of regime occur frequently with one clique replacing another. Additionally, within each country can be found ethnic, religious, and/or tribal minorities that reject the central government's authority and culture, seek the broadest possible autonomy, and often engage in rebellion. Central governments in Southeast Asia have only just begun to extend their authority to outlying areas where the minority groups usually live. Minorities, much more than revolutionary movements (except in Vietnam), pose the greatest challenge to national integration. The problem for governments is accentuated when, as in Burma, rebellious minority groups make contact with external forces or, as in the Thai-Malaysian and Thai-Lao border areas, the same minority groups living on opposite sides of a (to them, artificial) boundary join forces.

This political fragmentation has important foreign policy implications. Broadly speaking, it makes foreign policy vulnerable to domestic events. Personalism in politics means personalism in diplomacy. In the absence of a well-developed foreign affairs bureaucracy (here, Thailand is an exception), it becomes difficult for governments to maintain the continuity, form, and substance of foreign policy when leadership changes hands. Invitations to foreign powers to intervene are usually as much to preserve personal power as to protect national security. Moreover, foreign policy strength and credibility, in Southeast Asia as elsewhere, depend on a domestic consensus. Constant rebellions, revolutions, communal riots, and palace coups not only gravely weaken leadership, they also create opportunities for small or large powers to become involved.

A second important common element with foreign policy implications is nationalism. Expressed earlier in the century as anticolonialism, nationalism today means, among other things, opposition to undue dependence on foreign powers and antagonism toward the economic, military, and diplomatic access, or penetrability, that foreign allies have. The eras of Chinese, Western European, Japanese, and now great power exploitation and manipulation of Southeast Asians have left their mark. And it is crucial to point out that this kind of nationalism applies as much to North Vietnam as it does to Indonesia or Burma.

Nationalism, as a force in foreign policy, needs to be distinguished from ideology. Foreign policy objectives in Southeast Asia, even those of a government (Democratic Republic of Vietnam's) committed to Marxism-Leninism, are defined primarily by each country's history, politics, geography, and socio-economic circumstances. Ideology is a peculiarly western concept and preoccupation; it has little relevance in explaining the external (or internal) behavior of governments. Their decisions on how to relate to foreign powers and what overall foreign policy posture to adopt—whether it be called neutralism, nonalignment, anticommunism, antiimperialism, or self-reliance—are dictated above all by their national needs, their determination to retain sovereignty, and their subordinate place in world politics, rather than by any loyalty, expressed or implied, to a universalistic social and political philosophy. One major implication of this point is that Southeast Asian governments are likely to continue to experiment in foreign policy; they have a large capacity for adjusting, realigning, and accommodating, as indeed they must have to survive in a world dominated by the major powers.

Nationalism is also a key factor in the longstanding difficulties Southeast Asian states have experienced in getting along with one another. Rivalries between states in some instances are centuries old, such as between Thailand and Cambodia and between Cambodia and Vietnam. Disputes between Indonesia and Malaysia, and between Malaysia and the Philippines, are of more recent vintage. Differences over boundaries are accentuated by differences in culture, language, and politics. Their effects are to inhibit regional cooperation and bilateral understanding, although the recent phase of major power diplomacy has encouraged a breakdown of jealousies and decreased tensions between neighbors.

The problem of regional integration also stems from the limited interstate relations of Southeast Asian countries. It is a vast exaggeration to call Southeast Asia a state "system" when its members, because of the divisive policies of the western colonial powers, and for economic, cultural, political, and security reasons of more recent origin, have their principal contacts with states outside the region. Thus, Burma's primary relationships are with India; those of the Philippines, South Vietnam, and Cambodia are with the United States; North Vietnam with China and the Soviet Union; Thailand and Indonesia with the United States and Japan; and Malaysia and Singapore with Australia, New Zealand, and Great Britain.

This diverse pattern of interaction spotlights the dilemma of dependency for Southeast Asian governments: they cannot simultaneously pursue policies of independence and economic development. Their common desire to preserve their political independence and unique culture is threatened by their need to rely on external powers for aid, trade, and security. Although clearly the internal capabilities of individual states differ markedly—compare, for instance, Thailand's administrative and technical resources and economic productivity with Burma's—overall, Southeast Asian states do not possess the means of self-reliance. They are weak states in terms of their governments' ability to match resources with internal demands, hence another reason for their openness to penetration by external powers.

SOUTHEAST ASIAN RESPONSES TO
MAJOR POWER DIPLOMACY

Responses to the United States

To a degree that may be surprising, Southeast Asian governments—apart, obviously, from those of the two Vietnams—had a common concern about the Nixon Administration's troop withdrawals from South Vietnam and about the Nixon Doctrine. Quite simply, the concern was that a U.S. withdrawal from Vietnam should not presage a complete withdrawal from Southeast Asia. There was, to be sure, considerable disagreement among the region's governments about the timing and terms of withdrawal. Supporters of the American involvement, like the Thai government, argued against a precipitate withdrawal, while critics of the United States, like Prince Sihanouk when he ruled Cambodia, urged a rapid exit. But on the future U.S. role in the region, even Sihanouk contended that an American presence was desirable in order to offset the influences of China and other powers.

Sihanouk was expressing one widespread Southeast Asian viewpoint about America's future in the region, namely, that the United States continue to exercise a strategic function. By maintaining a visible and specifically military presence in or near Southeast Asia, the United States is believed capable of limiting any ambitions for hegemony that China or the Soviet Union may have. Southeast Asian statesmen seem to share Sihanouk's long-held opinion that there is virtue in a certain amount of superpower competition—a "certain" amount because once competition goes beyond the bounds of legitimate efforts to gain influence, the danger again arises of direct intervention and the conversion of Southeast Asia into a battleground. So long as intervention and confrontation can be avoided, an American presence is usually desired because U.S. power offsets or deters the power of the other actors and thereby lengthens the time available to smaller states to develop independently.

Differences have always existed, and exist today, over the way in which the United States should exercise this counterbalancing function. In particular, what attitude should Southeast Asian governments adopt toward U.S. bases in the region? One point of view is that the American strategic function can be performed without maintaining these bases, namely, by relying on sea and air power that originates outside Southeast Asia (in Japan, Guam, and Hawaii). As stated by Singapore's prime minister, Lee Kuan Yew, "I would like the U.S. to maintain a sufficient economic and strategic presence in the area to prevent any other single power, or any group of powers, from gaining complete hegemony over the area. But I don't think you need bases and troops to do that. The Russians don't have bases, and they are extending their influence all right." Governments allied with the United States, such as in Thailand and the Philippines, disagree. They have accepted large American military presences in order to manifest their contributions to the U.S. containment strategy. Yet in both countries the bases have aroused political dissension, because they are a convenient target of leftist movements and because they symbolize a foreign occupation. The Thai and Philippines governments recognize the political sensitivity of the U.S. bases, as evidenced by the fact that when they joined in August 1967 with Malaysia, Singapore, and Indonesia to form the Association of Southeast Asian Nations (ASEAN), they adopted the position that "all foreign bases are temporary . . . and are not intended to be used directly or indirectly to subvert the national independence and freedom of states in the area or prejudice the orderly processes of their national development." But in all probability the U.S. bases will continue to be accepted as a necessary evil for some years to come.

The direct involvement of the United States in Southeast Asia's security raises many more problems than does the American strategic function. No government, however friendly to the United States and however plagued by internal dissension, can blithely ignore the destructiveness of the American intervention in Indochina. The Nixon Doctrine's stress on Asian self-reliance in local defense thus finds its counterpart in Southeast Asian capitals, where U.S. allies—specifically, Thailand, Cambodia, and South Vietnam—are asking for the "tools" to do the "job" themselves. In theory, at least, the Southeast Asian balance of power will not keep internal warfare from happening, but it will reduce the directness of American involvement in behalf of its allies.

One characteristic of this less direct U.S. involvement is the deterioration of the alliance system so assiduously developed during the first Eisenhower Administration. SEATO, already of little utility in the 1960s, may now be considered defunct. Pakistan withdrew in 1972, the French government announced it would no longer contribute funds after June 1974, and the membership as a whole agreed in late 1973 to cut back sharply SEATO's military functions. Thailand, South Vietnam, and Cambodia—the latter two not being SEATO members but being embraced within it by virtue of a unilateral American protocol to the original 1954 treaty—rely for U.S. defense support on bilateral arrangements with the United States and not on provisions of the SEATO pact.

Apart from the controversial aspects of a future U.S. security role in Southeast Asia, there remains the American economic role. Here, there seems to be unanimous agreement among the region's governments that U.S. assistance, investments, and trade are desirable. On a bilateral basis, U.S. economic and military aid is being received in varying amounts by every Southeast Asian country except the Democratic Republic of Vietnam. (Recall, however, that American economic assistance to North Vietnam is part of the Paris Accords signed in January 1973, although whether or not Hanoi will ever receive such assistance is certainly questionable.) American investments in the region continue to rise, especially in Indonesia and in the offshore oil resources of the South China Sea. Within a multilateral framework, American capital is the major component of the Asian Development Bank, founded in 1965 with a $1 billion capitalization; of the international consortium of "Free World" creditors of Indonesia; and of international financial institutions such as the World Bank and the International Monetary Fund. Southeast Asian governments, like governments elsewhere in the Third World, cannot entirely separate economics from politics when dealing with the United States. But the new stage in the region's international relations may make that task easier than before, although the outcome will depend as always mainly on the flexibility of U.S. policy and the behavior of America's chief competitors.

Responses to the Soviet Union

Although the Southeast Asian states have not shown any serious interest in the Russian concept of "collective security," as indicated in Robert Horn's essay, the success of other Soviet diplomatic and economic initiatives indicates that the USSR is generally a welcome addition to the region's international politics. Like the Soviets themselves, the Southeast Asian governments seem to prefer dealing on a bilateral basis to becoming involved in new, potentially entangling, alliances. This preference would seem to be all the more advisable since the start of Sino-American détente. At a time when the United States has taken the lead in cultivating political and economic ties with China, no Southeast Asian government wants to be identified with an organization directly or indirectly influenced by China's number one enemy, the USSR.

Yet remembrance of the past and concern about the future of Chinese foreign policy in Southeast Asia probably accounts for the widespread interest among the region's governments in Soviet overtures for improved trade, cultural, and political relations. With the relative receding of the American presence, a Soviet presence has become more attractive—not because the Soviet Union is being regarded as a principal source of foreign aid or as a new protector against China, replacing the United States, but because the fact of cooperative ties with Moscow, and the potential for their further development, are believed in Southeast Asia to be useful forms of leverage against the Chinese, as well as against the Americans. In the past, Southeast Asian governments have proven highly adept at manipulating the anxieties of a major power (usually the United States) about contacts between local governments and other powers in order to win new pledges of aid and defense support. With the Soviet Union and Japan now actively bidding for Southeast Asia's favor, the opportunities for playing off one major power against one or more others would seem to be better than ever.

One additional reason why Southeast Asian capitals have generally been receptive to Soviet initiatives may be that Moscow, unlike Peking, lacks intimate and far-reaching contacts with revolutionary movements and overseas nationals. Moscow does not have Peking's presumed ability to turn insurgencies on and off, or at least to make them internal security threats even if not serious challengers for political power. Nor do the Russians have the equivalent of the overseas Chinese, whose economic power, communalism, and psychological ties to China make them politically suspect throughout Southeast Asia. Relations with the Soviet Union may, therefore, be considered far less risky than relations with China, simply because the Russians do not have available indigenous proxy or third forces capable of subverting local authority.

Responses to China

Of the four major powers, the relationship of Southeast Asia to China has undergone the most dramatic change. In 1969, when the Cultural Revolution ended, only the DRV and Laos were on good terms with Peking. Of the three other governments that had diplomatic relations with China, one (Indonesia) had officially suspended them, because of Communist Party involvement in an attempted coup in the fall of 1965; another (Cambodia) had very strained relations arising out of zealous propaganda activities by the Chinese embassy; and a third (Burma) had disrupted relations after anti-Chinese riots, precipitated again by the unseemly actions of the Chinese embassy, had led to violent criticisms of the Burmese government by Peking. China's image in

Southeast Asia was severely tarnished, and its diplomatic opportunities greatly weakened, by the Cultural Revolution. It took the end of that movement, acceptance of the People's Republic of China's representation in the United Nations, and most importantly the Sino-American diplomacy of 1971 and 1972 to make relations with China respectable and useful for most Southeast Asian governments.

Strictly in terms of diplomatic relations, the changed Southeast Asian perspective of China is not obvious. Relations with Burma were restored in 1971; but they remain suspended with Indonesia, and were broken with Cambodia on the removal of Sihanouk in 1970. Nevertheless, there has been considerable official and semiofficial movement toward normalizing relations with the People's Republic of China. Since 1971, various trade and cultural missions have visited between China and Thailand, Malaysia, Singapore, and the Philippines. In 1974, there are good prospects for additional progress toward formal state relations in each of these cases except the Philippines, where President Marcos' deep political difficulties, which have nothing to do with China, have put a halt to steps toward relaxing tensions with Peking. There are also signs that Chinese-Indonesian relations may soon be resumed.

How far and how fast the process of accommodation to China will go depends mainly on two factors: first, the Chinese attitude toward revolutionary movements in Southeast Asian countries; second, these countries' domestic political and economic stability. Governments such as Thailand's and Malaysia's want to get on the American-made bandwagon in achieving sound working relations with Peking; they don't want to be left behind, isolated. But they also want some assurance that China will phase out its verbal and (rather limited) material support of local communist parties and revolutionary movements. Those Southeast Asian governments that have long had hostile or unfriendly relations with China will not be easily convinced of Peking's good intentions. They are likely to move cautiously toward official relations, whether out of sincere concern about a Chinese presence (meaning, in the case of Malaysia and Singapore, that the establishment of a Chinese embassy might lead to subversive ties with the large local Chinese populations), or in the conviction that they can gain more by exaggerating the risks of contacts with China than by fully normalizing relations.

Even if China's attitude is constructive and its behavior proper, as has been the case since the end of the Cultural Revolution, events in the Philippines show that domestic upheaval in Southeast Asia promotes foreign policy insularity and inhibits flexibility. The fact that the major powers are playing balance-of-power politics does not guarantee cooperation by the smaller powers, whose foreign policy shifts require reasonable economic and social stability and a consensus of the political elites. Where these conditions are lacking, there is risk rather than incentive in normalizing relations with China, for unlike the American government, Southeast Asian governments cannot depend on diplomatic breakthroughs, especially with a major power that has been portrayed for years as aggressive, to bail them out of domestic difficulties or deflect political dissent.

Responses to Japan

The past probably affects far more profoundly Southeast Asian perceptions of Japan than of China. The Japanese occupation of much of the region during World War II has left a legacy of bitterness and suspicion among present-day political leaders. But the wartime experiences cannot suffice to explain the anti-Japanese rioting that occurred early in 1974 when Prime Minister Tanaka visited Thailand and Indonesia. The young people who did most of the demonstrating had no personal familiarity with the occupation period. Their anger, as illustrated in the essay by Alvin Coox, was directed at Japanese "imperialism" of a different kind: economic and cultural. As the Japanese government is well aware, it will take considerable effort and sensitivity to overcome the anxieties in Southeast Asia, which inevitably tend to be exaggerated, about the evolution of a new Co-Prosperity Sphere. Whatever their political orientation and economic structure, Southeast Asian governments want to avoid undue dependence on Japanese capital for their internal development and trade.

There is equal if not greater common opposition in the region to any suggestion, such as is sometimes heard in American quarters, of Japan's assumption of a security role beyond defense of the home islands. It is clearly within Japan's capacity to have air and sea forces able to range across the entire region. A far-flung Japanese navy, able to protect the sea routes on which Japan is dependent for Middle East oil, is often mentioned as one kind of military function in which a future government might be interested. But to date a Japanese security role in Southeast Asia, independently or as a backstop to American forces, has been repeatedly discounted by Tokyo, which prefers the more profitable influence of the yen. Indeed, Southeast Asian governments have found the Japanese hesitant to take decisive political stands on major regional issues, leaving other states to take the initiative. In the Asian and Pacific Council, for instance, the Japanese opposed the organization's taking a rigid anticommunist line, with respect to China and the Vietnam War, and resisted suggestions by some members that the organization assume military functions.

Present indications are that Japan's role in Southeast Asia will remain predominantly economic, in terms of further expanding trade, aid, and investments. The competition for political influence will be left for the United States to pursue while the Japanese compete for a bigger share of Asian markets. Only a fundamental American retreat from Southeast Asia would confront Japan with the need to consider political and possibly military means of protecting its economic stakes.

SOUTHEAST ASIAN INITIATIVES

The fact that responsiveness of individual governments to circumstances defined by the major powers continues to be the dominant motif of Southeast

Asia's international politics should not obscure some noteworthy collective activities. These got underway late in the 1960s as the region's governments sought to enhance their independence, self-reliance, and self-esteem. As one persistent spokesmen for regional cooperation, the long-time foreign minister of Thailand, Thanat Khoman, argued, it would not only promote progress on specific common problems but would also help insulate the region from the pressures of foreign powers:

> Outside nations, be they friendly or hostile, will find it more difficult to intrude and impose upon us their will as well as the primacy of their interests. . . . There is . . . a need for a more effective effort to neutralize any eventual interference or intervention on the part of others into our affairs and out interests. We shall not have to depend on the emotional instability and political whims of other peoples. We shall also take pride in being able to rely on our own efforts to further our national interests and objectives.[2]

The record of regional initiatives is spotty, but whatever the overall evaluation, its psychological and symbolic value for Southeast Asians should not be ignored. Cooperative acts between Asian states reflect a common desire that foreign powers be more responsive to those whose destiny they largely determine. And politically, there is the expectation that regional associations will afford bargaining power with foreign powers that individual governments lack.

Regional activity has primarily had economic purposes; political consultation and cultural exchange have been prominent but secondary motives. ASEAN, previously mentioned, was founded to "accelerate the economic growth, social progress and cultural development in the region through joint endeavour and partnership" and to "promote regional peace and stability." ASPAC has a broader membership with similar objectives. Its initially hard-line anticommunism has been greatly toned down over the years. The Mekong River Development Project, planning for which actually began in the early 1950s, has resulted in the completion or start of construction of several dams for irrigation and hydroelectric power in Thailand, Laos, Cambodia, and South Vietnam. These four states have contributed over 40 percent of the capital, with the United States, Japan, and several Western European nations contributing the remainder. Less well known are a number of specialized all-Asian associations devoted to research and technical exchange on education, tropical medicine, transportation, fisheries, rice-growing, and other matters of common concern.

Each of these groups has its problems. Territorial and political disputes have hindered cooperation in ASEAN and ASPAC. Fighting in Indochina has constantly plagued the work of the Mekong Project. Economic cooperation under ASEAN and the small functional groups it has sponsored has been limited by the competitive nature of the Southeast Asian economies. They lack the diversity that makes for natural trade partners, hence the need to look outside the region—and especially to Japan, the United States, and Western Europe—for technology and capital. A final consideration is that a fully regional membership has yet to be achieved. Although membership is available to them, China and the DRV have stayed away; so have Cambodia, Burma, and Laos, although for different reasons.

On the security side, there has been strong resistance to suggestions that some new military alliance be formed in Southeast Asia, one that would substitute for SEATO but not have American participation. However, sub-regional security cooperation has not been ruled out, and in November 1971 a Five-Power Agreement was concluded by Great Britain, Australia, New Zealand, Malaysia, and Singapore to prolong Britain's and Australia's commitment to the defense of that area. This agreement aside, it seems improbable, in the wake of Sino-American and Sino-Japanese diplomacy, that other security links will be forged. It is far more likely that old ones, such as SEATO, will further decline in importance or even be abolished outright. To the extent that military alliances still have relevance and credibility in Southeast Asia, bilateral agreements are considered more reliable than multilateral alliances.

Other means of enhancing security and reducing the risks of conflict have been found or considered. Thailand and Malaysia concluded arrangements in 1965 (expanded in 1970) for patrolling and cross-border police operations against guerillas. Malaysia and Indonesia began border cooperation in 1970. In November 1971 the Malaysian Government hosted a meeting of the five ASEAN member-states that endorsed the proposal of its prime minister for the neutralization of Southeast Asia and for the adoption of nonalignment as the cornerstone of foreign policy. (But movement from principle to practice has yet to occur; nonalignment and neutralization are dependent on the support of the major powers, support that has not materialized.) In 1973 and 1974, agreements were signed between Indonesia, Malaysia, and Thailand, and between Indonesia and Singapore, on the boundaries of the Strait of Malacca.

Southeast Asian governments thus prefer not being passive spectators to the balance-of-politics game. But their capacity for individually or collectively influencing the basic character of the game is clearly very limited. The major power governments are certain to remain the manipulators, treating Southeast Asia much like a chessboard and maneuvering the "pieces" in ways that best serve their respective global interests. Yet, as was remarked in Chapter 1, the classical European balance of power was constantly disrupted by political upheavals, and so may the present "balance" in Southeast Asia. In a negative sense, then, the region's small powers do have influence despite their weaknesses. Disputes between neighboring states, revolutions, civil wars, nationalistic outbursts against foreigners, sudden changes of government, and other forms of instability may, as in the past, attract the interest and involvement of the major powers.

Southeast Asia, after all, is unlike any other area of the world in that the interests of *all* the major powers are involved. The boundaries of their competition are fluid, and a common code of conduct has yet to be formulated. In these circumstances, there is no reason for optimism that the major powers will avoid direct confrontations or opt for restraint rather than intervention in order to preserve "stability." The peoples and cultures of Southeast Asia have, at increasing cost, survived the political systems imposed by major powers of the past. They will undoubtedly also survive the balance-of-power system of the 1970s, but whether the cost will be appreciably less this time is far from certain.

NOTES

1. See George Modelski, "Kautilya: Foreign Policy and International System in the Ancient Hindu World," *American Political Science Review,* 58, no. 3, September 1964, pp. 549-560.

2. Speech on "Building a Free Southeast Asia," 22 October 1968; Permanent Mission of Thailand to the United Nations, Press Release no. 62, same date.

Press Release No. 16 of the Permanent Mission of Thailand to the United Nations, August 8, 1967

The Presidium Minister for Political Affairs/Minister of Foreign Affairs of Indonesia, the Deputy Prime Minister of Malaysia, the Secretary of Foreign Affairs of the Philippines, the Minister for Foreign Affairs of Singapore and the Minister of Foreign Affairs of Thailand:

Mindful of the existence of mutual interests and common problems among the countries of South-East Asia and convinced of the need to strengthen further the existing bonds of regional solidarity and cooperation:

Desiring to establish a firm foundation for common action to promote regional cooperation in South-East Asia in the spirit of equality and partnership and thereby contribute towards peace, progress and prosperity in the region:

Conscious that in an increasingly interdependent world, the cherished ideals of peace, freedom, social justice and economic well-being are best attained by fostering good understanding, good neighbourliness and meaningful cooperation among the countries of the region already bound together by ties of history and culture:

Considering that the countries of South-East Asia share a primary responsibility for strengthening the economic and social stability of the region and insuring their peaceful and progressive national development, and that they are determined to ensure their stability and security from external interference in any form or manifestation in order to preserve their national identities in accordance with the ideals and aspirations of their peoples:

Affirming that all foreign bases are temporary and remain only with the expressed concurrence of the countries concerned and are not intended to be used directly or indirectly to subvert the national independence and freedom of states in the area or prejudice the orderly processes of their national development:

Do hereby declare:

First, the establishment of an association for regional cooperation among the countries of South-East Asia to be known as the Association of South-East Asian Nations (ASEAN)

Second, that the aims and purposes of the Association shall be:

1. To accelerate the economic growth, social progress and cultural development in the region through joint endeavours in the spirit of equality and partnership in order to strengthen the foundation for a prosperous and peaceful community of South-East Asian nations:

2. To promote regional peace and stability through abiding respect for justice and the rule of law in the relationship among countries of the region and adherence to the principles of the United Nations Charter:

3. To promote active collaboration and mutual assistance on matters of common interest in the economic, social, cultural, technical, scientific and administrative fields:

4. To provide assistance to each other in the form of training and research facilities in the educational, professional, technical and administrative spheres:

5. To collaborate more effectively for the greater utilization of their agriculture and industries, the expansion of their trade, including the study of the problems of international commodity trade, the improvement of their transportation and communication facilities and the raising of the living standards of their peoples:

6. To promote South-East Asian studies:

7. To maintain close and beneficial cooperation with existing international and regional organizations with similar aims and purposes, and explore all avenues for even closer cooperation among themselves.

Third, that, to carry out these aims and purposes, the following machinery shall be established:

A. Annual meeting of foreign ministers may be convened as required

B. A standing committee, under the chairmanship of the foreign minister of the host country or his representative and having as its members the accredited ambassadors of the other member countries, to carry on the work of the Association in between meetings of foreign ministers

C. Ad hoc committees and permanent committees of specialists and officials on specific subjects

D. A national secretariat in each member country to carry out the work of the Association on behalf of that country and to service the annual or special meetings of foreign ministers, the standing committee and such other committees as may hereafter be established

Fourth, that the Association is open for participation to all States in the South-East Asian region subscribing to the aforementioned aims, principles and purposes;

Fifth, that the Association represents the collective will of the nations of South-East Asia to bind themselves together in friendship and cooperation and, through joint efforts and sacrifices, secure for their peoples and for posterity the blessings of peace, freedom and prosperity.

Done in Bangkok on August 8, 1967

For Indonesia: (Signed) Adam Malik
                          Presidium Minister of Political Affairs,
                          Minister for Foreign Affairs

For Malaysia:	(Signed) Tun Abdul Razak
	Deputy Prime Minister, Minister of Defence
	and Minister of National Development
For the Philippines:	(Signed) Narciso Ramos
	Secretary of Foreign Affairs
For Singapore:	(Signed) S. Rajaratnam
	Minister for Foreign Affairs
For Thailand:	(Signed) Thanat Khoman
	Minister of Foreign Affairs

DOCUMENT 2
President Nixon's
Guam Doctrine,
July 1969

President Nixon stopped at Guam en route to Asia in July 1969. His remarks were paraphrased by reporters at his request. Excerpts below are from the New York Times, *26 July 1969, p. 8.*

Role In Asia

The United States is going to be facing, [Nixon] hoped before too long—no one can say how long, but before too long—a major decision. What will be its role in Asia and in the Pacific after the end of the war in Vietnam? We will be facing that decision, but also the Asian nations will be wondering about what that decision is, Mr. Nixon said.

When he talked to Prime Minister John G. Gorton, for example he indicated that in the conversations he had with a number of Asian leaders, they all wondered whether the United States, because of its frustration over the war in Vietnam, because of its earlier frustration over the war in Korea—whether the United States would continue to play a significat role in Asia or whether the United States, like the French before, and then the British, and, of course, the Dutch—whether it would withdraw from the Pacific and play a minor role.

This is a decision that will have to be made, of course, as the war comes to an end. But the time to develop the thinking that will go into that decision is now. Mr. Nixon said he thinks that one of the weaknesses in American foreign policy is that too often we react rather precipitously to events as they occur. We fail to have the perspective and the long-range view that is essential for a policy that will be viable.

As he sees it, even though the war in Vietnam has been, as we all know, a terribly frustrating one, and, as a result of that frustration, even though there would be a tendency for many Americans to say, "After we are through with that, let's not become involved in Asia," he is convinced that the way to avoid becoming involved in another war in Asia is for the United States to continue to play a significant role, the President said.

U.S. a Pacific Power

He said that whether we like it or not, geography makes us a Pacific power and when we consider, for example, that Indonesia and its closest point is only 14 miles from the Philippines, when we consider that Guam, where he was presently standing, of course, is in the heart of Asia, when we consider the interests of the whole Pacific as they relate to Alaska and Hawaii, we can all realize this.

Also, as we look over the historical perspective, while World War II began in Europe, for the United States it began in the Pacific. It came from Asia. The Korean war came from Asia. The Vietnamese war came from Asia.

So, as we consider our past history, Mr. Nixon said, the United States involvement in war so often has been tied to Pacific policy or lack of Pacific policy, as the case might be.

As we look at Asia today, the President observed, we see that the major world power that adopts a very aggressive attitude and a belligerent attitude in its foreign policy, Communist China, of course, is in Asia, and we find that the two minor world powers—minor, although they do have significant strength as we have learned—that most greatly threaten the peace of the world, that adopt the most belligerent foreign policy, are in Asia—North Korea, and, of course, North Vietnam.

When we consider those factors, we realize that if we are thinking down the road, down the long road—not just four years or five years, but 10, 15, or 20—that if we are going to have peace in the world, that potentially the greatest threat to that peace will be in the Pacific, the President said.

He did not mean to suggest that the Mideast is not a potential threat to the peace of the world and that there are not problems in Latin America that concern us, or in Africa and, of course, over it all, we see the great potential conflict between the United States and the Soviet Union, the East-West conflict between the two superpowers.

But as far as those other areas are concerned, he said, the possibility of finding some kind of solution is potentially greater than it was in the Asian area.

Pursuing that line of reasoning a bit further, he said he would like to put it in a more positive sense: When he looked at the problems in Asia, he said the threat to peace presented by the growing power of Communist China, the belligerence of North Korea and North Vietnam, should not obscure the great promise that was here.

Mr. Nixon declared that the fastest rate of growth in the world is occurring in non-Communist Asia. Japan, in the last ten years had trippled its G.N.P., South Korea had doubled its G.N.P., Taiwan had doubled its G.N.P., Thailand had doubled its G.N.P. The same was true of Singapore and of Malaysia.

The record in some of the other countries was not as impressive. But consider the Philippines, he said. The Philippines in 1953 was a major importer of rice. Today, as a result of miracle rice, it no longer had to import it. Some progress was being made in areas like that.

The President mentioned India and Pakistan and the terribly difficult and traumatic experience they have had. Because of their conflict with each other, more than with the problems they have had from the outside, that picture tends to be rather bleak.

But India's rate of growth as a result of two good crop years, and a reasonably good one this year, has been at 6 per cent, he said.

As far as Pakistan is concerned, Mr. Nixon said, they are emphasizing growth in manufacturing. They are growing at the rate of 10 per cent per year in manufacturing and from 1965 to 1970 their agricultural production will go up 21 per cent.

The poverty in these two countries, he said, strikes one with tremendous impact. But having seen what it was in 1953 and seeing what it was again in

1957, the amount of progress that has taken place, even in those countries where the rate has not been as high as others, was a very, very formidable thing to see, he asserted.

So, what he is trying to suggest is this, the President said: Look at Asia. It poses, in his view, over the long haul, looking down to the end of the century, the greatest threat to peace of the world, and, for that reason the United States should continue to play a significant role.

It also poses, he said, the greatest hope for progress in the world because of the ability, the resources, the ability of the people, the resources physically that are available in this part of the world, and for these reasons, we need policies that will see that we play a part and a part that is appropriate to the condition that we will find.

One other point he made very briefly was that in terms of this situation we must recognize that there are two great new factors which you will see, incidentally, particularly, when you arrive in the Philippines—something you will see there that we didn't see in 1953, to show you how quickly things change—a very great growth of nationalism, nationalism even in the Philippines, vis-à-vis the United States, as well as other countries in the world. And, also, at the same time that national pride is becoming a major factor, regional pride is becoming a major factor.

The second factor, he went on, is one that is going to have a major impact on the future of Asia, and it is something that we must take into account. Asians will say in every country that we visit that they do not want to be dictated to from the outside. Asia for the Asians. And that is what we want and that is the role we should play. We should assist it, but we should not dictate.

At this time, he said, the political and economic plans that they are gradually developing are very hopeful, we will give assistance to those plans. We, of course, will keep the treaty commitments we have.

But as far as our role is concerned, he said, we must avoid that kind of policy that will make countries in Asia so dependent upon us that we are dragged into conflicts such as the one that we have in Vietnam.

This is going to be a difficult line to follow. It is one, however, that he thinks, with proper planning, we can develop, he went on.

He said he would just answer some of the speculation about Rumania by pointing out that this trip to Rumania is not directed toward the Chinese or toward the Russians, but toward the Rumanians, Mr. Nixon said.

He said he did not believe that the President of the United States should be able to accept an invitation to visit a Western European country, but should automatically have to decline an invitation to visit an Eastern European country.

Mr. Nixon said that this was an era of negotiation rather than confrontation. It would be more difficult, of course, to develop the communication with Eastern European Communist countries than with Western European countries, but he thought it was time that a beginning be made.

But this trip under no circumstances, he said, should be interpreted as an affront to the Soviet Union or as a move toward China.

The President said he hoped that if the trip worked out it would set the stage for more openings of this type with countries in Eastern Europe where it would be mutually beneficial to the United States and the other countries involved.

The President was asked, on the question of United States military relationships in Asia, a hypothetical question: If a leader of one of the countries with which we have had close military relationships, either through SEATO or in Vietnam, should say, "Well, you are pulling out of Vietnam with your troops. We can read the newspapers. How can we know you will remain to play a significant role as you say you wish to do in the security arrangements in Europe?" What kind of approach would he take to that question?

The President replied that he had indicated that the answer to that question was not an easy one—not easy because we would be greatly tempted when that question is put to us to indicate that if any nation desires the assistance of the United States militarily in order to meet an internal or external threat we will provide it.

On Commitments, Two Points

However, he said he believed that the time had come when the United States, in its relations with all of its Asian friends, should be quite emphatic on two points: one, that we would keep our treaty commitments; our treaty commitments, for example, with Thailand under SEATO. And two, that as far as the problems of international security are concerned, as far as the problems of military defense, except for the threat of a major power involving nuclear weapons, that the United States was going to encourage and had a right to expect that this problem would be increasingly handled by, and the responsibility for it taken by, the Asian nations themselves.

He said he believed, from his preliminary conversations with several Asian leaders over the last few months, that they were going to be willing to undertake this responsibility. He said it would not be easy. But if the United States just continued down the road of responding to requests for assistance, of assuming the primary responsibility for defending these countries when they have international problems or external problems, they were never going to take care of themselves.

He added that, when he talked about collective security for Asia, he realized that at this time it looks like a weak reed. It actually was. But looking down the road—he said he was speaking now of five years from now, 10 years from now—he thought collective security, insofar as it deals with internal threats to any one of the countries, or insofar as it deals with a threat other than that posed by a nuclear power, was an objective that free Asian nations could see and which the United States should support.

The President was asked whether, when speaking of internal threats, he included threats internally assisted by a country from the outside, such as we have in Vietnam?

The President replied that, generally speaking, it was the kind of internal threat that we do have in the Asian countries. For example, in Thailand the threat was on that was indigenous to a certain extent to the northeast and the north, but that would not be too serious if it were not getting the assistance that it was from the outside. The same was true in several of the other Asian countries, he said.

The President was reminded of his hope that his meetings in Rumania would open the way to other meetings involving Eastern Europe. Was it his hope that he would eventually be invited to Moscow to talk with the Russians, perhaps within the next six months or so?

The President replied that as far as any meeting with the Soviet Union was concerned, summit meeting, he had stated his position previously. He thought it would be well to restate it.

He did not believe that any summit meeting with the Soviet Union was useful unless a subject of major interest to both powers was to be discussed with some promise of finding a solution or at least making progress on that particular problem.

He said he believed, for example, as he looked over the history of summitry with the Soviet Union, that while, in all administrations, we had the best of intentions, summitry had not been particularly helpful. He said this with regard to the spirit of Geneva, the spirit of Vienna and the spirit of Glassboro.

He felt that where the Soviet Union was concerned, for example today, there were three major areas where a summit meeting could be useful. If, for example, the time had come when we could make a breakthrough in the Mideast, and a summit meeting with the Soviet Union would play a significant part, he thought that could be considered.

The second area, Mr. Nixon said, is in the field of arms control. He said he had a long discussion with Mr. Smith just a few days ago, just before leaving, the day before leaving. As far as arms controls are concerned, at this time, the place and the forum in which the discussion should take place is at the ambassador level. There may come a time when a summit meeting may be the device that will make the breakthrough that we need in arms control.

Then at the top of the list he placed the problem of Vietnam where, if a summit meeting would serve a useful purpose insofar as Vietnam is concerned, naturally we would welcome that opportunity. That poses, however, Mr. Nixon said, a very significant problem because, whether the Soviet Union can be of assistance in Vietnam is somewhat dependent on its evaluation of whether such assistance should be so publicly provided as a summit, of course, would indicate. . . .

Issue of Withdrawal

The President was asked whether he anticipates in that connection that during his talks with the Asian leaders he is going to have to spend any significant amount of time perhaps convincing them that his plan for withdrawal of American forces from Vietnam will pose no threat to their security.

The President replied that one of the reasons for this trip is to leave no doubt in the minds of the leaders of non-Communist Asia that the United States is committed to a policy in the Pacific, a policy not of intervention but one that certainly rules out withdrawal, and regardless of what happens in Vietnam that we intend to continue to play a role in Asia to the extent that Asian nations bilaterally and collectively, desire us to play a role. . . .

Declines to Speculate

The President was reminded that he mentioned that he felt that perhaps five years or ten years from now the Asian nations could collectively take care of their regional security problems. What is our policy to be in the meantime, he was asked, if a Vietnam type situation does occur?

The President replied that he would rather not speculate about one occurring. Each of these countries poses an entirely different question. He would simply say we are going to handle each country on a case-by-case basis.

But attempting to avoid that creeping involvement that eventually simply submerges you, he knows that we can learn from past experiences and we must avoid that kind of involvement in the future. . . .

The President was reminded that the last time he met with reporters he mentioned that it was his hope that we might be able to withdraw all our combat troops in South Vietnam by the end of next year. In the light of that, he was asked if he had any plans for withdrawing the troops that we now have, or some percentage of them, from Thailand, and could he tell what he is going to tell the Thais about that?

Will Tell Thais First

The President replied that he would tell the Thais first. But it is, of course, a proper question, he said.

He is reviewing not only our civilian personnel abroad, where he announced a cut a few weeks ago, but our military personnel abroad, including Thailand.

This is a matter, however, which will be discussed with the Thais, but it would not be appropriate to make any announcement as to what we were going to do until we have discussed it.

The President was asked whether in looking at the situation in post-Vietnam, and in countries other than Vietnam, it seemed to him that in terms of our military strength, the military men that we put into these other countries to help them, or military assistance or economic assistance, that in Asia, generally, we would have more or less of this type of assistance and aid in the years down the road than we have now.

The President replied less, if he got the question correctly, would there be more or less of military type of assistance?

He was asked about both in military and nonmilitary, since there are really two parts to this assistance problem, the economic part and the military part. Did he see us having a greater expenditure and a greater involvement in those respects or a lessened involvement as we look down the road?

The President replied that the military involvement, the military assistance, the military aid program and the rest, and particularly the commitments of military personnel, that that type of program would recede.

Economic Aid Stressed

However, as far as economic programs are concerned, and particularly those of a multilateral character—and here he had some new ideas that he will be expanding on in the months ahead—he would say that the level of United States activity would be adequate to meet the challenge as it develops, because it is very much in our interest in terms of economic assistance, economic assistance through loans and other programs, to help build the economies of free Asia, Mr. Nixon said. . . .

Pact With Thailand

The President was asked about quite a bit of speculation in the papers lately—both here and in Washington and in Thailand—as to whether or not there exists some sort of secret defense agreements with any other countries that might commit us beyond what his hopes might be?

The President replied that there is no secret defense agreement with Thailand. We, of course, have the SEATO treaty. We will keep our commitments under that treaty. We had the Rusk-Thanat communique, which simply spelled out the treaty.

We will, of course, keep our commitments set forth there as well, Mr. Nixon said.

But as far as any secret commitments are concerned, we not only have none in any of these nations, he will make none—and incidentally, he told Senator J. W. Fulbright that the other day, too.

The President was asked to give an evaluation of Red China's economic-political capability of inspiring further wars of liberation in the Asian nations. Are they able to continue that?

The President replied that Red China's capacity in this respect is much less than it was five years ago, even ten years ago. Because of its internal problems, Red China is not nearly as effective in exporting revolution as it was then. He thinks a pretty good indication of that is the minimal role that Red China is playing in Vietnam as compared with the Soviet Union, the President remarked.

Three years ago, Red China was furnishing over 50 per cent of the military equipment, the hardware, for the North Vietnamese. Now it is approximately 80-20 the other way round, he said.

Problems Within China

There may be other reasons for that coming about, and part of it is that Red China has enough problems within.

Another point he would make in that respect that bears on this: How things have changed since 1953, in country after country that he visited—and he was in every one that we are visiting here and all the others as well. The ones that Secretary William P. Rogers is going to visit on his trip—among most of the intellectual leaders and among many Government leaders, there was a real question as to what was the best path for progress, a question as to whether Communism, as it was developing in Red China, a Communist system was a better way to progress or whether a non-Communist system was the better way.

Now, Mr. Nixon said, one of the significant developments that has occurred over these last 16 years, with all the bad things that have occurred, including the war in Vietnam, has been that that situation has reversed itself. The appeal of the Communist philosophy for example, in Pakistan, in India, in Indonesia, in Japan, in any one of these countries, is less today than it was 16 years ago, 10 years ago, 5 years ago.

On the other hand, he would have to say that the effectiveness of subversive activities in many of these countries has not abated to the same extent. It can be on the upsurge. But as we look at the whole of Asia today, it is significant to note that what we have going for us more than anything else is this enormous rate of growth in non-Communist Asia as compared to Communist Asia. You compare Hong Kong with Communist China, you compare Taiwan with Communist China, you look at Japan with 100 million people, with a greater G.N.P. that China with 700 million people. Looking clear around the perimeter, from Japan through India, we find that free Asia's record of growth is a very significant factor in affecting the thinking of those who have to make the determination as to which path they are going to take, Mr. Nixon said.

No More Vietnam

The President was asked when he said that the United States was going to continue to play a major role in Asia and that this was one message that he intended to take with him on this trip, whether another message was that there would be no more Vietnams.

The President replied that certainly the objective of any American administration would be to avoid another war like Vietnam any place in the world. He recalled he had said it and so had his opponent, Mr. Humphrey, during the campaign—that we should develop a policy that would avoid other Vietnams.

Mr. Nixon said it was very easy to say that. But he said that to develop the policies to avoid that was taking an enormous amount of his time and that of his associates.

But what he said he could do was to learn from the mistakes of the past. He believed that we have, if we examine what happened in Vietnam, how we became so deeply involved—that we have a good chance of avoiding that kind of involvement in the future, he said.

Troop Withdrawals Discussed

Mr. Nixon was asked whether he intended to make it clear to the Asian leaders that if the lull in Vietnam continues, he would announce a substantial withdrawal of United States forces in August.

The President replied that he would not make any announcement and no decision on troop withdrawals on this trip, and, of course, he would not make any disclosures of plans in that respect to Asian leaders prior to the time that he had discussed it with the government of South Vietnam and then made the announcement jointly. . . .

DOCUMENT 3
Chairman Brezhnev's Reference to Collective Security

Reported in Pravda, *June 8, 1969.*

Despite the pressing problems of the present international situation we do not push into the background more long-range tasks, especially the creation of a system of collective security in those parts of the world where the threat of the unleashing of a new world war and the unleashing of armed conflicts is centered. Such a system is the best substitute for the existing military-political groupings.

The communist and workers' parties of Europe, boh the parties in power and those in the continent's capitalist countries, at their Karlovy Vary conference drew up a joint program of struggle for ensuring security in Europe. The Warsaw Pact member states have come out with a concrete security program for the peoples of Europe, the stability of borders and peaceful cooperation among the European states. The C.P.S.U. and the Soviet Union will do everything they can to implement that program.

We think that the course of events also places on the agenda the task of creating a system of collective security in Asia.

A Soviet Commentary on
Foreign Bases in Southeast Asia

The article below was written for the official Moscow News-paper, Izvestia, *May 29, 1969, by V. Matreyer. Translation from U.S. Foreign Broadcast Information Service,* Daily Report: USSR *June 3, 1969.*

India, Pakistan, Afghanistan, Burma, Cambodia, and Singapore—these and other Asian countries are making efforts to maintain their sovereignty and strengthen their economic independence. They cannot be interested in having foreign forces intervening in their domestic affairs. Hence the question of foreign military bases for these and other countries striving to protect their national interests from the intrigues of the imperialist expansionist forces can be considered on the same plane: The more areas of the Asian continent are rid of such bases, the better!

It is common knowledge that it is not only Britain that is maintaining its military forces in a number of countries of this vast region. American military bases are located in many areas of the Far East and Southeast Asia. The Australian Government, urged on by Washington, has recently been taking on itself the role of uninvited guardian of Asian peoples. Some people in Japan would have no objection to gaining a foothold on Asian soil similarly. Judging by statements in the Chinese press, Mao Tse-tung and his associates have very decided views on a number of countries of this region when they support the notorious thesis of the power "vacuum."

Peking progapanda solemnly declares that not a single Chinese solider is found outside CPR boundaries. But what about the northern regions of Burma? Reports of CPR military detachments there are not denied in Peking. The most important thing is that the numerous Chinese communities in a number of Asian countries are being increasingly used by the Maoists for purposes which have nothing in common with the sovereignty of these countries. This leads to complications and incidents.

The independent states that have risen on the ruins of colonial empires do not need any guardians. They have the opportunities and means of defending their own interests, including the interests of security. The liquidation of foreign military bases in this part of the globe would provide the prerequisites for creating bases of collective security, and then those very countries which have defended their freedom will, by their joint efforts, strengthen peace and repel any intrigues of the forces of imperialism and expansionism.

The Soviet Union and other socialist countries, in developing attitudes of friendship, equality, and mutual aid with countries defending their national independence, have done and will continue to do everything that helps make peace and security in Asia more reliable and lasting, notwithstanding the antipopular considerations of militant reaction.

DOCUMENT 5
A Soviet Analysis of Chinese Policy Toward the Third World

The following article, "Maoist Intrigues in the 'Third World,' " by V. Shelepin, appeared in the Moscow newspaper, Novoye Vremya, *on June 27, 1969. Translation from U.S. Foreign Broadcast Information Service,* Daily Report: USSR, *July 3, 1969.*

Speaking on 7 June at the international conference of communist and workers parties in Moscow, CPSU Central Committee General Secretary L. I. Brezhnev spoke of the necessity of analyzing the international aspects of the present Chinese leadership's policy.

Comrade Brezhnev said: "It is all the more important to speak about this matter, since a certain part of progressive public opinion still believes in the revolutionary strivings of the present Chinese leadership and its assertions that it is leading the struggle against imperialism. . . ."

In reality, Peking's policy is primarily determined by the hegemonic ambitions of Mao Tse-tung and his supporters. The Maoists are implanting and rousing great-power sentiments in the poeple and are publicizing the idea that China and its "great helmsman" can rid the peoples of the world of all evils. The well-defined aim of gaining world hegemony is concealed behind this phraseology.

The strategy of affirming Peking's great-power positions is copied from Mao's well-known theory about the "people's war:" To seize the most accessible objectives, to build up forces in the countryside, and then to make one's offensive on the cities and the fortified places. On a world scale, by "cities" the Peking strategists mean the economically developed countries (it is immaterial whether they are capitalist or socialist). The "countryside" is the so-called "third world." Here the Chinese leadership is mainly banking on the vast regions of Asia and Africa, which are characterized by economic backwardness, predominance of peasant population, the maintenance of the vestiges of pre-capitalist social formations, and the remnants of the colonial or semicolonial past.

During the "cultural revolution," the Maoists' excesses within the country and the provocations in the international arena fundamentally undermined their position in Asia and Africa. After Indonesia, Chinese influence was undermined in such countries as Burma, Nepal, Cambodia, Ghana, Tunisia, Kenya, Burundi, the Central African Republic, Dahomey, Nigeria, and Laos. However, this does not mean that Peking is ready to give up its plans. On the contrary, the materials of the Ninth CCP Congress confirmed that Peking is striving as before to win a dominant position in the "third world" and to use its people in the global struggle for its own hegemony.

The present Chinese leaders, not without reason, consider the countries of the socialist community and primarily the Soviet Union as the main obstacle on the path to achieve their hegemonistic aims in Asia and Africa. The Maoists' activity is directed toward forming an ideological and even a political anti-Soviet bloc in the "third world." They are using all means to achieve this aim: The authority of the Chinese revolution and objective factors which draw the economically backward countries closer; the political immaturity of the peasant masses; and the petit-bourgeois illusions of certain leaders of the national liberation movement.

There is a double task facing the Peking propaganda machine: To slander and compromise the Soviet Union in the eyes of the peoples, and at the same time to impose on them the vicious Maoist methods of political struggle and economic building.

Today in the countries of the "third world" the Maoists only consider as their friends those who oppose the Soviet Union, the socialist community, and the international communist movement, if only on certain questions. They consider all the rest in the "revisionist" camp and declare war on them.

The Chinese leadership is trying to undermine the young Asian and African states' links with the socialist countries. It is quite obvious that this is fraught with the danger not only of slowing down economic progress in the "third world" but also of weakening the advanced social forces' positions in the young countries. Peking's policy is objectively clearing the way for the forces of reaction and neocolonialism and the military-bureaucratic dictators. Thus, imperialism, in striving to undermine the national liberation movement, has found an active ally in the Maoists. In Indonesia, Chana, and certain other countries, the Chinese policy has become one of the causes of reactionary coups and the removal of governments pursuing an anti-imperialist policy. . . .

The Ninth CCP Congress [April 1969] laid down a new stage in the evolution of Maoism's political tenets. Today, Chinese propaganda openly states the intention "to hoist the banner of Mao's ideas over the whole glcbe." In the "third world" countries these notorious ideas more often than not are exported in the guise of primitive ultrarevolutionary slogans. . . .

As the facts show, Peking, in summoning the peoples to arms, is acting not in the interests of national liberation but entirely for its own mercenary motives. In the Chinese leaders' opinion, any armed conflict of whatever character creates favourable soil for spreading Maoism. On their lips, the formula "the gun engenders power" means the absolutization of the armed struggle and the propagation of the belief in force. They are stirring up and inflaming national ethnic contradictions, as in the recent events in Malaysia, and are supplying arms to the Nigerian dissidents from Biafra. In the Near East, the Maoists are trying to prevent a peaceful political settlement by every means. . . .

"Revolutionary" phraseology does not prevent the Maoists from co-operating with the bitterest enemies of the national liberation movement—U.S. imperialism and the reactionary regimes of Asia and Africa. Thus, certain facts suggest that Chinese proposals to the United States about "holding talks on peaceful coexistence" presuppose, in particular, an attempt to divide Asia into spheres of influence. . . .

The Maoists' intrigues in the Asian and African countries confirm the evaluation of their political policy given at the Moscow international conference of communist and workers parties by the head of the CPSU delegation. As L. I. Brezhnev said: "Facts show that the Chinese leaders only talk about the struggle against imperialism, while in fact they are directly or indirectly aiding it. . . . With the passage of time, it becomes increasingly obvious that the peoples of the young countries and their leaders distrust Peking's maneuvers. In the main, they reject the Chinese dogmas."

*The following remarks are excerpted from a speech by Chair-
man Brezhnev at the World Congress of Peace Forces, October
26, 1973. Translated in* New Times, *no. 44, November 1973, p.
8.*

It is common knowledge that the Soviet Union is advocating the consolidation of peace on the Asian continent by collective effort. We conceive of
this as the progressive development of all aspects of mutually beneficial and
mutually enriching relations and peaceful co-operation between all the Asian
states, as the consolidation in these relations of the well-known principles
proclaimed by the Asian states at Bandung of peaceful co-existence with strict
observance of the soveriegnty and independence of each country. The peoples
of Asia most certainly need lasting peace and constructive co-operation no less
than, say, the peoples of Europe. It is probably safe to say that the people of
Tokyo and Tashkent, of Hanoi and Teheran, Peking and Rangoon, Delhi and
Colombo—all the hundreds of millions of inhabitants of the world's largest
continent—have an equal stake in lasting peace and tranquil peaceful labour.
This, I am convinced, is in the interest of them all.

It is often said that the idea of creating and ensuring security in Asia by
collective effort is directed against China and all but pursues the perfidious aim
of "surrounding" or "isolating" China. But these contentions are either the
product of morbid suspicion or a reluctance to face the facts.

And the facts are that the Soviet Union and the other states favouring
collective efforts to ensure peace and security in Asia have always maintained
that all the states of the Asian continent without exception should take part in
this big and important undertaking if they so desire. Nobody has ever raised the
question of China's non-participation or, much less, "isolation" (not to speak
of the fact that it would be ludicrous to think of "isolating" such a big
country). As for the Soviet Union, it would welcome the participation of the
People's Republic of China in carrying out measures aimed at strengthening
Asian security.

Dear friends, of course, we would be going against the facts if we
pretended that China's present actions on the international scene are consonant
with the task of strengthening peace and peaceful co-operation between countries. For reasons they alone know, China's leaders refuse to halt their attempts
to poison the international climate and heighten international tensions. They
continue to make absurd territorial claims on the Soviet Union, which,
naturally, we reject categorically. They doggedly repeat the timeworn inven-
tions of anti-communist propaganda about a "Soviet threat," about "a threat
from the North," and, while dismissing all reasonable proposals for a settlement
and for a treaty of non-aggression, continue to keep their people in an
artificially created feverish atmosphere of war preparations. And all this is

accompanied by the dissemination of preposterous, slanderous accusations against the USSR and other countries, by brazen attempts to interfere in our—and, in fact, not only our—internal affairs.

What strikes one is the total lack of principle in the foreign policy of the Chinese leaders. They say that they are working for socialism and peaceful co-existence, but in fact they go out of their way to undermine the international positions of the socialist countries and encourage the activity of the aggressive military blocs and closed economic groups of capitalist states. They style themselves proponents of disarmament, but in fact try to block all the practical steps designed to restrict and slow down the arms race and, defying world public opinion, continue to pollute the earth's atmosphere by testing nuclear weapons. They assert that they support the just struggle of the Arabs for the return of the territories seized by the aggressor and for the establishment of a just peace in the Middle East, but at the same time are doing their utmost to discredit the real assistance rendered to the victims of aggression by their true friends, the Soviet Union and the other countries of the socialist community. They call themselves revolutionaries, but cordially shake the hand of a representative of the fascist junta of Chilean reactionaries, a hand stained with the blood of thousands of heroes of the revolution, the sons and daughters of the working class, of the working people of Chile.

Of course, a policy of this kind does not help to strengthen peace and security. It injects an element of dangerous instability into international affairs. But the possibility of changing this policy depends wholly and entirely on the Chinese leaders. As regards the Soviet Union, we, I repeat, would welcome a constructive contribution by China to improving the international atmosphere and promoting true and equitable peaceful co-operation between states.

Richard M. Nixon, U.S. Foreign Policy for the 1970's: Building
for Peace *(Washington, D.C.: Government Printing Office, February 25, 1971), pp. 10-21.*

It is not my belief that the way to peace is by giving up our
friends or letting down our allies. On the contrary, our aim is to
place America's international commitments on a sustainable, long-term basis, to encourage local and regional initiatives, to foster
national independence and self-sufficiency, and by so doing to
strengthen the total fabric of peace.

> Address to the United Nations
> General Assembly
> September 18, 1969

This Administration began with the conviction that a global structure of
peace requires a strong but redefined American role. In other countries there
was growing strength and autonomy. In our own there was nascent isolationism
in reaction to overextension. In the light of these changed conditions, we could
not continue on the old path.

We need to replace the impulses of the previous era: both our instinct that
we knew what was best for others and their temptation to lean on our prescriptions. We need to head off possible overreactions in the new era: a feeling on our
part that we need not help others, and a conclusion on their part that they cannot
count on America at all. We need to strengthen relations with allies and friends,
and to evoke their commitment to their own future and to the international system.

Perception of the growing imbalance between the scope of America's role
and the potential of America's partners thus prompted the Nixon Doctrine. It
is the key to understanding what we have done during the past two years, why
we have done it, and where we are going.

The Doctrine seeks to reflect these realities:

- that a major American role remains indispensable.
- that other nations can and should assume greater responsibilities, for
their sake as well as ours.
- that the change in the strategic relationship calls for new doctrines.
- that the emerging polycentrism of the Communist world presents
different challenges and new opportunities.

Toward New Forms of Partnership

The tangible expression of the new partnership is in greater material
contributions by other countries. But we must first consider its primary
purpose—to help make a peace that belongs to all.

For this venture we will look to others for a greater share in the definition of policy as well as in bearing the costs of programs. This psychological reorientation is more fundamental than the material redistribution; when countries feel responsible for the formulation of plans they are more apt to furnish the assets needed to make them work.

For America this could be the most critical aspect of the Doctrine. To continue our predominant contribution might not have been beyond our physical resources—though our own domestic problems summoned them. But it certainly would have exceeded our psychological resources. For no nation has the wisdom, and the understanding, and the energy required to act wisely on all problems, at all times, in every part of the world. And it asks too much of a people to understand—and therefore support—sweeping and seemingly permanent overseas involvement in local problems, particularly when other countries seem able to make greater efforts themselves.

The intellectual adjustment is a healthy development for other nations as well as for us. It requires them to think hard about some issues that had been removed, or had never appeared, on their national agendas. It is no more in their interest than in ours to place on the United States the onus for complicated decisions—the structure of an army, the outline of a development plan, the components of an economic policy, the framework of a regional alliance.

The Nixon Doctrine, then, should not be thought of primarily as the sharing of burdens or the lightening of our load. It has a more positive meaning for other nations and for ourselves.

In effect we are encouraging countries to participate fully in the creation of plans and the designing of programs. They must define the nature of their own security and determine the path of their own progress. For only in this manner will they think of their fate as truly their own.

This new sharing requires a new, more subtle form of leadership. Before, we often acted as if our role was primarily one of drawing up and selling American blueprints. Now, we must evoke the ideas of others and together consider programs that meet common needs. We will concentrate more on getting other countries engaged with us in the formulation of policies; they will be less involved in trying to influence American decisions and more involved in devising their own approaches.

More than ever before in the period since World War II, foreign policy must become the concern of many rather than few. There cannot be a structure of peace unless other nations help to fashion it. Indeed, in this central fact lie both its hope and its elusiveness: it cannot be built except by the willing hands—and minds—of all.

It was in this context that at Guam in the summer of 1969, and in my November 3, 1969, address to the Nation, I laid out the elements of new partnership.

"First, the United States will keep all of its treaty commitments." We will respect the commitments we inherited—both because of their intrinsic merit, and because of the impact of sudden shifts on regional or world stability. To desert those who have come to depend on us would cause disruption and invite aggression. It is in everyone's interest, however, including those with whom we have ties, to view undertakings as a dynamic process. Maintaining the integrity of commitments requires relating their tangible expression, such as troop deployments or financial contributions, to changing conditions.

The concrete results vary. In South Korea fewer U.S. troops are required, but Korean forces must receive more modern equipment. In NATO a continuing level of U.S. forces and greater European contributions are in order. The best way of maintaining stable relationships with our allies is jointly to reach common conclusions and jointly to act on them.

In contemplating new commitments we will apply rigorous yardsticks. What precisely is our national concern? What precisely is the threat? What would be the efficacy of our involvement? We do not rule out new commitments, but we will relate them to our interests. For as I said in last year's report:

> Our objective, in the first instance, is to support our interests over the long run with a sound foreign policy. The more that policy is based on a realistic assessment of our and others' interests, the more effective our role in the world can be. We are not involved in the world because we have commitments; we have commitments because we are involved. Our interests must shape our commitments, rather than the other way around.

"Second, we shall provide a shield if a nuclear power threatens the freedom of a nation allied with us or of a nation whose survival we consider vital to our security." Nuclear power is the element of security that our friends either cannot provide or could provide only with great and disruptive efforts. Hence, we bear special obligations toward non-nuclear countries. Their concern would be magnified if we were to leave them defenseless against nuclear blackmail, or conventional aggression backed by nuclear power. Nations in a position to build their own nuclear weapons would be likely to do so. And the spread of nuclear capabilities would be inherently destabilizing, multiplying the chances that conflicts could escalate into catastrophic exchanges.

Accordingly, while we maintain our nuclear force, we have encouraged others to forego their own under the Non-Proliferation Treaty. We have assured those signing the NPT that they would not be subject to nuclear blackmail or nuclear aggression. The Soviet Union has done so as well.

"Third, in cases involving other types of aggression we shall furnish military and economic assistance when requested in accordance with our treaty commitments. But we shall look to the nation directly threatened to assume the primary responsibility of providing the manpower for its defense." No President can guarantee that future conflicts will never involve American personnel—but in some theaters the threshold of involvement will be raised and in some instances involvement will be much more unlikely. This principle, first applied to security matters, applies as well to economic development. Our economic assistance will continue to be substantial. But we will expect countries receiving it to mobilize themselves and their resources; we will look to other developed nations to play their full role in furnishing help; and we will channel our aid increasingly through multilateral channels.

We will continue to provide elements of military strength and economic resources appropriate to our size and our interests. But it is no longer natural or possible in this age to argue that security or development around the globe is primarily America's concern. The defense and progress of other countries must be first their responsibility and second, a regional responsibility. Without the foundations of self-help and regional help, American help will not succeed. The United States can and will participate, where our interests dictate, but as a weight—not the weight—in the scale.

The Process of Implementation

Policy becomes clearer only in the process of translation into programs and actions.

In this process the Nixon Doctrine seeks to reflect the need for continuity as well as the mandate for change. There are two concurrent challenges:

- to carry out our new policy so as to maintain confidence abroad.
- to define our new policy to the American people and to elicit their support.

This transition from bearing the principal burdens to invoking and supporting the efforts of others is difficult and delicate.

Some vestiges of the past consist of essentially sound relationships and valid practices. They should be preserved.

Others must be liquidated, but the method is crucial. Clearly, we could not have continued the inherited policy on Vietnam. Just as clearly, the way in which we set about to resolve this problem has a major impact on our credibility abroad and our cohesion at home. The same is true in other areas where our military presence remained too large, or our economic burden disproportionate, or our attitude paternalistic.

The challenge is not merely to reduce our presence, or redistribute our burden, or change our approach, but to do so in a way that does not call into question our very objectives.

Others judge us—and set their own course—by the steadiness of our performance as well as the merit of our ideas. Abrupt shifts in our policies—no matter how sound in concept—are unsettling, particularly for those who may have committed themselves to past practices at United States urging. For their own political future is involved. If we acquired a reputation for unsteadiness, we would isolate ourselves. We must avoid practicing either consistency or novelty for its own sake.

For the mood among many of our friends is ambivalent. They seek autonomy but still presume American initiative. They at once realize the need for their new independent role, welcome it, and are apprehensive about its responsibilities. The Nixon Doctrine recognizes that we cannot abandon friends, and must not transfer burdens too swiftly. We must strike a balance between doing too much and thus preventing self-reliance, and doing too little and thus undermining self-confidence.

This balance we seek abroad is crucial. We only compound insecurity if we modify our protective or development responsibilities without giving our friends the time and the means to adjust, materially and psychologically, to a new form of American participation in the world.

Precipitate shrinking of the American role would not bring peace. It would not reduce America's stake in a turbulent world. It would not solve our problems, either abroad or at home.

The need for steadiness overseas has a domestic corollary. While striking a balance in the world it is also necessary, and in some ways even more difficult, to find the proper balance at home.

For the American people have grown somewhat weary of 25 years of international burdens. This weariness was coming in any event, but the anguish of the Vietnam war hastened it, or at least our awareness of it. Many Americans, frustrated by the conflict in Southeast Asia, have been tempted to draw the wrong conclusions. There are lessons to be learned from our Vietnam experience—about unconventional warfare and the role of outside countries, the nature of commitments, the balance of responsibilities, the need for public understanding and support. But there is also a lesson not to be drawn: that the only antidote for undifferentiated involvement is indiscriminate retreat.

Our experience in the 1960's has underlined the fact that we should not do more abroad than domestic opinion can sustain. But we cannot let the pendulum swing in the other direction, sweeping us toward an isolationism which could be as disastrous as excessive zeal.

Thus, while lowering our overseas presence and direct military involvement, our new policy calls for a new form of leadership, not abdication of leadership. This policy must not only reflect a changed public will. It must shape a new consensus for a balanced and positive American role.

While cutting back overseas forces prudently, we must resist the automatic reduction of the American presence everywhere without regard to consequences. While trimming our defense budget where possible and adjusting defenses to modern realities, we must resist ritualistic voting against defense spending. Mere scaling down is not an end in itself. We need to determine the proper role for our forces abroad; the level of assistance for allied forces; and the shape of our respective budgets.

The Nixon Doctrine will enable us to remain committed in ways that we can sustain. The solidity of domestic support in turn will reverberate overseas with continued confidence in American performance.

The Record of Implementation

Different national and regional circumstances dictate variations in style, speed, and substance in implementing the Nixon Doctrine. This past year the sharing of responsibilities was reflected in various ways.

In some areas the Nixon Doctrine resulted in reduced American presence:

• In Vietnam, we progressively transferred combat burdens in an on-going war. Vietnamization produced substantial improvement in South Vietnamese forces, the withdrawal of some 260,000 Americans by May 1 of this year, and a decline in American casualties in 1970 to a level 70% below 1968.

• In South Korea, we moved to a more supportive role in the continuing process of deterring a new war. We announced a reduction of 20,000 in the authorized American troop ceiling together with modernization of Korean forces through expanded military assistance.

• Elsewhere in Asia we cut back our forces to reflect our declining involvement in Vietnam and the increased capabilities of our allies. Troop reductions and base consolidations by this July will lower the U.S. presence by some 12,000 in Japan, 5,000 in Okinawa, 16,000 in Thailand and 9,000 in the Philippines.

• Worldwide we cut back the U.S. official presence, civilian and military, for a more efficient and less conspicuous approach. A program begun in November 1969 reduced our government personnel abroad by about 86,000.

In other cases our new approach took different forms:

• In Europe we enlisted greater material and intellectual contributions from our allies. We jointly reviewed NATO strategy and agreed to a realistic defense in which the European conventional share will be relatively larger. For the ongoing SALT negotiations we stayed in close touch with our allies not only because of their interest but also for their ideas.

• In the Western Hemisphere we have shifted from paternalism to a more balanced partnership. We sought the ideas and initiatives of our neighbors and together strengthened the mechanisms for sharing responsibilities in hemispheric development and diplomacy.

• Our foreign assistance program enabled us to help countries who were helping themselves. Congressional passage of a $1 billion supplemental appropriation at year's end was encouraging recognition that the Nixon Doctrine requires substantial American assistance.

• In our proposals for a new approach to foreign aid we emphasized multilateral institutions and collaboration. We will work more with, and ask more of, others in the development process.

In 1970 there were also examples of policies which belied oversimplified interpretations of the Nixon Doctrine as a formula for heedless withdrawal:

• The Cambodian sanctuary operations were not inconsistent with the plan for American disengagement. Rather they furthered the strategic purpose of insuring the Vietnamization and withdrawal programs.

• Maintaining the present level of U.S. forces in Europe does not contradict the principle of self-help and burden sharing in Asia. Rather it is the best means of eliciting greater partnership in the European theater, while recognizing the reality of the security problem.

• The discreet projection of American presence in the Mediterranean during the Jordanian crisis did not increase the chances of outside intervention. Rather it served as a reminder that outside intervention carried great risks.

The Nixon Doctrine applies most directly to our dealings with allies and friends. But it animates all areas of our new foreign policy.

• In our economic posture. We look towards increased U.S. economic and military assistance in certain areas to help our friends make full use of their

resources and move on to greater self-reliance. International trade and monetary policies will demand mutual accommodations and adjustment.

• In our defense posture. We will provide the nuclear shield of the Nixon
Doctrine. Our general purpose forces are more and more keyed to our partners'
capabilities, to provide truly flexible response when our commitments are
involved. And our security assistance program will provide indispensable support to our friends, especially where there are reductions in U.S. manpower.

• In our negotiating posture. When we conduct bilateral negotiations with
the USSR, as in SALT, partnership involves close consultations with our allies
both to protect their interests and solicit their views. In turn partnership
requires our allies, in their negotiations, to pursue their course within a
framework of common objectives. And there are areas of multilateral negotiations in which partnership is most immediately involved.

• In our global posture. Nonpolitical world problems call for cooperation
that transcends national rivalries. Here, more comprehensively than in traditional realms, there is a need for shared approaches and shared participation.

The Necessity for Dialogue

The Nixon Doctrine, then, is a means to fulfill our world responsibilities
on a sustained basis by evoking both the contributions of our friends and the
support of our own people. Its very nature calls for continuing dialogue abroad
and at home.

We recognize that the Doctrine, like any philosophic attitude, is not a
detailed design. In this case ambiguity is increased since it is given full meaning
through a process that involves other countries. When other nations ask how
the Doctrine applies to them in technical detail, the question itself recalls the
pattern of the previous period when America generally provided technical
prescriptions. The response to the question, to be meaningful, partly depends
on them, for the Doctrine's full elaboration requires their participation. To
attempt to define the new diplomacy completely by ourselves would repeat the
now presumptuous instinct of the previous era and violate the very spirit of our
new approach.

In coming years we will therefore be engaged in a broad and deep
discussion with others concerning foreign policy and the nature of our respective roles. To define and assume new modes of partnership, to discover a new
sense of participation, will pose a great intellectual challenge for our friends
and ourselves.

At home the challenge is comparable.

It is always a requirement of American leadership to explain, as clearly as
possible, its overall approach. We must convincingly demonstrate the relationship between our specific actions and our basic purposes. In turn, the leadership can ask the American people for some degree of trust, and for acknowl-
edgement of the complexities of foreign policy. This does not mean a
moratorium on criticism. It means listening to the rationale for specific actions
and distinguishing attacks on the broad policy itself from attacks on tactical
judgments.

This dialogue between the government and the people is all the more imperative in this transitional era. Gone for Americans is a foreign policy with the psychological simplicity of worrying primarily about what we want for others. In its place is a role that demands a new type of sustained effort with others.

To further this dialogue overseas and in America is the principal objective of this annual review.

To promote this dialogue is to improve the prospects that America, together with others, will play its vital part in fashioning a global structure of peace. A peace that will come when all have a share in its shaping. A peace that will last when all have a stake in its lasting.

Ministry of Foreign Affairs, Malaysia, Foreign Affairs Malaysia
4, no. 4, December 1971.

We the Foreign Ministers of Indonesia, Malaysia, the Philippines, Singapore and the Special Envoy of the National Executive Council of Thailand:

Firmly believing in the merits of regional co-operation which has drawn our countries to co-operate together in the economic, social and cultural fields in the Association of Southeast Asian Nations;

Desirous of bringing about a relaxation of international tension and of achieving a lasting peace in Southeast Asia;

Inspired by the worthy aims and objectives of the United Nations, in particular by the principles of respect for the sovereignty and territorial integrity of all States, abstention from the threat or use of force, peaceful settlement of international disputes, equal rights and self-determination and non-interference in the internal affairs of States;

Believing in the continuing validity of the "Declaration on the Promotion of World Peace and Co-operation" of the Bandung Conference of 1955, which, among others, enunciates the principles by which States may co-exist peacefully;

Recognizing the right of every State, large or small, to lead its national existence free from outside interference in its internal affairs as this interference will adversely affect its freedom, independence and integrity;

Dedicated to the maintenance of peace, freedom and independence unimpaired;

Believing in the need to meet present challenges and new developments by co-operating with all peace and freedom loving nations, both within and outside the region, in the furtherance of world peace, stability and harmony;

Cognizant of the significant trend towards establishing nuclear-free zones, as in the "Treaty for the Prohibition of Nuclear Weapons in Latin America" and the Lusaka Declaration proclaiming Africa a nuclear-free zone, for the purpose of promoting world peace and security by reducing the areas of international conflicts and tensions;

Reiterating our commitment to the principle in the Bangkok Declaration which established ASEAN in 1967, "that the countries of Southeast Asia share a primary responsibility for strengthening the economic and social stability of the region and ensuring their peaceful and progressive national development, and that they are determined to ensure their stability and security from external interference in any form or manifestation in order to preserve their national identities in accordance with the ideals and aspirations of their peoples";

Agreeing that the neutralization of Southeast Asia is a desirable objective and that we should explore ways and means of bringing about its realization, and

Convinced that the time is propitious for joint action to give effective expression to the deeply felt desire of the peoples of Southeast Asia to ensure the conditions of peace and stability indispensable to their independence and their economic and social well-being;

Do hereby state

1. that Indonesia, Malaysia, the Philippines, Singapore and Thailand are determined to exert initially necessary efforts to secure the recognition of, and respect for, Southeast Asia as Zone of Peace, Freedom and Neutrality, free from any form or manner of interference by outside Powers;
2. that Southeast Asian countries should make concerted efforts to broaden the areas of co-operation which would contribute to their strength, solidarity and closer relationship.

The Chinese Proposal for a
Peaceful Coexistence Agreement
with the United States,
November 1968

The following proposal, made by the PRC Ministry of Foreign Affairs on 26 November 1968, was the last point of a statement that, overall, was sharply critical of the U.S. Government for cancelling a Sino-American meeting of ambassadors scheduled for that day in Warsaw, Poland. The context of the proposal is important: It occurred soon after the election of Richard Nixon, in the early months of the Paris peace talks on Indochina, only three months after the Soviet invasion of Czechoslovakia, and in the aftermath of the Chinese leadership's reassertion of political order throughout the mainland. Reprinted from Peking Review, *no. 48, November 29, 1968, p. 31.*

Over the past 13 years, the Chinese Government has consistently adhered to the following two principles in the Sino-U.S. ambassadorial talks: First, the U.S. Government undertakes to immediately withdraw all its armed forces from China's territory Taiwan Province and the Taiwan Straits area and dismantle all its military installations in Taiwan Province; second, the U.S. Government agrees that China and the United States conclude an agreement on the Five Principles of Peaceful Coexistence. But in the past 13 years, while refusing all along to reach an agreement with the Chinese Government on these two principles, the U.S. Government, putting the cart before the horse, has kept on haggling over side issues. The Chinese Government has repeatedly told the U.S. side in explicit terms that the Chinese Government will never barter away principles. If the U.S. side continues its current practice, no result whatsoever will come of the Sino-U.S. ambassadorial talks no matter which administration assumes office in the United States.

DOCUMENT 10
Excerpts on China from President Nixon's
Foreign Policy Report to Congress,
February 1971

Richard M. Nixon, U.S. Foreign Policy for the 1970's: Building for Peace *(Washington, D.C.: Government Printing Office, February 25, 1971), pp. 105-109.*

The Peoples Republic of China faces perhaps the most severe problem of all in adjusting her policies to the realities of modern Asia. With a population eight times greater than that of Japan, and possessing a much greater resource base, Mainland China nonetheless sees the free Japanese economy producing a gross national product two and a half times that of her own. The remarkable success of the Chinese people within the free economic setting of Taiwan and Singapore, and the contributions of the overseas Chinese to growth elsewhere in Asia, stands as an eloquent rebuttal to Peking's claim of unique insight and wisdom in organizing the talents of the Chinese people.

The Peoples Republic of China is making a claim to leadership of the less developed portions of the world. But for that claim to be credible, and for it to be pursued effectively, Communist China must expose herself to contact with the outside world. Both require the end of the insulation of Mainland China from outside realities, and therefore from change.

The twenty-two year old hostility between ourselves and the Peoples Republic of China is another unresolved problem, serious indeed in view of the fact that it determines our relationship with 750 million talented and energetic people.

It is a truism that an international order cannot be secure if one of the major powers remains largely outside it and hostile toward it. In this decade, therefore, there will be no more important challenge than that of drawing the Peoples Republic of China into a constructive relationship with the world community, and particularly with the rest of Asia.

We recognize that China's long historical experience weighs heavily on contemporary Chinese foreign policy. China has had little experience in conducting diplomacy based on the sovereign equality of nations. For centuries China dominated its neighbors, culturally and politically. In the last 150 years it has been subjected to massive foreign interventions. Thus, China's attitude toward foreign countries retains elements of aloofness, suspicion, and hostility. Under Communism these historically shaped attitudes have been sharpened by doctrines of violence and revolution, proclaimed more often than followed as principles in foreign relations.

Another factor determining Communist Chinese conduct is the intense and dangerous conflict with the USSR. It has its roots in the historical development of the vast border areas between the two countries. It is aggravated by contemporary ideological hostility, by power rivalry and nationalist antagonisms.

A clash between these two great powers is inconsistent with the kind of stable Asian structure we seek. We, therefore, see no advantage to us in the hostility between the Soviet Union and Communist China. We do not seek any. We will do nothing to sharpen that conflict—nor to encourage it. It is absurd to believe that we could collude with one of the parties against the other. We have taken great pains to make it clear that we are not attempting to do so.

At the same time, we cannot permit either Communist China or the USSR to dictate our policies and conduct toward the other. We recognize that one effect of the Sino-Soviet conflict could be to propel both countries into poses of militancy toward the non-Communist world in order to validate their credentials as revolutionary centers. It is also possible that these two major powers, engaged in such a dangerous confrontation, might have an incentive to avoid further complications in other areas of policy. In this respect, we will have to judge China, as well as the USSR, not by its rhetoric but by its actions.

We are prepared to establish a dialogue with Peking. We cannot accept its ideological precepts, or the notion that Communist China must exercise hegemony over Asia. But neither do we wish to impose on China an international position that denies its legitimate national interests.

The evolution of our dialogue with Peking cannot be at the expense of international order or our own commitments. Our attitude is public and clear. We will continue to honor our treaty commitments to the security of our Asian allies. An honorable relationship with Peking cannot be constructed at their expense.

Among these allies is the Republic of China. We have been associated with that government since its inception in 1911, and with particular intimacy when we were World War II allies. These were among the considerations behind the American decision to assist the Government of the Republic of China on Taiwan with its defense and economic needs.

Our present commitment to the security of the Republic of China on Taiwan stems from our 1954 treaty. The purpose of the treaty is exclusively defensive, and it controls the entire range of our military relationship with the Republic of China.

Our economic assistance to the Republic of China has had gratifying results. Beginning in 1951, the U.S. provided $1.5 billion in economic assistance. Its effective and imaginative use by the Government of the Republic of China and the people of Taiwan made it possible for us to terminate the program in 1965.

I am recalling the record of friendship, assistance, and alliance between the United States and the Government of the Republic of China in order to make clear both the vitality of this relationship and the nature of our defense relationship. I do not believe that this honorable and peaceful association need constitute an obstacle to the movement toward normal relations between the United States and the Peoples Republic of China. As I have tried to make clear since the beginning of my Administration, while I cannot foretell the ultimate resolution of the differences between Taipei and Peking, we believe these differences must be resolved by peaceful means.

In that connection, I wish to make it clear that the United States is prepared to see the Peoples Republic of China play a constructive role in the family of nations. The question of its place in the United Nations is not, however, merely a question of whether it should participate. It is also a question of whether Peking should be permitted to dictate to the world the terms of its participation. For a number of years attempts have been made to deprive the Republic of China of its place as a member of the United Nations and its Specialized Agencies. We have opposed these attempts. We will continue to oppose them.

The past four years have been a period of internal turmoil and upheaval in Mainland China. A calmer mood now seems to be developing. There could be new opportunities for the Peoples Republic of China to explore the path of normalization of its relations with its neighbors and with the world, including our own country.

For the United States the development of a relationship with Peking embodies precisely the challenges of this decade: to deal with, and resolve, the vestiges of the postwar period that continue to influence our relationship, and to create a balanced international structure in which all nations will have a stake. We believe that such a structure should provide full scope for the influence to which China's achievements entitle it.

We continue to believe that practical measures on our part will, over time, make evident to the leaders in Peking that we are prepared for a serious dialogue. In the past year we took several such steps:

• In January and February of 1970, two meetings were held between our representatives in Warsaw, thus restoring an important channel of communication. The subsequent cancelling of the scheduled May meeting was at Chinese initiative.

• In April, we authorized the selective licensing of goods for export to the Peoples Republic of China.

• In August, certain restrictions were lifted on American oil companies operating abroad, so that most foreign ships could use American-owned bunkering facilities on voyages to and from mainland Chinese ports.

• During 1970, the passports of 270 Americans were validated for travel to the Peoples Republic of China. This brought to nearly 1,000 the number so validated. Regrettably, only three holders of such passports were permitted entry to China.

In the coming year, I will carefully examine what further steps we might take to create broader opportunities for contacts between the Chinese and American peoples, and how we might remove needless obstacles to the realization of these opportunities. We hope for, but will not be deterred by a lack of, reciprocity.

We should, however, be totally realistic about the prospects. The Peoples Republic of China continues to convey to its own people and to the world its determination to cast us in the devil's role. Our modest efforts to prove otherwise have not reduced Peking's doctrinaire enmity toward us. So long as this is true, so long as Peking continues to be adamant for hostility, there is little we can do by ourselves to improve the relationship. What we can do, we will.

DOCUMENT 11
The U.S.-China Communiqué
at the Conclusion of
President Nixon's Visit to China
February 1972

*The Chinese and U.S. sides reached agreement on a joint com-
muniqué on February 27, 1972 in Shanghai. Following is the
full text, reprinted from* Peking Review *no. 9, March 3, 1972,
pp. 4-5.*

President Richard Nixon of the United States of America visited the
People's Republic of China at the invitation of Premier Chou En-lai of the
People's Republic of China from February 21 to February 28, 1972. Accom-
panying the President were Mrs. Nixon, U.S. Secretary of State William Rogers,
Assistant to the President Dr. Henry Kissinger, and other American officials.

President Nixon met with Chairman Mao Tsetung of the Communist Party
of China on February 21. The two leaders had a serious and frank exchange of
views on Sino-U.S. relations and world affairs.

During the visit, extensive, earnest and frank discussions were held between President Nixon and Premier Chou En-lai on the normalization of
relations between the United States of America and the People's Republic of
China, as well as on other matters of interest to both sides. In addition,
Secretary of State William Rogers and Foreign Minister Chi Peng-fei held talks
in the same spirit.

President Nixon and his party visited Peking and viewed cultural, industrial and agricultural sites, and they also toured Hangchow and Shanghai
where, continuing discussions with Chinese leaders, they viewed similar places
of interest.

The leaders of the People's Republic of China and the United States of
America found it beneficial to have this opportunity, after so many years
without contact, to present candidly to one another their views on a variety of
issues. They reviewed the international situation in which important changes
and great upheavals are taking place and expounded their respective positions
and attitudes.

The Chinese side stated: Wherever there is oppression, there is resistance.
Countries want independence, nations want liberation and the people want
revolution—this has become the irresistible trend of history. All nations, big or
small, should be equal; big nations should not bully the small and strong
nations should not bully the weak. China will never be a superpower and it
opposes hegemony and power politics of any kind. The Chinese side stated that
it firmly supports the struggles of all the oppressed people and nations for
freedom and liberation and that the people of all countries have the right to
choose their social systems according to their own wishes and the right to
safeguard the independence, sovereignty and territorial integrity of their own
countries and oppose foreign aggression, interference, control and subversion.
All foreign troops should be withdrawn to their own countries. The Chinese
side expressed its firm support to the peoples of Viet Nam, Laos and Cambodia

in their efforts for the attainment of their goal and its firm support to the seven-point proposal of the Provisional Revolutionary Government of the Republic of South Viet Nam and the elaboration of February this year on the two key problems in the proposal, and to the Joint Declaration of the Summit Conference of the Indochinese Peoples. It firmly supports the eight-point program for the peaceful unification of Korea put forward by the Government of the Democratic People's Republic of Korea on April 12, 1971, and the stand for the abolition of the "U.N. Commission for the Unification and Rehabilitation of Korea". It firmly opposes the revival and outward expansion of Japanese militarism and firmly supports the Japanese people's desire to build an independent, democratic, peaceful and neutral Japan. It firmly maintains that India and Pakistan should, in accordance with the United Nations resolutions on the India-Pakistan question, immediately withdraw all their forces to their respective territories and to their own sides of the ceasefire line in Jammu and Kashmir and firmly supports the Pakistan Government and people in their struggle to preserve their independence and sovereignty and the people of Jammu and Kashmir in their struggle for the right of self-determination.

The U.S. side stated: Peace in Asia and peace in the world requires efforts both to reduce immediate tensions and to eliminate the basic causes of conflict. The United States will work for a just and secure peace: just, because it fulfills the aspirations of peoples and nations for freedom and progress; secure, because it removes the danger of foreign aggression. The United States supports individual freedom and social progress for all the peoples of the world, free of outside pressure or intervention. The United States believes that the effort to reduce tensions is served by improving communication between countries that have different ideologies so as to lessen the risks of confrontation through accident, miscalculation or misunderstanding. Countries should treat each other with mutual respect and be willing to compete peacefully, letting performance be the ultimate judge. No country should claim infallibility and each country should be prepared to reexamine its own attitudes for the common good. The United States stressed that the peoples of Indochina should be allowed to determine their destiny without outside intervention; its constant primary objective has been a negotiated solution; the eight-point proposal put forward by the Republic of Viet Nam and the United States on January 27, 1972 represents a basis for the attainment of that objective; in the absence of a negotiated settlement the United States envisages the ultimate withdrawal of all U.S. forces from the region consistent with the aim of self-determination for each country of Indochina. The United States will maintain its close ties with and support for the Republic of Korea; the United States will support efforts of the Republic of Korea to seek a relaxation of tension and increased communication in the Korean peninsula. The United States places the highest value on its friendly relations with Japan; it will continue to develop the existing close bonds. Consistent with the United Nations Security Council Resolution of December 21, 1971, the United States favors the continuation of the ceasefire between India and Pakistan and the withdrawal of all military forces to within their own territories and to their own sides of the ceasefire line in Jammu and Kashmir; the United States supports the right of the peoples of South Asia to shape their own future in peace, free of military threat, and without having the area become the subject of great power rivalry.

There are essential differences between China and the United States in their social systems and foreign policies. However, the two sides agreed that countries, regardless of their social systems, should conduct their relations on the principles of respect for the sovereignty and territorial integrity of all states, non-aggression against other states, non-interference in the internal affairs of other states, equality and mutual benefit, and peaceful coexistence. International disputes should be settled on this basis, without resorting to the use of threat of force. The United States and the People's Republic of China are prepared to apply these principles to their mutual relations.

With these principles of international relations in mind the two sides stated that:

- progress toward the normalization of relations between China and the United States is in the interests of all countries;
- both wish to reduce the danger of international military conflict;
- neither should seek hegemony in the Asia-Pacific region and each is opposed to efforts by any other country or group of countries to establish such hegemony; and
- neither is prepared to negotiate on behalf of any third party or to enter into agreements or understandings with the other directed at other states.

Both sides are of the view that it would be against the interests of the peoples of the world for any major country to collude with another against other countries, or for major countries to divide up the world into spheres of interest.

The two sides reviewed the long-standing serious disputes between China and the United States. The Chinese side reaffirmed its position: The Taiwan question is the crucial question obstructing the normalization of relations between China and the United States; the Government of the People's Republic of China is the sole legal government of China; Taiwan is a province of China which has long been returned to the motherland; the liberation of Taiwan is China's internal affair in which no other country has the right to interfere; and all U.S. forces and military installations must be withdrawn from Taiwan. The Chinese Government firmly opposes any activities which aim at the creation of "one China, one Taiwan", "one China, two governments", "two Chinas", and "independent Taiwan" or advocate that "the status of Taiwan remains to be determined".

The U.S. side declared: The United States acknowledges that all Chinese on either side of the Taiwan Strait maintain there is but one China and that Taiwan is a part of China. The United States Government does not challenge that position. It reaffirms its interest in a peaceful settlement of the Taiwan question by the Chinese themselves. With this prospect in mind, it affirms the ultimate objective of the withdrawal of all U.S. forces and military installations from Taiwan. In the meantime, it will progressively reduce its forces and military installations on Taiwan as the tension in the area diminishes.

The two sides agreed that it is desirable to broaden the understanding between the two peoples. To this end, they discussed specific areas in such fields as science, technology, culture, sports and journalism, in which people-to-people contacts and exchanges would be mutually beneficial. Each side undertakes to facilitate the further development of such contacts and exchanges.

Both sides view bilateral trade as another area from which mutual benefit can be derived, and agreed that economic relations based on equality and mutual benefit are in the interest of the peoples of the two countries. They agree to facilitate the progressive development of trade between their two countries.

The two sides agreed that they will stay in contact through various channels, including the sending of a senior U.S. representative to Peking from time to time for concrete consultations to further the normalization of relations between the two countries and continue to exchange views on issues of common interest.

The two sides expressed the hope that the gains achieved during this visit would open up new prospects for the relations between the two countries. They believe that the normalization of relations between the two countries is not only in the interest of the Chinese and American peoples but also contributes to the relaxation of tension in Asia and the world.

President Nixon, Mrs. Nixon and the American party expressed their appreciation for the gracious hospitality shown them by the Government and people of the People's Republic of China.

DOCUMENT 12
The China-Japan Agreement
to Normalize Relations,
October 1972

Reprinted from Peking Review, *no. 40, October 6, 1972, pp. 12-13.*

At the invitation of Premier Chou En-lai of the State Council of the People's Republic of China, Prime Minister Kakuei Tanaka of Japan visited the People's Republic of China from September 25 to 30, 1972. Accompanying Prime Minister Kakuei Tanaka were Foreign Minister Massayoshi Ohira, Chief Cabinet Secretary Susumu Nikaido and other government officials.

Chairman Mao Tsetung met Prime Minister Kakuei Tanaka on September 27. The two sides had an earnest and friendly conversation.

Premier Chou En-lai and Foreign Minister Chi Peng-fei had an earnest and frank exchange of views with Prime Minister Kakuei Tanaka and Foreign Minister Masayoshi Ohira, all along in a friendly atmosphere, on various matters between the two countries and other matters of interest to both sides, with the normalization of relations between China and Japan as the focal point, and the two sides agreed to issue the following joint statement of the two Governments:

China and Japan are neighbouring countries separated only by a strip of water, and there was a long history of traditional friendship between them. The two peoples ardently wish to end the abnormal state of affairs that has hitherto existed between the two countries. The termination of the state of war and the normalization of relations between China and Japan—the realization of such wishes of the two peoples will open a new page in the annals of relations between the two countries.

The Japanese side is keenly aware of Japan's responsibility for causing enormous damages in the past to the Chinese people through war and deeply reproaches itself. The Japanese side reaffirms its position that in seeking to realize the normalization of relations between Japan and China, it proceeds from the stand of fully understanding the three principles for the restoration of diplomatic relations put forward by the Government of the People's Republic of China. The Chinese side expresses its welcome for this.

Although the social systems of China and Japan are different, the two countries should and can establish peaceful and friendly relations. The normalization of relations and the development of good-neighbourly and friendly relations between the two countries are in the interests of the two peoples, and will also contribute to the relaxation of tension in Asia and the safeguarding of world peace.

1. The abnormal state of affairs which has hitherto existed between the People's Republic of China and Japan is declared terminated on the date of publication of this statement.

2. The Government of Japan recognizes the Government of the People's Republic of China as the sole legal government of China.

3. The Government of the People's Republic of China reaffirms that Taiwan is an inalienable part of the territory of the People's Republic of China. The Government of Japan fully understands and respects this stand of the Government of China and adheres to its stand of complying with Article 8 of the Potsdam Proclamation.

4. The Government of the People's Republic of China and the Government of Japan have decided upon the establishment of diplomatic relations as from September 29, 1972. The two Governments have decided to adopt all necessary measures for the establishment and the performance of functions of embassies in each other's capitals in accordance with international law and practice and exchange ambassadors as speedily as possible.

5. The Government of the People's Republic of China declares that in the interest of the friendship between the peoples of China and Japan, it renounces its demand for war indemnities from Japan.

6. The Government of the People's Republic of China and the Government of Japan agree to establish durable relations of peace and friendship between the two countries on the basis of the principles of mutual respect for sovereignty and territorial integrity, mutual non-aggression, non-interference in each other's internal affairs, equality and mutual benefit and peaceful coexistence.

In keeping with the foregoing principles and the principles of the United Nations Charter, the Governments of the two countries affirm that in their mutual relations, all disputes shall be settled by peaceful means without resorting to the use or threat of force.

7. The normalization of relations between China and Japan is not directed against third countries. Neither of the two countries should seek hegemony in the Asia-Pacific region and each country is opposed to efforts by any other country or group of countries to establish such hegemony.

8. To consolidate and develop the peaceful and friendly relations between the two countries, the Government of the People's Republic of China and the Government of Japan agree to hold negotiations aimed at the conclusion of a treaty of peace and friendship.

9. In order to further develop the relations between the two countries and broaden the exchange of visits, the Government of the People's Republic of China and the Government of Japan agree to hold negotiations aimed at the conclusion of agreements on trade, navigation, aviation, fishery, etc., in accordance with the needs and taking into consideration the existing non-governmental agreements.

(Signed) Chou En-lai Premier of the State Council of the Peo- ple's Republic of China	(Signed) Kakuei Tanaka Prime Minister of Japan
(Signed) Chi Peng-fei Minister of Foreign Affairs of the Peo- ple's Republic of China	(Signed) Masayoshi Ohira Minister for Foreign Affairs of Japan

Reprinted from the New York Times, *May 30, 1972, p. 18.*

The United States of America and the Union of Soviet Socialist Republics,

Guided by their obligations under the Charter of the United Nations and by a desire to strengthen peaceful relations with each other and to place these relations on the firmest possible basis,

Aware of the need to make every effort to remove the threat of war and to create conditions which promote the reduction of tensions in the world and the strengthening of universal security and international cooperation,

Believing that the improvement of U.S.-Soviet relations and their mutually advantageous development in such areas as economics, science and culture will meet these objectives and contribute to better mutual understanding and businesslike cooperation without in any way prejudicing the interests of third countries,

Conscious that these objectives reflect the interests of the peoples of both countries,

Have agreed as follows:

First, they will proceed from the common determination that in the nuclear age there is no alternative to conducting their mutual relations on the basis of peaceful coexistence. Differences in ideology and in the social systems of the U.S.A. and the U.S.S.R. are not obstacles to the bilateral development of normal relations based on the principles of sovereignty, equality, noninterference in internal affairs and mutual advantage.

Second, the U.S.A. and the U.S.S.R. attach major importance to preventing the development of situations capable of causing a dangerous exacerbation of their relations. Therefore, they will do their utmost to avoid military confrontations and to prevent the outbreak of nuclear war. They will always exercise restraint in their mutual relations, and will be prepared to negotiate and settle differences by peaceful means, Discussions and negotiations on outstanding issues will be conducted in a spirit of reciprocity, mutual accommodations and mutual benefit.

Both sides recognize that efforts to obtain unilateral advantage at the expense of the other, directly or indirectly, are inconsistent with these objectives.

The prerequisites for maintaining and strengthening peaceful relations between the U.S.A. and the U.S.S.R. are the recognition of the security interests of the parties based on the principle of equality and the renunciation of the use or threat of force.

Third, the U.S.A. and the U.S.S.R. have a special responsibility, as do other countries which are permanent members of the United Nations Security Council, to do everything in their power so that conflicts or situations will not arise which would serve to increase international tensions. Accordingly they will seek to promote conditions in which all countries will live in peace and security and will not be subject to outside interference in their internal affairs.

Fourth, the U.S.A. and the U.S.S.R. intend to widen the juridical basis of their mutual relations and to exert the necessary efforts so that bilateral agreements to which they are jointly parties are faithfully implemented.

Fifth, the U.S.A. and the U.S.S.R. reaffirm their readiness to continue the practice of exchanging views on problems of mutual interest and, when necessary, to conduct such exchanges at the highest level, including meetings between leaders of the two countries.

The two Governments welcome and will facilitate an increase in productive contacts between representatives of the legislative bodies of the two countries.

Sixth, the parties will continue their efforts to limit armaments on a bilateral as well as on a multilateral basis. They will continue to make special efforts to limit strategic armaments. Whenever possible, they will conclude concrete agreements aimed at achieving these purposes.

The U.S.A. and the U.S.S.R. regard as the ultimate objective of their efforts the achievement of general and complete disarmament and the establishment of an effective system of international security in accordance with the purposes and principles of the United Nations.

Seventh, the U.S.A. and the U.S.S.R. regard commercial and economic ties as an important and necessary element in the strengthening of their bilateral relations and thus will actively promote the growth of such ties. They will facilitate cooperation between the relevant organizations and enterprises of the two countries and the conclusion of appropriate agreements and contracts, including long-term ones.

The two countries will contribute to the improvement of maritime and air communications between them.

Eighth, the two sides consider it timely and useful to develop mutual contacts and cooperation in the fields of science and technology. Where suitable, the U.S.A. and the U.S.S.R. will conclude appropriate agreements dealing with concrete cooperation in these fields.

Ninth, the two sides reaffirm their intention to deepen cultural ties with one another and to encourage fuller familiarization with each other's cultural values. They will promote improved conditions for cultural exchanges and tourism.

Tenth, the U.S.A. and the U.S.S.R. will seek to insure that their ties and cooperation in all the above mentioned fields and in any others in their mutual interest are built on a firm and long-term basis. To give a permanent character to these efforts, they will establish in all fields where this is feasible joint commissions or other joint bodies.

Eleventh, the U.S.A. and the U.S.S.R. make no claim for themselves and would not recognize the claims of anyone else to any special rights or advantages in world affairs. They recognize the sovereign equality of all states.

The development of U.S.-Soviet relations is not directed against third countries and their interests.

Twelfth, the basic principles set forth in this document do not affect any obligations with respect to other countries earlier assumed by the U.S.A. and the U.S.S.R.

Moscow, May 29, 1972

For the United States of America   For the Union of Soviet Socialist Republics
Richard Nixon   Leonid I. Brezhnev
President of the United States   General Secretary of the
of America   Central Committee, C.P.S.U.

DOCUMENT 14
Chinese Commentary on
International Relations,
1972

The following newspaper editorial, written to commemorate China's National Day (October 1), affords an official overview of the state of the world in the aftermath of the Nixon and Tanaka visits. The editorial's title is "Strive for New Victories." Reprinted from Peking Review, *no. 40, October 6, 1972, pp. 9-10.*

Twenty-three years have passed since the founding of the People's Republic of China. Over these years the Chinese people, led by the great leader Chairman Mao, have fought victoriously along the revolutionary road of socialism. The people of all nationalities of China are filled with joy as they celebrate the glorious festival today in an excellent domestic and international situation.

The world has witnessed great changes in the past year. There have been new developments in the revolutionary struggles of the people of various countries. People's struggles to achieve national liberation and safeguard national independence are deepening and surging higher in Indochina and the Middle East, and throughout Asia, Africa and Latin America. It has become the common demand of the people of various countries to oppose the power politics and hegemony of the superpowers. More and more countries in the first as well as the second intermediate zone are joining forces in different forms and on a varying scale to engage in struggles against one or two superpowers. The third world is playing an increasingly important role in international affairs. Even some countries under fairly tight control of Soviet revisionism or U.S. imperialism are striving to free themselves from their dictate. Egypt's announcement of the sending away of Soviet military experts and part of the Soviet officers and men, the enlargement of the West European Common Market, the formation of the 17-nation free trade zone, and the new diplomatic moves of Japan and some other countries—all this shows that international relations are undergoing new readjustments and changes.

During the past year, China has continued to carry out Chairman Mao's revolutionary line in foreign affairs in an all-round way. We have further developed our relations of friendship, mutual assistance and co-operation with the other socialist countries. We have firmly supported the people of Viet Nam, Laos and Cambodia in their struggle against U.S. aggression and for national salvation, and supported the people of other Asian, African and Latin American countries in their just struggles to achieve and safeguard national independence and defend state sovereignty. We insist on peaceful coexistence with countries having different social systems on the basis of the Five Principles and strive for the relaxation of international tension. This is what we have done towards Asian, African and Latin American countries as well as towards countries in the second intermediate zone. Even if a country previously adopted a policy hostile to China, we would hold talks with it for the improvement of relations between the two countries when it indicates its readiness to change that policy. We uphold our principle and, at the same time, adopt a flexible attitude which is permissible and necessary for carrying out our principle. Our foreign policy has won ever wider sympathy and support in the world. Our friendly exchanges with other peoples have increased. We have finally regained our legitimate rights in the United Nations after being deprived of them for more than 20 years, and the Chiang Kai-shek clique has been driven out of this world body. Twenty more countries have established or restored diplomatic relations with China in the past year. Heads of state and government, foreign ministers and government delegations from many countries have visited our country. After relations between China and the United States had been suspended for more than 20 years, U.S. President Richard Nixon visited China last February, and the leaders of the two countries held earnest, frank and beneficial talks on Sino-U.S. relations and world affairs. The gate to friendly contacts between the people of the two countries is now open. Japanese Prime Minister Kakuei Tanaka has just visited China on invitation, and the leaders of the two countries held friendly talks and reached agreement on the important question of normalization of Sino-Japanese relations. The termination of the state of war and the establishment of diplomatic relations between China and Japan have fulfilled a long-time desire of the Chinese and Japanese people and opened a new page in the relations between the two countries. This will exert a positive influence on the relaxation of tension in Asia and the safeguarding of world peace. As a result of the great achievements of Chairman Mao's line in foreign affairs, the policy of those who dreamt of isolating China has gone bankrupt and the still extant counter-revolutionary schemes to encircle China are falling apart.

The world today is far from peaceful. U.S. imperialism is still waging a bloody war in Viet Nam and the rest of Indochina. It has not yet withdrawn all its aggressor troops and those of its vassals from there, but instead has been reinforcing its naval and air forces engaged in the bombing and blockading of Viet Nam. The situation remains tense in the South Asian subcontinent, the Middle East and other areas as a result of contention between Soviet revisionism and U.S. imperialism. Though the two superpowers, the Soviet Union and the United States, have conducted negotiations and concluded certain agreements, their superficial compromise and ease-off only serve to prepare for a new fight. The Soviet Union and the United States signed in Moscow an agreement on the so-called limitation of strategic offensive arms, but before the ink was dry one stepped up the testing and manufacturing of new nuclear weapons and the other increased its military expenditures enormously. Thus they entered a new stage of nuclear arms race. While maintaining a no-war-no-peace situation in the Middle East, they have stepped up open and covert struggles to increase their control over Arab countries and suppress the Palestinian revolutionary movement. Soviet revisionism has exerted itself to play up the so-called European security question only to pinpoint Europe as the main area of its contention with U.S. imperialism.

In the course of this contention, the Soviet revisionist renegade clique has further revealed its true colours of social-imperialism. With a growing appetite, it is reaching out its hands everywhere. It is even more deceitful than old-line imperialist countries, and therefore more dangerous. Social-imperialism is, as Lenin pointed out, "Socialism in words, imperialism in deeds, the growth of opportunism into imperialism." While obviously pursuing a policy of military expansion, Soviet revisionist social-imperialism clamours for "peace" and "security." While obviously pushing neocolonialism in a big way in Asia, Africa and Latin America, it advertises "support to the national-liberation movement." While obviously stepping up its arms expansion and war preparations, it raises a hue and cry about "disarmament." At the current U.N. General Assembly Session, Soviet revisionism has talked glibly about so-called "permanent prohibition of the use of nuclear weapons," just so much humbug with which it intends to avoid committing itself to the complete prohibition and thorough destruction of nuclear weapons and to maintain its nuclear monopoly. But sham is sham. It may deceive some people for some time, but not for ever. Soviet revisionism is still being condemned for its military occupation of Czechoslovakia; by instigating India to launch a war of aggression against Pakistan, it once again revealed its expansionist ambitions; its schemes to control the Arab countries have been further exposed; its subversive activities in many countries have been frustrated one after another. These ugly facts have helped people to see things much more clearly. The aggression and expansion by Soviet revisionism has not only evoked stronger and stronger opposition from the people of various countries, but also aggravated its domestic crises, thus placing it in an increasingly difficult position both at home and abroad.

Chairman Mao teaches: "With regard to the question of world war, there are but two possibilities: One is that war will give rise to revolution and the other is that revolution will prevent the war." "The danger of a new world war exists, and the people of all countries must get prepared. But revolution is the main trend in the world today." The prospects of the world people's revolutionary movement are bright, while the road has twists and turns. Victory in the revolutionary struggle of the people of a country depends mainly on the people themselves gradually raising their political consciousness and sense of organization in the course of struggle and gradually combining the universal truth of Marxism-Leninism with the concrete practice of revolution in their own country. We always support people's revolutionary struggles; we place hope on the people. The development of our relations with countries having different social systems on the basis of the Five Principles of Peaceful Coexistence and the increase of our friendly exchanges with other peoples are not only conducive to the easing of international tension but are in the interests of the revolutionary struggles of the people of various countries. That is why the Five Principles of Peaceful Coexistence set forth by China have found their way ever deeper into the hearts of the people.

In this excellent international situation we should further implement in an all-round way Chairman Mao's revolutionary line and policies in foreign affairs. We must unite with the other socialist countries and the working class throughout the world, with all oppressed people and oppressed nations and with all peace-loving countries and people who are against power politics, to firmly oppose the policy of aggression and war of imperialism and social-imperialism, especially to expose the Soviet revisionist scheme of sham relaxation but real expansion, and strive for the easing of international tension and the maintenance of world peace. Our doing so conforms to the fundamental interests of the people of China and the world. And only by doing so can international tension be truly eased and world peace safeguarded. . . .

Chinese Commentary on
International Relations,
1973

The comments below are by Ch'iao Kuan-hua, chairman of the PRC delegation to the United Nations and a vice-minister of foreign affairs. He spoke on October 2, 1973 to the U.N. General Assembly. Reprinted from Peking Review, *no. 40, October 5, 1973, pp. 10-17.*

1. What is the Characteristic of the Present World Situation?

The Chinese Government has long held that our world is now going through a process of great turbulence, great division and great realignment. The basic contradictions in the world are all sharpening, and in particular the contradictions between imperialism and colonialism on the one hand and the oppressed nations and peoples on the other and the contradictions among the imperialist countries, especially those between the two superpowers. Although no new world war has broken out since World War II, local wars resulting from imperialist aggressions have never ceased. The great victory of the heroic Vietnamese people's war of resistance against U.S. aggression and for national salvation has once again proved that imperialism and all reactionaries are paper tigers. A small nation can defeat a big one and a weak nation can defeat a strong one, so long as they dare to struggle, are good at struggle and persevere in struggle. It is not the people who fear imperialism; it is imperialism which fears the people. Revolution is the main trend in the world today. Now that the war in Viet Nam has ended, can it be assumed that the world will henceforth be tranquil? Obviously not. When the Korean war was ended in 1953, some people thought that no more gun-shots would be heard in the world. Not long afterwards, however, the Suez war broke out and then the Viet Nam war started. And even today, the war in Indochina has not stopped completely, for there is still fighting in Cambodia. Tension in the Middle East has not relaxed in the least. The colonialists and racists are carrying out armed suppression against the African people, and the African people are developing armed resistance against them. The aggression, subversion, control and interference against countries in Africa, Asia and Latin America by the superpowers are continuing without end. A recent case in point is the military coup d'etat in Chile. President Salvador Allende died a martyr at his post. We express profound condolences on his heroic death. At the same time, we hold one should not forget how harmful the absurd theory of so-called "peaceful transition" is to the anti-imperialist revolutionary struggles of the Asian, African and Latin American people, a theory which has been advocated by another superpower. To dismember a sovereign country by armed force and to legalize and perpetuate the division of a country have also become a tendency on the part of the big powers in their attempt to dominate the world. In the economic field, the gap is widening between the rich and developed countries and the poor and developing countries, and even among the developed countries there exist many contradictions, and hence detente among them is far from being the case. The recent Fourth Conference of the Heads of State and Government of Non-Allied Countries strongly condemned racism, Zionism, colonialism, imperialism and hegemonism and strongly demanded a change in the present state of affairs in the world, demonstrating a further awakening of the Asian, African and Latin American peoples. In a word, we consider that the characteristic of the present situation is one of great disorder throughout the world and not tranquillity. And the main trend amidst this great disorder is that countries want independence, nations want liberation, and the people want revolution.

2. Why Is There No Tranquillity in the World Today?

We have always held that all countries in the world, big or small, should be equal; that all countries, irrespective of their social systems, should establish normal state relations on the Five Principles of mutual respect for territorial integrity and sovereignty, mutual non-aggression, non-interference in each other's internal affairs, equality and mutual benefit, and peaceful co-existence; and that international disputes should be settled peacefully on the basis of these principles without resorting to the use or threat of force. This should apply to relations between big powers, to relations between a big power and a small country, and all the more so to relations between a strong and a weak, or between a rich and a poor country. It was on these principles that China started to improve her relations with the United States and established diplomatic relations with Japan. In their joint communique issued in Shanghai, China and the United States further declared that they should not seek hegemony in the Asia-Pacific region and were opposed to efforts by any other country or group of countries to establish such hegemony. The same principle was reaffirmed in the Sino-Japanese statement on the establishment of diplomatic relations between them. In our view, the above-mentioned principles are the minimum critiera of equality of all countries in international relations and indicate the correct way to the relaxation of international tension.

As sovereign states, the United States and the Soviet Union are fully entitled to take measures they deem appropriate to improve and develop their bilateral relations. However, we cannot but point out that the agreement on the prevention of nuclear war signed by them goes far beyond the scope of bilateral relations. One may ask: Who has given them the right to enter into what they call "urgent consultations" in case of a dispute between either of the parties and other countries and even between any other two countries? The phrase about disputes which "appear to involve the risk of a nuclear conflict" is open to any interpretation, and their so-called "urgent consultations" are bound to be followed by actions dictated by their own interests. Does not this mean that they may interfere at will in the relations among all countries on the strength of the huge numbers of nuclear weapons in their possession? China absolutely will not go begging for nuclear protection from any country, nor is she afraid of nuclear threat from any country. But we feel duty bound to state our views on this matter since it concerns all the people of the world.

The signing of such an agreement by the Soviet Union and the United States is by no means accidental but is derived from the so-called principle which they agreed upon in 1972 that the Soviet Union and the United States have "security interests based on the principle of equality." What is meant by "security interests based on the principle of equality"? To put it bluntly, it means rivalry for world hegemony—wherever one goes, the other will do the same. What they have done is simply to wrap up this content in the form of an agreement.

In fact, this agreement is a mere scrap of paper. It contains no explicit undertaking on the non-use of nuclear weapons, still less does it envisage the complete prohibition and thorough destruction of nuclear weapons. The U.S. Government was more frank when it stated that the agreement was only a general statement of policy which did not involve any particular positive actions that either side had to take, and pointed out that agreements were not always maintained and there was nothing self-enforcing about this document.

However, the Soviet leaders have made a great fanfare, lauding this agreement to the skies, alleging that it ushered in "a new era" in international relations and opened up "historical vistas for strengthening universal security as a whole," and that it was "indeed of historic importance for all mankind." They have their motives for so eulogizing the agreement. One may recall Khrushchov's famous remarks: "Even a tiny spark can cause a world conflagration," and "we (the Soviet Union and the United States) are the strongest countries in the world, and if we unite for peace there can be no war. Then if any madman wanted war, we would but have to shake our fingers to warn him off." In this way, if the Soviet Union could be bound together with the United States, would not the whole world have to cringe to them? However, in our view, things may not necessarily turn out that way.

It is not so easy for the Soviet Union to bind herself to the United States. Shortly after the signing of the agreement, the Soviet Union pressed forward with her underground nuclear tests and hastened the development of missiles with multiple warheads. The United States will not take this lying down. Why? Because the desperate struggle for nuclear superiority and world hegemony still goes on. The contention between the Soviet Union and the United States now extends all over the world. A vivid proof can be found in the recent subversion of a government in Asia and another in South America. Their scramble is becoming increasingly fierce. This is the reason why there is no tranquillity in the world today. So, what peaceful coexistence is there to speak of? There is only a travesty of peaceful coexistence; the substance is coexistence in rivalry. But whether such coexistence can last is of course another question.

The Soviet leaders noisily proclaim that as a "socialist" state, the Soviet Union is the "natural and surest ally" of the developing countries. In the past, some people in China also believed this. Because they saw the Soviet Union as the homeland of the great Lenin and the Chinese revolution a continuation of the October Revolution. Therefore, how could the Soviet Union, as a socialist state, fail to give the developing countries wholehearted internationalist assistance? But since Khrushchov rose to power, thanks to the long and direct experience we gained as a result of the Soviet Union's demand for the establishment of a joint fleet in the China Sea, withdrawal of experts, tearing up of contracts, border intrusions, subversions, etc., we came to realize that this was not the case, and that what the Soviet Union practised was not internationalism, but great-power chauvinism, national egoism and territorial expansionism. Therefore, we will not blame those friends who have so far failed to see this for lack of experience. How can a socialist turn into an imperialist? There is in fact nothing strange about it if one goes a little into the history of the international communist movement. Wasn't Karl Kautsky once a somewhat well-known Marxist? But he later betrayed Marxism and capitulated to imperialism. It was Lenin who passed the final historical verdict on Kautsky in his well-known pamphlet *The Proletarian Revolution and the Renegade Kautsky*. People can change, so can a state. It has changed, and what can you do about it?

Lenin pointed out: "We judge a person not by what he says or thinks of himself but by his actions." This applies to a state as well. What has the Soviet Government done to other countries in these years? This is clear to the broad masses of the people of Czechoslovakia, Egypt and Pakistan, to the people of Cambodia who are fighting dauntlessly, and to other peoples who have been subjected to its aggression, subversion, control, interference or bullying. The actions of the Soviet Government have amply shown that it is "socialist in words, imperialist in deeds," as Lenin said.

The Soviet-U.S. agreement on the prevention of nuclear war cannot hoodwink many people or intimidate the peoples of the world, but can only arouse indignation, misgivings and disillusionment. The tide is mounting against the hegemonism and power politics practised by the superpowers. . . .

* * * *

4. The Cambodian Question

The Chinese Government resolutely denounces the U.S. Government for continuing to support in various ways the puppet regime in Phnom Penh and wantonly interfere in the affairs of Cambodia. The regime of the traitorous Lon Nol clique, which is now installed in Phnom Penh, was imposed on the Khmer people by the U.S. imperialists and their allies and has been illegal from its very inception. The Royal Government of National Union of Cambodia under the leadership of Head of State Prince Norodom Sihanouk is the sole legal government of Cambodia. The People's Armed Forces of National Liberation of Cambodia under its leadership have liberated over 90 per cent of Cambodia's territory with over 80 per cent of the population. The Royal Government of National Union of Cambodia has been recognized by nearly 50 countries. The participants of the recent Conference of Non-Aligned Countries in Algiers have declared that the Royal Government of National Union under the leadership of Prince Norodom Sihanouk is the only legal government of Cambodia, and earnestly requested all countries which love peace and justice to give it formal recognition. This is a voice of justice. The Chinese Government holds that the continued usurpation by the traitorous Lon Nol clique of the seat in the United Nations is a contempt (disgrace) for all countries that uphold justice, and for the Fourth Conference of Non-Aligned Countries and for the United Nations itself. The Chinese Government firmly maintains that the present session of the

General Assembly should take a decision immediately to expel the representatives of the traitorous Lon Nol clique from the United Nations and restore to the Royal Government of National Union of Cambodia under the leadership of Head of State Prince Norodom Sihanouk its rightful seat in the United Nations. . . .

* * * *

Mr. President,
The People's Republic of China is taking part in the activities of the United Nations for the third year. We wish to say frankly that what we have experienced in the United Nations has caused us to become worried. Speeches are multiplying and resolutions piling up in the United Nations, yet it has not been able to look into matters which it ought to (for instance, the question of the prevention of nuclear war) and is impotent in the solution of many major issues (for instance, the Middle East question). If things continue this way, what future is there for the United Nations? However, we are not disheartened. We believe that the present conditions in the United Nations should be changed and the Charter should be revised. How can the United Nations go on working in the same old way it did more than twenty years ago, when the world has already changed? The Third World has risen up. The United Nations must be able to give expression to the desires of the numerous small and medium-sized countries, truly give effect to the principle of equality of all countries, big or small, and cease to be controlled by the superpowers and their small number of followers if it is to be worthy of its name. China is ready to work together with all countries which love peace and uphold justice for the achievement of this noble aim.
Thank you, Mr. President!

Source: U.S. Department of State, Bureau of Public Affairs, News Release, January 24, 1973.

Agreement on Ending the War
And
Restoring Peace in Vietnam

The Parties participating in the Paris Conference on Vietnam,

With a view to ending the war and restoring peace in Vietnam on the basis of respect for the Vietnamese people's fundamental national rights and the South Vietnamese people's right to self-determination, and to contributing to the consolidation of peace in Asia and the world,

Have agreed on the following provisions and undertake to respect and to implement them:

Chapter I

The Vietnamese People's
Fundamental National Rights

Article 1

The United States and all other countries respect the independence, sovereignty, unity, and territorial integrity of Vietnam as recognized by the 1954 Geneva Agreements on Vietnam.

Chapter II

Cessation of Hostilities—Withdrawal of Troops

Article 2

A cease-fire shall be observed throughout South Vietnam as of 2400 hours G.M.T., on January 27, 1973.

At the same hour, the United States will stop all its military activities against the territory of the Democratic Republic of Vietnam by ground, air and naval forces, wherever they may be based, and end the mining of the territorial waters, ports, harbors, and waterways of the Democratic Republic of Vietnam.

The United States will remove, permanently deactivate or destroy all the mines in the territorial waters, ports, harbors, and waterways of North Vietnam as soon as this Agreement goes into effect.

The complete cessation of hostilities mentioned in this Article shall be durable and without limit of time.

Article 3

The parties undertake to maintain the cease-fire and to ensure a lasting and stable peace.

As soon as the cease-fire goes into effect:

(a) The United States forces and those of the other foreign countries allied with the United States and the Republic of Vietnam shall remain in-place pending the implementation of the plan of troop withdrawal. The Four-Party Joint Military Commission described in Article 16 shall determine the modalities.

(b) The armed forces of the two South Vietnamese parties shall remain in-place. The Two-Party Joint Military Commission described in Article 17 shall determine the areas controlled by each party and the modalities of stationing.

(c) The regular forces of all services and arms and the irregular forces of the parties in South Vietnam shall stop all offensive activities against each other and shall strictly abide by the following stipulations:

- All acts of force on the ground, in the air, and on the sea shall be prohibited;
- All hostile acts, terrorism and reprisals by both sides will be banned.

Article 4

The United States will not continue its military involvement or intervene in the internal affairs of South Vietnam.

Article 5

Within sixty days of the signing of this Agreement, there will be a total withdrawal from South Vietnam of troops, military advisers, and military personnel, including technical military personnel and military personnel associated with the pacification program, armaments, munitions, and war material of the United States and those of the other foreign countries mentioned in Article 3 (a). Advisers from the above-mentioned countries to all paramilitary organizations and the police force will also be withdrawn within the same period of time.

Article 6

The dismantlement of all military bases in South Vietnam of the United States and of the other foreign countries mentioned in Article 3 (a) shall be completed within sixty days of the signing of this Agreement.

Article 7

From the enforcement of the cease-fire to the formation of the government provided for in Articles 9 (b) and 14 of this Agreement, the two South Vietnamese parties shall not accept the introduction of troops, military advisers, and military personnel including technical military personnel, armaments, munitions, and war material into South Vietnam.

The two South Vietnamese parties shall be permitted to make periodic replacement of armaments, munitions and war material which have been destroyed, damaged, worn out or used up after the cease-fire, on the basis of piece-for-piece, of the same characteristics and properties, under the supervision of the Joint Military Commission of the two South Vietnamese parties and of the International Commission of Control and Supervision.

Chapter III

The Return of Captured Military Personnel and Foreign Civilians, and Captured and Detained Vietnamese Civilian Personnel

Article 8

(a) The return of captured military personnel and foreign civilians of the parties shall be carried out simultaneously with and completed not later than the same day as the troop withdrawal mentioned in Article 5. The parties shall exchange complete lists of the above-mentioned captured military personnel and foreign civilians on the day of the signing of this Agreement.

(b) The parties shall help each other to get information about those military personnal and foreign civilians of the parties missing in action, to determine the location and take care of the graves of the dead so as to facilitate the exhumation and repatriation of the remains, and to take any such other measures as may be required to get information about those still considered missing in action.

(c) The question of the return of Vietnamese civilian personnel captured and detained in South Vietnam will be resolved by the two South Vietnamese parties on the basis of the principles of Article 21 (b) of the Agreement on the Cessation of Hostilities in Vietnam of July 20, 1954. The two South Vietnamese parties will do so in a spirit of national reconciliation and concord, with a view to ending hatred and enmity, in order to ease suffering and to reunite familites. The two South Veitnamese parties will do their utmost to resolve this question within ninety days after the cease-fire comes into effect.

Chapter IV

The Exercise of the South Vietnamese People's Right to Self-Determination

Article 9

The Government of the United States of America and the Government of the Democratic Republic of Vietnam undertake to respect the following principles for the exercise of the South Vietnamese people's right to self-determination:

(a) The South Vietnamese people's right to self-determination is sacred, inalienable, and shall be respected by all countries.

(b) The South Vietnamese people shall decide themselves the political future of South Vietnam through genuinely free and democratic general elections under international supervision.

(c) Foreign countries shall not impose any political tendency or personality on the South Vietnamese people.

Article 10

The two South Vietnamese parties undertake to respect the cease-fire and maintain peace in South Vietnam, settle all matters of contention through negotiations, and avoid all armed conflict.

Article 11

Immediately after the cease-fire, the two South Vietnamese parties will:

- achieve national reconciliation and concord, end hatred and enmity, prohibit all acts of reprisal and discrimination against individuals or organizations that have collaborated with one side or the other;
- ensure the democratic liberties of the people: personal freedom, freedom of speech, freedom of the press, freedom of meeting, freedom of organization, freedom of political activities, freedom of belief, freedom of movement, freedom of residence, freedom of work, right to property ownership, and right to free enterprise.

Article 12

(a) Immediately after the cease-fire, the two South Vietnamese parties shall hold consultations in a spirit of national reconciliation and concord, mutual respect, and mutual non-elimination to set up a National Council of National Reconciliation and Concord of three equal segments. The Council shall operate on the principle of unanimity. After the National Council of National Reconciliation and Concord has assumed its functions, the two South Vietnamese parties will consult about the formation of councils at lower levels. The two South Vietnamese parties shall sign an agreement on the internal matters of South Vietnam as soon as possible and do their utmost to accomplish this within ninety days after the cease-fire comes into effect, in keeping with the South Vietnamese people's aspirations for peace, independence and democracy.

(b) The National Council of National Reconciliation and Concord shall have the task of promoting the two South Vietnamese parties' implementation of this Agreement, achievement of national reconciliation and concord and ensurance of democratic liberties. The National Council of National Reconciliation and Concord will organize the free and democratic general elections provided for in Article 9 (b) and decide the procedures and modalities of these general elections. The institutions for which the general elections are to be held will be agreed upon through consultations between the two South Vietnamese parties. The National Council of National Reconciliation and Concord will also decide the procedures and modalities of such local elections as the two South Vietnamese parties agree upon.

Article 13

The question of Vietnamese armed forces in South Vietnam shall be settled by the two South Vietnamese parties in a spirit of national reconciliation and concord, equality and mutual respect, without foreign interference, in accordance with the postwar situation. Among the questions to be discussed by the two South Vietnamese parties are steps to reduce their military effectives and to demobilize the troops being reduced. The two South Vietnamese parties will accomplish this as soon as possible.

Article 14

South Vietnam will pursue a foreign policy of peace and independence. It will be prepared to establish relations with all countries irrespective of their political and social systems on the basis of mutual respect for independence and sovereignty and accept economic and technical aid from any country with no political conditions attached. The acceptance of military aid by South Vietnam in the future shall come under the authority of the government set up after the general elections in South Vietnam provided for in Article 9 (b).

Chapter V

The Reunification of Vietnam and the
Relationship Between North and South Vietnam

Article 15

The reunification of Vietnam shall be carried out step by step through peaceful means on the basis of discussions and agreements between North and South Vietnam, without coercion or annexation by either party, and without foreign interference. The time for reunification will be agreed upon by North and South Vietnam.

Pending reunification:

(a) The military demarcation line between the two zones at the 17th parallel is only provisional and not a political or territorial boundary, as provided for in paragraph 6 of the Final Declaration of the 1954 Geneva Conference.

(b) North and South Vietnam shall respect the Demilitarized Zone on either side of the Provisional Military Demarcation Line.

(c) North and South Vietnam shall promptly start negotiations with a view to reestablishing normal relations in various fields. Among the questions to be negotiated are the modalities of civilian movement across the Provisional Military Demarcation Line.

(d) North and South Vietnam shall not join any military alliance or military bloc and shall not allow foreign powers to maintain military bases, troops, military advisers, and military personnel on their respective territories, as stipulated in the 1954 Geneva Agreements on Vietnam.

Chapter VI

The Joint Military Commissions, the International Commission of Control and Supervision, the International Conference

Article 16

(a) The Parties participating in the Paris Conference on Vietnam shall immediately designate representatives to form a Four-Party Joint Military Commission with the task of ensuring joint action by the parties in implementing the following provisions of this Agreement:

• The first paragraph of Article 2, regarding the enforcement of the cease-fire throughout South Vietnam;

• Article 3 (a), regarding the cease-fire by U.S. forces and those of the other foreign countries referred to in that Article;

• Article 3 (c), regarding the cease-fire between all parties in South Vietnam;

• Article 5, regarding the withdrawal from South Vietnam of U.S. troops and those of the other foreign countries mentioned in Article 3 (a);

• Article 6, regarding the dismantlement of military bases in South Vietnam of the United States and those of the other foreign countries mentioned in Article 3 (a); . . .

Chapter VII

Regarding Cambodia and Laos

Article 20

(a) The parties participating in the Paris Conference on Vietnam shall strictly respect the 1954 Geneva Agreements on Cambodia and the 1962

Geneva Agreements on Laos, which recognized the Cambodian and the Lao peoples' fundamental national rights, i.e., the independence, sovereignty, unity, and territorial integrity of these countries. The parties shall respect the neutrality of Cambodia and Laos.

The parties participating in the Paris Conference on Vietnam undertake to refrain from using the territory of Cambodia and the territory of Laos to encroach on the sovereignty and security of one another and of other countries.

(b) Foreign countries shall put an end to all military activities in Cambodia and Laos, totally withdraw from and refrain from reintroducing into these two countries troops, military advisers and military personnel, armaments, munitions and war material.

(c) The internal affairs of Cambodia and Laos shall be settled by the people of each of these countries without foreign interference.

(d) The problems existing between the Indochinese countries shall be settled by the Indochinese parties on the basis of respect for each other's independence, sovereignty, and territorial integrity, and non-interference in each other's internal affairs.

Chapter VIII

The Relationship Between
the United States and
the Democratic Republic of Vietnam

Article 21

The United States anticipates that this Agreement will usher in an era of reconciliation with the Democratic Republic of Vietnam as with all the peoples of Indochina. In pursuance of its traditional policy, the United States will contribute to healing the wounds of war and to postwar reconstruction of the Democratic Republic of Vietnam and throughout Indochina.

Article 22

The ending of the war, the restoration of peace in Vietnam, and the strict implementation of this Agreement will create conditions for establishing a new, equal and mutually beneficial relationship between the United States and the Democratic Republic of Vietnam on the basis of respect for each other's independence and sovereignty, and non-interference in each other's internal affairs. At the same time this will ensure stable peace in Vietnam and contribute to the preservation of lasting peace in Indochina and Southeast Asia.

DOCUMENT 17
India's Call for
Asian Self-Reliance

India's Prime Minister Mrs. Indira Gandhi addressed the One-Asia Assembly in New Delhi on February 6, 1973. In her remarks she expressed reservations about the "new balance of power" and stressed that future self-reliance should be the major goal of Asian nations. Source: Embassy of India, India News (Washington, D.C., February 16, 1973).

This year India is celebrating the 25th Anniversary of her Independence. Our freedom marked the beginning of a period of decolonisation during which many other countries of Asia, Africa and the Caribbeans have attained political independence. In a parallel process has taken place the rebirth of China. Some of the problems which you are discussing in depth, problems of hunger and nutrition, economic development and education, are a consequence of the long-period spent under subjection. Any kind of mercantile, industrial and intellectual enterprise which was inconvenient to the colonial rulers was discouraged and the evolution from within our traditional societies was perforce inhibited. Some other problems—which are not on your discussion papers—arise from the relationships between ourselves and from the changing relationships between our nations on one side and the world's dominant military and economic powers on other. The advance of technology brings a third set of problems which disturb our society no less than that of the advanced nations.

Asian Diversity

Asia is a continent vaster and older—not in geology but in terms of remembered and recorded history—a continent of extraordinary cultural diversity, of a variety of historical experiences which are difficult to grasp. Europe had the benefit of three or four major unifying factors—Greco-Roman tradition, Christian church, colonising thrust and industrial revolution. Marxism itself was a response to these conditioning factors and incorporated major features of Western thought and outlook. Asia has had no comparable unifying factors. Buddhism and Islam, remarkable as their spread was, did not pervade the whole of the continent.

The experience of Western domination should have given the nations of Asia a new awareness of a common destiny and of the importance of working together in overcoming their problems. It is possible today to speak of the emergence of a common Asian quest. Asian goals include economic development, modernisation of traditional societies and the assertion of national sovereignty and identity.

Neo-Colonialism and Nationalism

Except in a few known and glaring instances Western nations have withdrawn as colonial powers but their political or military presence continues on our continent. This has been done in the name of filling a vacuum or to wage a crusade against communism or other doctrines. In India, we have always rejected what we consider a rather naive theory of political vacuums. Europe shed its colonies, not out of altruism or caprice but because of rising pressure of Asian nationalism. With this assertive nationalism, how can there be a vacuum? The very theory of a power vacuum is thus a continuation of the colonial outlook in another garb.

The West has not been able to assess the power of nationalism even when forced to yield to it. This explains the paradox of the West's involvement and failure in Asia in the past two decades. Various alliances which were forged seem rather pointless now. Forces, which were sought to be eliminated through these alliances, are still in evidence and since the policy and methods adopted were such obvious failures, there is now an effort to build bridges with the very nations whom they had sought to contain.

We welcome any effort towards peace and understanding. We are glad of the belated confirmation of the views expressed by the non-aligned nations. But we are aware of the dangers which still hover over us. Detente should not become an occasion to build new balances of power and to redraw the spheres of influence or to reinforce the opinion of certain big powers that they alone can be responsible for shaping the destinies of small nations.

I cannot help feeling that the very manner of ending the Vietnam war may create new tensions. The cease-fire should not lull us into the comfort that there will be peace all the way. To many nations peace itself has often been war by other means.

But the truce in Vietnam has opened up new opportunities which we must avail of to devise and to take concerted steps. It is unrealistic to talk of any move towards normalisation in Asia when military action continues in any part of Indochina. The Vietnam truce should also extend to Laos and Cambodia. All countries of Asia must cooperate with the nations of Indochina in their immense tasks of reconstruction.

Indian tradition has always spoken of one world—I have grown up in this belief and I abhor chauvinistic nationalism or racialism of any color and type but I would like to ask a question? Would this sort of war or the savage bombing which has taken place in Vietnam have been tolerated for so long had the people been European?

The interests of trade and commerce and of the manufacturers of armaments do not distinguish between ideologies and have no compunction about making an about turn should it suit them to do so. A declaration of love for democracy does not seem to be incompatible with open admiration for dictatorship. While this attitude remains, can there be clear thinking or positive action for real peace?

Problems of Economic Development

Discussions in this Assembly have ranged over the problems of economic development—I am specially glad to see that the distinguished author of the "Asian Drama" is also present among us. Most experts equate development with the prototype of affluent countries of the West. In the middle of the 19th century, scientists evolved concepts of natural selection which were adopted by political theorists to justify exploitation of one class by another, one race by another and one country by another. In the last part of this century, certain new economic, technological and biological theories have been put forward which would consign a large number of nations to perpetual backwardness. They imply that a late starter could never catch up. Many of our own political and economic scholars in Asian countries seem to be converted to this opinion, reiterating that the rate of growth is all important, that progress is synonymous with urbanisation, with established patterns of industrialisation and production and an advertisement-and-acquisition-oriented society. Do they really justify all that has occurred in the advanced countries as desirable and worthy of emulation by the poorer countries? Ideas of drugs and diet—value of proteins or calories, for instance—have fluctuated but each in its time has been held as indisputable. Advance in modern medicine has provided cures for many old diseases but such treatment is becoming increasingly expensive and new ailments have appeared. Pesticides eradicate insects but also affect the health of human beings. The list is a long one. There is blind reverence for the written word. But has literacy increased comprehension or brought any kind of wisdom? . . .

*This Joint Resolution was passed by both Houses of Congress,
over the veto of President Nixon, on November 7, 1973.*

**Public Law 93-148; 87 Stat. 555
(H. J. Res. 542)
Joint Resolution Concerning the War Powers of Congress and the President**

Resolved that by the Senate and House of Representatives of the United States of America in Congress assembled, That:

Short Title

Section 1. This joint reolution may be cited as the "War Powers Resolution".

Purpose and Policy

Sec. 2. (a) It is the purpose of this joint resolution of fulfill the intent of the framers of the Constitution of the United States and insure that the collective judgment of both the Congress and the President will apply to the introduction of the United States Armed Forces into hostilities, or into situations where imminent involvement in hostilities is clearly indicated by the circumstances, and to the continued use of such forces in hostilities or in such situations.

(b) Under article I, section 8, of the Constitution, it is specifically provided that the Congress shall have the power to make all laws necessary and proper for carrying into execution, not only its own powers but also all other powers vested by the Constitution in the Government of the United States, or in any department or officer thereof.

(c) The constitutional powers of the President as Commander-in-Chief to introduce United States Armed Forces into hostilities, or into situations where imminent involvement in hostilities is clearly indicated by the circumstances, are exercised only pursuant to (1) a declaration of war, (2) specific statutory authorization, or (3) a national emergency created by attack upon the United States, its territories or possessions, or its armed forces.

Consultation

Sec. 3. The President in every possible instance shall consult with Congress before introducing United States Armed Forces into hostilities or into situations where imminent involvement in hostilities is clearly indicated by the

179

circumstances, and after every such introduction shall consult regularly with the Congress until United States Armed Forces are no longer engaged in hostilities or have been removed from such situations.

Reporting

Sec. 4. (a) In the absence of a declaration of war, in any case in which United States Armed Forces are introduced—

1. into hostilities or into situations where imminent involvement in hostilities is clearly indicated by the circumstances;

2. into the territory, airspace or waters of a foreign nation, while equipped for combat, except for deployments which relate solely to supply, replacement, repair, or training of such forces; or

3. in numbers which substantially enlarge United States Armed Forces equipped for combat already located in a foreign nation;

the President shall submit within 48 hours to the Speaker of the House of Representatives and to the President pro tempore of the Senate a report, in writing, setting forth—

A. the circumstances necessitating the introduction of United States Armed Forces;

B. the constitutional and legislative authority under which such introduction took place; and

C. the estimated scope and duration of the hostilities or involvement.

(b) The President shall provide such other information as the Congress may request in the fulfillment of its constitutional responsibilities with respect to committing the Nation to war and to the use of United States Armed Forces abroad.

(c) Whenever United States Armed Forces are introduced into hostilities or into any situation described in subsection (a) of this section, the President shall, so long as such armed forces continue to be engaged in such hostilities or situation, report to the Congress periodically on the status of such hostilities or situation as well as on the scope and duration of such hostilities or situation, but in no event shall he report to the Congress less often than once every six months.

Congressional Action

Sec. 5. (a) Each report submitted pursuant to section 4(a)(1) shall be transmitted to the Speaker of the House of Representatives and to the President pro tempore of the Senate on the same calendar day. Each report so transmitted shall be referred to the Committee on Foreign Affairs of the House of Representatives and to the Committee on Foreign Relations of the Senate for appropriate action. If, when the report is transmitted, the Congress has adjourned sine die or has adjourned for any period in excess of three calendar days, the Speaker of the House of Representatives and the President pro tempore of the Senate, if they deem it advisable (or if petitioned by at least 30 percent of the membership of their respective Houses) shall jointly request the President to convene Congress in order that it may consider the report and take appropriate action pursuant to this section.

(b) Within sixty calendar days after a report is submitted or is required to be submitted pursuant to section 4(a)(1), whichever is earlier, the President shall terminate any use of United States Armed Forces with respect to which such report was submitted (or required to be submitted), unless Congress (1) has declared war or has enacted a specific authorization for such use of United States Armed Forces, (2) has extended by law such sixty-day period, or (3) is physically unable to meet as a result of an armed attack upon the United States. Such sixty-day period shall be extended for not more than an additional thirty days if the President determines and certifies to the Congress in writing that unavoidable military necessity respecting the safety of United States Armed Forces requires the continued use of such armed forces in the course of bringing about a prompt removal of such forces.

(c) Notwithstanding subsection (b), at any time that United States Armed Forces are engaged in hostilities outside the territory of the United States, its possessions and territories without a declaration of war or specific statutory authorization, such forces shall be removed by the President if the Congress so directs by concurrent resolution.

Congressional Priority Procedures for Joint Resolution or Bill

Sec. 6. (a) Any joint resolution or bill introduced pursuant to section 5(b) at least thirty calendar days before the expiration of the sixty-day period specified in such section shall be referred to the Committee on Foreign Affairs of the House of Representatives or the Committee on Foreign Relations of the Senate, as the case may be, and such committee shall report one such joint resolution or bill, together with its recommendations, not later than twenty-four calendar days before the expiration of the sixty-day period specified in such section, unless such House shall otherwise determine by the yeas and nays.

(b) Any joint resolution or bill so reported shall become the pending business of the House in question (in the case of the Senate the time for debate shall be equally divided between the proponents and the opponents), and shall be voted on within three calendar days thereafter, unless such House shall otherwise determine by yeas and nays.

(c) Such a joint resolution or bill passed by one House shall be referred to the committee of the other House named in subsection (a) and shall be reported out not later than fourteen calendar days before the expiration of the sixty-day period specified in section 5(b). The joint resolution or bill so reported shall become the pending business of the House in question and shall be voted on within three calendar days after it has been reported, unless such House shall otherwise determine by yeas and nays.

(d) In the case of any disagreement between the two Houses of Congress with respect to a joint resolution or bill passed by both Houses, conferees shall be promptly appointed and the committee of conference shall make and file a report with respect to such resolution or bill not later than four calendar days before the expiration of the sixty-day period specified in section 5(b). In the event the conferees are unable to agree within 48 hours, they shall report back to their respective Houses in disagreement. Notwithstanding any rule in either House concerning the printing of conference reports in the Record or concerning any delay in the consideration of such reports, such report shall be acted on by both houses not later than the expiration of such sixty-day period.

Congressional Priority Procedures for Concurrent Resolution

Sec. 7. (a) Any concurrent resolution introduced pursuant to section 5(c) shall be referred to the Committee on Foreign Affairs of the House of Representatives or the Committee on Foreign Relations of the Senate, as the case may be, and one such concurrent resolution shall be reported out by such committee together with its recommendations within fifteen calendar days, unless such House shall otherwise determine by the yeas and nays.

(b) Any concurrent resolution so reported shall become the pending business of the House in question (in the case of the Senate the time for debate shall be equally divided between the proponents and the opponents) and shall be voted on within three calendar days thereafter, unless such House shall otherwise determine by yeas and nays.

(c) Such a concurrent resolution passed by one House shall be referred to the committee of the other House named in subsection (a) and shall be reported out by such committee together with its recommendations within fifteen calendar days and shall thereupon become the pending business of such House and shall be voted upon within three calendar days, unless such House shall otherwise determine by yeas and nays.

(d) In the case of any disagreement between the two Houses of Congress with respect to a concurrent resolution passed by both Houses, conferees shall be promptly appointed and the committee of conference shall make and file a report with respect to such concurrent resolution within six calendar days after the legislation is referred to the committee of conference. Notwithstanding any rule in either House concerning the printing of conference reports in the Record or concerning any delay in the consideration of such reports, such report shall be acted on by both Houses not later than six calendar days after the conference report is filed. In the event the conferees are unable to agree within 48 hours, they shall report back to their respective Houses in disagreement.

Interpretation of Joint Resolution

Sec. 8. (a) Authority to introduce United States Armed Forces into hostilities or into situations wherein involvement in hostilities is clearly indicated by the circumstances shall not be inferred—

(1) from any provision of law (whether or not in effect before the date of the enactment of this joint resolution), including any provision contained in any appropriation Act, unless such provision specifically authorizes the introduction of United States Armed Forces into hostilities or into such situations and states that it is intended to constitute specific statutory authorization within the meaning of this joint resolution; or

(2) from any treaty heretofore or hereafter ratified unless such treaty is implemented by legislation specifically authorizing the introduction of United States Armed Forces into hostilities or into such situations and stating that it is

intended to constitute specific statutory authorization within the meaning of this joint resolution.

(b) Nothing in this joint resolution shall be construed to require any further specific statutory authorization to permit members of the United States Armed Forces to participate jointly with members of the armed forces of one or more foreign countries in the headquarters operations of high-level military commands which were established prior to the date of enactment of this joint resolution and pursuant to the United Nations Charter or any treaty ratified by the United States prior to such date.

(c) For purposes of this joint resolution, the term "introduction of United States Armed Forces" includes the assignment of members of such armed forces to command, coordinate, participate in the movement of, or accompany the regular or irregular military forces of any foreign country or government when such military forces are engaged, or there exists an imminent threat that such forces will become engaged, in hostilities.

(d) Nothing in this joint resolution—

(1) is intended to alter the constitutional authority of the Congress or of the President, or the provisions of existing treaties; or

(2) shall be construed as granting any authority to the President with respect to the introduction of United States Armed Forces into hostilities or into situations wherein involvement in hostilities is clearly indicated by the circumstances which authority he would not have had in the absence of this joint resolution.

Separability Clause

Sec. 9. If any provision of this joint resolution or the application thereof to any person or circumstance is held invalid, the remainder of the joint resolution and teh application of such provision to any other person or circumstance shall not be affected thereby.

Effective Date

Sec. 10. The joint resolution shall take effect on the date of its enactment.

Passed over Presidential veto Nov. 7, 1973.

SELECTED BIBLIOGRAPHY

INTERNATIONAL RELATIONS AND SOUTHEAST ASIA

Badgley, John. *Asian Development: Problems and Prognosis*. New York: Free Press, 1971.

Brecher, Michael. *The New States of Asia: A Political Analysis*. New York: Oxford University Press, 1963.

Brzezinski, Zbigniew. "The Balance of Power Delusion." *Foreign Policy* 7 (Summer 1972): 54-59.

Buchan, Alastair. "A World Restored?" *Foreign Affairs* 1, 4 (July 1972): 644-659.

Bull, Hedley. "The New Balance of Power in Asian and the Pacific." *Foreign Affairs* 49, 4 (July 1971): 669-681.

Claude, Inis L., Jr. *Power and International Relations*. New York: Random House, 1962.

Gordon, Bernard K. *The Dimensions of Conflict in Southeast Asia*. Englewood Cliffs, N.J.: Prentice-Hall, 1966.

Gulick, Edward Vose. *Europe's Classical Balance of Power*. New York: Norton, 1955.

Hoffman, Stanley. "Weighing the Balance of Power." *Foreign Affairs* 50, 4 (July 1972): 618-643.

_____. "Will the Balance Balance at Home?" *Foreign Policy* 7 (Summer 1972): 60-86.

Kaplan, Morton A. *System and Process in International Politics*. New York: Wiley, 1957.

Kissinger, Henry A. *A World Restored*. Boston: Houghton Mifflin, 1957.

Leifer, Michael. *Dilemmas of Statehood in Southeast Asia*. Vancouver: University of British Columbia Press, 1972.

Levi, Werner. *The Challenge of World Politics in South and Southeast Asia*. Englewood Cliffs, N.J.: Prentice-Hall, 1968.

Lyon, Peter. *War and Peace in Southeast Asia*. London: Oxford University Press, 1969.

Morgenthau, Hans J. *Politics Among Nations*. 4th ed. New York: Knopf, 1967.

Osborne, Milton. *Region of Revolt: Focus on Southeast Asia*. Victoria: Australia Pelican Books, 1971.

Scalapino, Robert A. *Asia and the Major Powers: Implications for the International Order.* Washington, D.C.: American Enterprise Institute for Public Policy Research, 1972.

Solomon, Robert L. "Boundary Concepts and Practices in Southeast Asia." *World Politics* 23, 1 (October 1970): 1-23.

Steinberg, David Joel, ed. *In Search of Southeast Asia: A Modern History*. New York: Praeger Publishers, 1971.

Taylor, A. J. P. *The Struggle for Mastery in Europe, 1848-1918*. London: Oxford University Press, 1954.

Tilman, Robert O., ed. *Man, State, and Society in Contemporary Southeast Asia*. New York: Praeger Publishers, 1969.

Wilcox, Wayne, Leo E. Rose, and Gavin Boyd, eds. *Asia and the International System*. Cambridge, Mass.: Winthrop, 1972.

THE UNITED STATES AND SOUTHEAST ASIA

Friedman, Edward and Mark Seldon, eds. *America's Asia: Dissenting Essays on Asian American Relations*. New York: Vintage Books, 1971.

Gardner, Lloyd C., ed. *The Great Nixon Turnaround*. New York: New Viewpoints, 1973.

Greene, Fred. *U.S. Policy and the Security of Asia*. New York: McGraw Hill, 1968.

Gregg, Robert W. and Charles W. Kegley, Jr. *After Vietnam: The Future of American Foreign Policy*. New York: Doubleday, 1970.

Hoffman, Stanley. *Gulliver's Troubles: or the Setting of American Foreign Policy*. New York: McGraw Hill, 1968.

Hoopes, Townsend. "Legacy of the Cold War in Indochina." *Foreign Affairs* 48, 4 (July 1970): 601-617.

Kissinger, Henry. "The Vietnam Negotiations," *Foreign Affairs* 47, 2 (January 1969): 211-234.

Landau, David. *Kissinger: The Uses of Power*. Boston: Houghton Mifflin, 1972.

Nixon, Richard. *U.S. Foreign Policy for the 1970's*. Washington, D.C.: Government Publications Office, 1971.

————. "Asia After Vietnam," *Foreign Affairs* 46, 1 (October 1967): 111-126.

Ravenol, Earl C., ed. *Peace With China?: U.S. Decisions For Asia*. New York: Liveright, 1971.

Reischauer, Edwin O. *Beyond Vietnam—The U.S. and Asia*. New York: Vintage Books, 1968.

Spanier, John. *American Foreign Policy Since World War II*. New York: Praeger Publishers, 1973.

The New York *Times. The Pentagon Papers*. New York: Bantam Books, 1971.

Zachar, Mark W. and R. S. Milne, eds. *Conflict and Stability in Southeast Asia*. New York: Doubleday, 1974.

THE SOVIET PERSPECTIVE

Duncan, W. Raymond, ed. *Soviet Policy in Developing Countries*. Waltham, Mass.: Ginn-Blaisdell, 1970.

Gurtov, Melvin. "Sino-Soviet Relations and Southeast Asia: Recent Developments and Future Possibilities." *Pacific Affairs* 43, 4 (Winter 1970-1971): 491-505.

Horn, Robert C. "Changing Soviet Policies and Sino-Soviet Competition in Southeast Asia." *ORBIS* 17, 2 (Summer 1973): 493-526.

Joshua, Wynfred and Stephen P. Gibert. *Arms for the Third World: Soviet Military Aid Diplomacy*. Baltimore: Johns Hopkins Press, 1969.

Jukes, Jeoffrey. *The Soviet Union in Asia*. Berkeley: University of California Press, 1973.

McLane, Charles B. *Soviet Strategies in Southeast Asia. An Exploration of Eastern Policy Under Lenin and Stalin*. Princeton: Princeton University Press, 1966.

_____. *Soviet-Third World Relations*. New York: Columbia University Press, 1974.

Ra'anan, Uri. *The USSR Arms the Third World. Case Studies in Soviet Foreign Policy*. Cambridge, Mass.: M.I.T. Press, 1969.

THE CHINESE PERSPECTIVE

Barnett, A. Doak. *Communist China and Asia: A Challenge to American Policy*. New York: Vintage Books, 1960.

Butwell, Richard. *Southeast Asia Today—and Tomorrow: Problems of Political Development*. 2nd ed. New York: Praeger Publishers, 1969.

Fitzgerald, Stephen. *China and the Overseas Chinese*. Cambridge: Cambridge University Press, 1972.

Gurtov, Melvin. *China and Southeast Asia. The Politics of Survival: A Study of Foreign Policy Interactions*. Lexington, Mass.: D. C. Heath, 1971.

Hinton, Harold C. *Communist China in World Politics*. London: MacMillan, 1966.

_____. *China's Turbulent Quest. An Analysis of China's Foreign Relations Since 1949*. Bloomington: Indiana University Press, 1972.

Lambert, Richard D., ed. *China in the World Today*. Philadelphia: The Annals of the American Academy of Political and Social Science, July 1972.

Ohja, Ishwer C. *Chinese Foreign Policy in an Age of Transition: The Diplomacy of Cultural Despair*. 2nd ed. Boston: Beacon Press, 1969.

Osborne, Milton. *Region of Revolt: Focus on Southeast Asia*. Harmondsworth, England: Penguin Books, 1970.

Robinson, Thomas W. "Future Domestic and Foreign Policy Choices for Mainland China." *Journal of International Affairs* 26, 2, (1972).

Van Ness, Peter. *Revolution and Chinese Foreign Policy: Peking's Support for Wars of National Liberation*. Berkeley: University of California Press, 1971.

THE JAPANESE PERSPECTIVE

Auer, James E. *The Postwar Rearmament of Japanese Maritime Forces, 1945-71*. New York: Praeger Publishers, 1973.

Axelbank, Albert. *Black Star Over Japan: Rising Forces of Militarism*. New York: Hill and Wang, 1972.

Chomchai, Prachoom and Masahide Shibusawa. *Asia in the World Community*. Tokyo: East-West Seminar, 1973.

Emmerson, John K. and Leonard A. Humphreys. *Will Japan Rearm? A Study in Attitudes*. Washington, D.C., and Stanford, Calif.: American Enterprise Institute for Public Policy Research, 1973.

Hellman, Donald C. *Japan and East Asia: The New International Order*. New York: Praeger Publishers, 1972.

Japan in Current World Affairs, 1970-1972. Tokyo: Kajima Institute of International Peace, 1972.

Walker, Richard L., ed. *Prospects in the Pacific*. Washington, D.C.: HELDREF Publications, 1972.

Wu, Yuan-li. *Raw Material Supply in a Multipolar World*. New York: National Strategy Information Center, 1973.

THE INDIAN PERSPECTIVE

Barnds, William J. *India, Pakistan, and the Great Powers*. New York: Praeger Publishers, 1972.

Donaldson, Robert H. "India: The Soviet Stake in Stability." *Asian Survey* 12, 6 (June 1972).

Dutt, V. P. "India and China: Betrayal, Humiliation and Reappraisal." *Policies Toward China: Views from Six Continents*. N.p. and n.d.

Galbraith, John Kenneth. *Ambassador's Journal: A Personal Account of the Kennedy Years*. Boston: Houghton Mifflin, 1969.

Gandhi, Indira. "India and the World." *Foreign Affairs* 49, 1 (October 1972).

Graham, Ian C. C. "The Indo-Soviet MIG Deal and Its International Repercussions." *Asian Survey* 4, 5 (May 1964).

Jain, A. P., ed. *Shadow of the Bear, the Indo-Soviet Treaty*. New Delhi: P. K. Deo, 1971.

Jukes, Geoffrey. "The Soviet Union and the Indian Ocean." *Survival* 13, 11 (November 1971).

Kavic, Lorne J. *India's Quest for Security: Defense Policies, 1947-1965*. Berkeley: University of California Press, 1967.

Millar, T. B. "Soviet Policies South and East of Suez." *Foreign Affairs* 49, 1 (October 1970).

———. "The Indian and Pacific Oceans: Some Strategic Considerations." *Adelphi Paper No. 57*. London: Institute of Strategic Studies, 1969.

Palmer, Norman D. *South Asia and United States Policy*. Boston: Houghton Mifflin, 1966.

Rajan, M. S. "Chinese Aggression and the Future of India's Nonalignment Policy." *International Studies* 5 (July-October 1963).

SarDesai, D. R. *Indian Foreign Policy in Cambodia, Laos, and Vietnam, 1947-1964*. Berkeley: University of California Press, 1968.

———. "South Asia and the Vietnam War." *United Asia* 20, 4 (July-August 1968).

Sen Gupta, Bhabhani. *The Fulcrum of Asia: Relations Among China, India, and Pakistan and the U.S.S.R.* New York: Pegasus, 1970.

Sondhi, M. L. "India and Nuclear China." *Pacific Community* 5, 4 (January 1973).

Stein, Arthur. *India and the Soviet Union*. Chicago: University of Chicago Press, 1969.

Subrahmanyam, K. *The Asian Balance of Power in the Seventies: An Indian View*. New Delhi: The Institute for Defense Studies and Analyses, 1968.

Thien, Ton That. *India and Southeast Asia, 1947-1960*. Geneva: Librairie Droz, 1963.

Van Eekelen, W. F. *Indian Foreign Policy and the Border Dispute with China*. The Hague: Martinus Nijhoff, 1964.

Wilcox, Wayne. *The Emergence of Bangla Desh*. Washington, D.C.: American Enterprise Institute for Public Policy Research, 1973.

Williams, Shelton. *The U.S., India, and the Bomb*. Baltimore: The Johns Hopkins Press, 1969.

INDEX

Adjitorop, J., 36
Aeroflot, 46
Africa, 53, 72, 94
Afro-Asian bloc, 54, 70, 96
Afro Asian conference. See Bandung conference.
Akasaka, T., 88
Algiers summit conference, 43
America (*see* United States)
Americans, 27-28, 69, 70
Andaman Islands, 104
Annam, 81
Arab-Israeli War (1973), 76
Arthashastra, 106
Asahi Shimbun, 87
Asia, 43-44, 52, 53, 54, 55, 56, 68; peoples of, 57, 94
Asian and Pacific Council (ASPAC), 25, 113, 114
Asian Development Bank, 86, 110
Asian Monroe Doctrine, 57
Asian states, 31, 55
Association of Southeast Asian Nations (ASEAN), 47, 48, 87, 89, 103, 109, 114
Australia, 80, 88, 108

balance of power: concept, policies, practices, 1-8, 18, 24, 28, 74, 94, 112; in Asia, 6-7, 17, 52; in East Asia, 53; in Southeast Asia, 53, 57, 58, 59, 75, 76-77, 95, 115; in the world, 52, 71, 94, 101
Bandung Conference, 30, 61, 70, 95, 96, 97
Bangkok, 25, 81, 84, 91
Bangladesh, 2, 4, 6, 33, 75, 100, 101, 102, 104
Bataan, 81
Belgrade, 96, 97
Bengal (Bay of), 100
Bismarck, 9
Borneo, 80
Brezhnev, 2, 31, 40, 47, 103; Brezhnev doctrine, 33, 102
Britain, 25, 95, 102, 108
Brunei, 81
Buchan, A., 7
Bulgaria, 46
Bull, H., 99-100
Burma, 48, 55-56, 59, 61, 64, 70, 80, 102, 107, 111-112; relations with China and

the USSR, 37-38

Cambodia, 5, 10, 14, 59, 60, 97, 108, 109, 111, 112; relations with U.S., 26
Canada, 97
Celebes Islands, 80
Central Intelligence Agency (CIA), 20-21, 84
China (People's Republic of), 1, 2, 4, 5, 6, 10, 11, 30-31, 40, 48; and the communist parties in Southeast Asia, 65-67; and the overseas Chinese, 64-65; Commission of Cultural Relations with foreign countries, 60; of Economic Relations with foreign countries, 60; of Overseas Chinese Affairs, 60, 65; relations with Africa, 72; with Burma, 63, 68, 77, 111-112; with Cambodia, 62-63, 111-112; with India, 96-97, 99; with Indonesia, 63, 68, 72, 111-112; with Japan, 76, 88; with Malaysia-Singapore, 77; with South Asia, 69; with the U.S., 51, 75, 94
China (Imperial), 56
China (Nationalist), 6, 19, 55-56, 70, 71, 74, 90, 99; relations with the U.S., 21-22
Chinese aid, 51, 62, 63; atom bomb, 72; communist party, 73; communities (*see* overseas Chinese); cultural policy in Southeast Asia, 63; economic policy in Southeast Asia, 60-62; foreign policy objectives, 54-58; communism and revolution, 54, 55, 66
Chou En-lai, 2, 16, 30, 47, 54, 60, 69, 70, 73, 77
Clark Air Base, 22
Clark, G., 87
Claude, I.L., 5
cold war, 51, 52, 57, 67, 68, 82, 90
collective security, 47, 48, 110-111
Colombo, 103; Colombo Conference, 95
Commonwealth, 99
Communism, 11, 44, 45; anti-communism, 83, 107
Communist parties in Asia, 69; in Southeast Asia, 58, 59, 77
Communist insurrections in Asia, 68; in Burma, 77; in Cambodia, 77; in Malaya, 64, 66, 77
Confucius, 75
Congo, 96

SUDERSHAN CHAWLA is Professor of Political Science at California State University, Long Beach. He served for one year as Research Associate at the Center for International Studies, Massachusetts Institute of Technology. He was also associated with the Peace Corps India Projects at Ohio State University and the University of Illinois.

Dr. Chawla did his graduate work at the Ohio State University. He spent 1971-72 in India and parts of Southeast Asia gathering data.

ALVIN D. COOX is Professor of History at California State University, San Diego, and is Director of the Center for Asian Studies. He was previously Senior Historian of the Operations Research Office, Johns Hopkins University, 1949-54; Historian, Japanese Research Division, U.S. Army, Japan, 1955-57; Managing Editor, Orient/West Magazine, Tokyo, 1958-64; and Lecturer in History, University of Maryland, Far East Division, 1963-64.

Dr. Coox received his M.A. and Ph.D. from Harvard University. He is the author of several publications, among them *Year of the Tiger* (1964) and *Japan: The Final Agony* (1970).

MELVIN GURTOV is Associate Professor of Political Science at the University of California, Riverside. He is the author of *The First Vietnam Crisis: Chinese Communist Strategy and United States Involvement, 1953-54* (1967); *Southeast Asia Tomorrow: Problems and Prospects for U.S. Policy* (1970); and *China and Southeast Asia: The Politics of Survival* (1971), and coauthor of *The Cultural Revolution in China* (1971).

ROBERT C. HORN is Associate Professor of Political Science and Asian Studies at California State University, Northridge. He previously taught at the University of Massachusetts (Boston) after receiving two Master's degrees and his Ph.D. from the Fletcher School of Law and Diplomacy, Medford, Mass. He has published numerous articles on Soviet foreign policy and Southeast Asian politics in such journals as *Survey*, *Orbis*, and *Pacific Affairs*.

ALAIN G. MARSOT is Associate Professor of Political Science at California State University, Long Beach, and was, until recently, Director of the Center for Asian Studies.

Dr. Marsot, born in Saigon (Vietnam), lived in India and Thailand for several years and traveled extensively in other Asian countries. His main scholarly interests and publications are in the field of China and Southeast Asia and the overseas Chinese. He was educated at the Universities of Paris and Oxford and has previously taught in France, England, and Egypt.

D. R. SARDESAI is Associate Professor of History at the University of California, Los Angeles. He was Acting Chairman and Professor of History at the University of Bombay during 1971-73. Dr. SarDesai, who did his graduate work at UCLA, was the recipient of a Ford Foundation Research Grant, 1968-69, a Watumull Foundation Scholarship, 1961-62, and an American Institute of Indian Studies Research Fellowship, 1963-64.

Dr. SarDesai is the author of several publications, among them *Indian Foreign Policy in Cambodia, Laos and Vietnam, 1947-1964* (1968) and *Trade and Empire in Malaya and Singapore, 1869-1874* (1970); he is coauthor of *India Through the Ages* (1969) and *Text-Book of World History* (1958).

CHINA AND THE GREAT POWERS: Relations with the
U.S., the USSR, and Japan
edited by Francis O. Wilcox

CHINA AND SOUTHEAST ASIA: Peking's Relations with
Revolutionary Movements
John J. Taylor

EDUCATION, MANPOWER, AND DEVELOPMENT IN
SOUTH AND SOUTHEAST ASIA
Muhammad Shamsul Huq

THE NEUTRALIZATION OF SOUTHEAST ASIA
Dick Wilson

SINO-AMERICAN DETENTE AND ITS POLICY IMPLICA-
TIONS*
edited by Gene T. Hsiao

*Also available in paperback as a PSS Student Edition.